ATTRA

EXPLAINED

When it comes to relationships, there's no shortage of advice from self-help 'experts', pick-up artists, and glossy magazines. But modern-day myths of attraction often have no basis in fact or – worse – are rooted in little more than misogyny. In *Attraction Explained*, psychologist Viren Swami debunks these myths and draws on cutting-edge research to provide a ground-breaking and evidence-based account of relationship formation.

At the core of this book is a very simple idea: there are no 'laws of attraction', no foolproof methods or strategies for getting someone to date you. But this isn't to say that there's nothing to be gained from studying attraction. Based on science rather than self-help clichés, *Attraction Explained* looks at how factors such as geography, appearance, personality, and similarity affect who we fall for and why.

Viren Swami is Professor of Social Psychology at Anglia Ruskin University in the UK. He is an international expert on attraction and body image, and has written and edited several books on these topics. He is also the founder of Plug In Your Brain, a public engagement initiative to promote the wider understanding of psychology.

'This is a beautifully written book, more like a novel than an academic textbook. But don't be misled: the author is a world authority on the topic. Professor Swami has made sure the book is scrupulously accurate and that all assertions are research-based. It is really unputdownable.'

– **Adrian Furnham**, Department of Psychology and Language Sciences, University College London, UK

'I trusted this author at once because, unlike the psychobabblers, he says from the start that there are no "laws" of attraction and no foolproof methods for getting someone to date you, let alone jump into bed with you. That isn't to say there is nothing to be gained from studying the processes involved in what draws us together. It's just a lot trickier than most self-help books would suggest. But with precision and no small wit – I found myself frequently laughing out loud – he explores the four key factors that shape the formation of most relationships: proximity, appearance, reciprocity and similarity. As he shows, studying attraction or relationships scientifically, far from destroying the magic and mystery of it all, can actually be helpful, whether you aspire to be lover or friend. He also satisfyingly nails my biggest bête noire: that "treat 'em mean" is any sort of relationship advice.'

– **Suzie Hayman**, agony aunt, relationship counsellor, accredited TripleP (Positive Parenting Programme) parenting educator, broadcaster and author

ATTRACTION
EXPLAINED

THE SCIENCE OF HOW WE FORM RELATIONSHIPS

VIREN SWAMI

Routledge
Taylor & Francis Group

LONDON AND NEW YORK

First published 2016
by Routledge
2 Park Square, Milton Park, Abingdon, Oxon, OX14 4RN

and by Routledge
711 Third Avenue, New York, NY 10017

Routledge is an imprint of the Taylor & Francis Group, an informa business

British Library Cataloguing in Publication Data
A catalogue record for this book is available from the British Library

Library of Congress Cataloging-in-Publication Data
A catalog record for this book has been requested

ISBN: 978-1-138-93700-0 (hbk)
ISBN: 978-1-138-93703-1 (pbk)
ISBN: 978-1-315-67650-0 (ebk)

Typeset in Minion Pro
by Apex CoVantage, LLC

Printed and bound by CPI Group (UK) Ltd,
Croydon, CR0 4YY

Christa: For a long time, in my life from before, I had forgotten how to dream. Then, one night in January, I saw you floating, so I photographed you into my heart. Later, when I awoke, I saw you looking back at me and I thought, I'm glad you exist in real life.

CONTENTS

COPYRIGHT NOTES

1

CUPID'S ARROW

OR, A BRIEF HISTORY OF ATTRACTION THEORIES, SOME DUMB SHIT OTHER PEOPLE HAVE SAID, AND WHAT THIS BOOK IS ALL ABOUT

The first time Scott sees the delivery-woman on rollerblades, at the Wychwood Branch of the Toronto Public Library, he's lovestruck. For those of you who don't know him, Scott Pilgrim (age: 23; rating: awesome) is a jobless slacker living with his cool gay roommate Wallace Wells (age: 25; rating: 7.5/10) in a one-room basement apartment in Toronto. Scott plays bass guitar in a band called Sex Bob-omb with his friends Stephen Stills (guitar) and Kim Pine (drums), who he once dated in high school. Oh, and Scott hates smoking and considers anyone who smokes to be evil. Still carrying some baggage from a previous bad breakup, Scott has begun dating

Knives Chau (age: 17), a high-schooler, mainly because he finds the relationship easy – all they do is ride the bus together and talk about her school. Despite Scott's questionable relationship choices, for some time now he's felt an increasing sense of loneliness, a feeling that something isn't quite right.

Anyway, back to the story. Scott is at the Toronto Public Library one day when he spots a mysterious pink-haired woman on rollerblades delivering a package. He's instantly smitten. Later, he finds he can't stop thinking about her. The strange 'ninja delivery girl' even appears in his dreams, skating away before he has a chance to ask her anything. Life just isn't the same for Scott anymore. He's distracted when on dates with Knives and band practice is frequently interrupted by Scott's daydreams. Luckily, he's at a party not long later where he sees the pink-haired woman again. Asking around, he finds out that her name is Ramona Flowers and that she's just moved from New York to Toronto, where she now works as a delivery-woman for the online retailer Amazon. Scott goes up to her and, failing rather spectacularly in his attempts to chat her up, promises to leave her alone forever... but then stalks her until she leaves the party (not cool, Scott).

The next day, completely ~~forgetting~~ ignoring his (pseudo) relationship with Knives, Scott orders some CDs from amazon.ca, hoping to get another chance to meet Ramona. Sure enough, Ramona arrives a few days later with Scott's package. Not missing a beat, he asks her out. Umming and ahhing, Ramona reveals that the reason Scott has been dreaming about her is because she's been using the Subspace Highway running through his head as a shortcut for her deliveries. She finally agrees to go on a date with him as compensation for using his mind as a shortcut. This is the moment we've been waiting for: the start of Scott Pilgrim's long journey to win Ramona's love. Along the way, he has to – among other things – defeat Ramona's seven evil exes, find closure over his past relationships, earn various swords and power-ups, and learn self-acceptance through struggle. Should be easy.

These scenes, which I've borrowed from the first of Bryan Lee O'Malley's six graphic novels about Scott Pilgrim,* set up one of the most common and powerful tropes in popular culture: the formation of a relationship between two people. But understanding this process can sometimes be tricky. What is it that draws Scott to Ramona? Why Ramona and not anyone else? What shapes the extent to which that attraction is mutual? What specifically determines whether Scott and Ramona might form some sort of relationship? And how do two people, complete strangers to each other, go on to consider each other special and unique, to form a lasting relationship with each other?

Unsurprisingly, attempts to answer these sorts of questions have a rather long history. It fascinated the Roman poet Ovid in about 1 AD. His *Metamorphoses*, a fifteen-book narrative poem that has been described as containing 'many large-scale psychological studies,'[1] presents one of the earliest attempts at explaining romantic attraction. In the very first erotic adventure of the *Metamorphoses*, Apollo the archer boasts of his prowess in overcoming the monstrous Python, but makes the mistake of provoking Cupid, the god of attraction and love:

> Thou lascivious boy,
> Are arms like these for children to employ?
> Know, such achievements are my proper claim;
> Due to my vigour, and unerring aim:

---

* There's also a film adaptation of the series, *Scott Pilgrim vs. the World*, starring Michael Cera as Scott and Mary Elizabeth Winstead as Ramona. FYI, in case it isn't obvious, Scott and Ramona aren't real people. But we can still learn a lot about relationship formation from these fictional characters, so they'll crop up quite a bit over the course of this book. Oh, and you should get yourself O'Malley's graphic novels – you won't be disappointed.

Resistless are my shafts, and Python late
In such a feather'd death, has found his fate.*

The love-god's arrows, Apollo claims, have no place in an epic. Instead, Cupid should be content with stirring the concealed fires of romance with his burning torch. Cupid's reply is to shoot two arrows. One, with a sharp golden point, strikes Apollo and he immediately falls in love with Daphne:

So burns the God, consuming in desire,
And feeding in his breast a fruitless fire:
Her well-turn'd neck he view'd (her neck was bare)
And on her shoulders her dishevel'd hair;
Oh were it comb'd, said he, with what a grace
Wou'd every waving curl become her face!
He view'd her eyes, like heav'nly lamps that shone,
He view'd her lips, too sweet to view alone,
Her taper fingers, and her panting breast;
He praises all he sees, and for the rest
Believes the beauties yet unseen are best.†

---

* If, like me, you find the Early Modern English difficult, Anthony Kline's translation might help: 'Impudent boy, what are you doing with a man's weapons? That one is suited to my shoulders, since I can hit wild beasts of a certainty, and wound my enemies, and not long ago destroyed with countless arrows the swollen Python that covered many acres with its plague-ridden belly.'

† Kline's translation: '... so the god was altered by the flames, and all his heart burned, feeding his useless desire with hope. He sees her disordered hair hanging about her neck and sighs, 'What if it were properly dressed?' He gazes at her eyes sparkling with the brightness of starlight. He gazes on her lips, where mere gazing does not satisfy. He praises her wrists and hands and fingers, and her arms bare to the shoulder: whatever is hidden, he imagines more beautiful.'

But Cupid isn't finished yet. He shoots another arrow at Daphne, only this one is lead-tipped and blunt – an antaphrodisiac – and 'swift as the wind, the damsel fled away'.[2] Cupid's retaliation is striking because, with Apollo's own weapon of choice, Cupid demonstrates his superiority in *gloria* – it is Cupid that is supreme among all gods. But there's a deeper significance in Ovid's telling of this myth: attraction is literally an act of god. To be attracted to another is reduced to the scheming of an arrow-wielding love-god. Later depictions of Cupid even portrayed him as blind, not so much in the sense of being sightless, but rather as blinkered and arbitrary. Hasty, childlike Cupid shoots his arrows and anyone lucky (or unlucky) enough to be struck is spurred to love.

By the Middle Ages, Cupid's arrow had begun to be reinterpreted in terms of developments in optical theory. In *Cligés*, a poem by the medieval French poet Chrétien de Troyes from around 1176, two characters – Alexander and Soredamors – have fallen painfully in love with each other and reflect on their source of their suffering. While Soredamors blames herself, reproaching herself for her lack of self-control, Alexander entertains a more elaborate series of explanations. He proposes that he has been shot through the heart by Love's arrow,* but is confused by how it might have reached his heart without leaving a mark. His conclusion? That the arrow pierced his eyes... although this raises an even more difficult question: how did the arrow pierce his eyes without leaving a wound there either?

Having considered things some more, Alexander comes to the conclusion that the 'arrow' is actually an image of Soredamors. His eyes rely on their transparency to convey or reflect the image of Soredamors to his heart, where it is interpreted and 'sets the

---

* In medieval poetry, it wasn't always clear where the darts came from, whether they were shot by Cupid, released by the person being gazed upon, or emerged from some other place entirely.

heart on fire'.[3] In this interpretation, the eyes are a mirror for the heart and the arrow is a sensation or a sense impression. So the passage of the arrow from the eye to heart becomes, in *Cligés*, a metaphor for the reception of an image, harmless until it is comprehended by the heart. It is the heart, and not the eyes or even the brain, that judges the images it receives, liking or disliking them, falling in love or not. But of the many images that Alexander's eyes receive, why is it the image of Soredamors in particular that leads him to fall in love? The image of Soredamors, he says, was deceptively beautiful, an inaccurate representation of the world, causing his heart to be led astray.

CUPID'S STORY, UPDATED FOR THE TWENTY-FIRST CENTURY

There's something comical in the image of Alexander, the hapless lover blaming his eyes and heart for deceiving him into falling in love. But it's also in the pages of *Cligés* that we find one of the earliest attempts at understanding attraction and relationship formation from a scientific basis.[4] In assimilating the emerging science of perception and optics into his poetry, Chrétien not only provided Cupid with a newfound relevance, he also attempted one of the earliest scientific explanations of how we form relationships with other people. But progress was slow. By the mid-nineteenth century, the seat of perception had moved from the heart to the brain, but the process of attraction itself continued to be explained largely in terms of visual imagery and its effects. Part of the reason for this was the belief that studying attraction or relationships scientifically destroys the magic and mystery of it all.

The notion of relationship formation as mysterious and magical is one that remains popular. In the late 1980s, the psychologist Arthur Aron and his colleagues invited university students to take part in a study about their experiences of being attracted to another person and falling in love. The participants, all of whom had 'become strongly attracted' or 'fallen in love' in the eight months before the study, were asked to think about their experiences before writing in detail about the situation in which they first felt that attraction. When the participants' accounts were analysed, the researchers found that almost 10 per cent of respondents believed that the attraction had been sparked by 'mystery' – either something mysterious about the other person or in the situation itself. When a larger group of university students were asked to rate a list of items that they believed had influenced their feelings of attraction, 30 per cent said mystery had a strong positive impact.[5]

The desire to retain some of that mystery by keeping scientists away is perhaps understandable. When lonely, eccentric scientists with their odd-looking hair* come along, there's a real fear that they will destroy the magic of attraction, reducing everything to formulas and numbers. Except, there's no real evidence that studying attraction scientifically makes it any less enthralling. In fact, a scientific approach to attraction and relationships often raises new questions that need answering, uncovering mystery among everyday or mundane behaviours. Nor will a scientific approach be able to explain everything about relationship formation. In the study I just mentioned by Aron and his colleagues, respondents frequently highlighted very specific, idiosyncratic cues – some characteristic of the other person, such as their voice or posture – that were sufficient to elicit a strong attraction. The scientific study of attraction can help us understand some of those idiosyncrasies, but it is unlikely to be able to explain every such case.

---

* When children are asked to draw a scientist, they typically draw a White man, wearing a lab coat, with strange-looking hair and crazy sideburns. Adults, too, have similar stereotypic perceptions of scientists.

A different critique of a science of attraction and relationships comes from those who say that scientists have very little to add beyond what we already know through common sense. When I tell people that I am a psychologist, I'm almost always asked if I can read their minds.* Once that minefield has been safely navigated and I tell them I'm interested in the study of attraction and the formation of relationships, I'm then usually met by incredulous stares. I know what they're going to say: 'Surely studying attraction scientifically will only tell us what we already know'. My response is that common sense about attraction is often wrong and sometimes dangerously so. To demonstrate this point, humour me a moment and answer this question: do you think opposites attract? Do you think that people who are opposite from each other in their personalities or values or beliefs are more likely to be attracted to each other?

If you said yes, opposites do attract, you're not alone. In one study, my colleagues and I asked British university students to indicate whether they believed in the idea that opposites attract (along with forty-nine other common-held beliefs related to psychology). Just over 48 per cent thought it was true. In the same study, about a fifth of respondents from among the public in central Europe also believed that opposites attract, whereas among North American undergraduates the figure rises to whopping 77 per cent.[6] If so many people believe in this seemingly commonsensical idea, that must make it correct, right? Well, no. It turns out that, when it comes to relationship formation, opposites very rarely attract. As we'll see in Chapter 6, the evidence from science indicates that there's a much greater tendency for similar people to be attracted to one another, but the belief that opposites attract remains widespread – so widespread, in fact, that it has been included in a list of fifty of the most popular myths of psychology.[7]

---

* I can, but only when I'm wearing my mind-reading hat and cloak.

Of course, I'm not suggesting that all commonsensical beliefs about attraction are wrong or unscientific. The theories that non-scientists come up with are an attempt to explain and predict how relationships are formed and, in that sense, they have the same aims as scientists. And, sometimes, studying commonsensical ideas allows scientists to generate new ideas or uncover new ways of thinking about a topic.* The trouble is that, more often than not, common sense ideas about attraction offer only a partial account of how relationships are formed. And when those commonsensical ideas are misleading or false, they can have damaging consequences.

For my birthday a few years ago, I was given a book called *Top Tips for Girls*, in which journalist and author Kate Reardon has collected 'real advice for real women for real life'.[8] I'm fairly certain I was given the book as a joke given that I'm not a girl in need of 'real' advice (I'm less certain whether the book itself is a joke, though it is marketed as 'Non-fiction/Reference'), but the sections on dating and relationships did catch my attention. To say I was dumbfounded by some of the recommendations would be an understatement. Here's one example of a top tip from the book, on 'how to get your boyfriend to commit':

> Consolidate his mind by dumping him... if he is the right one, he will come and get you. If he doesn't, you have done the right thing.

I'd be interested to know whether this dating tactic has ever worked, but I'm fairly confident it's an astonishingly bad

---

* It was a commonsensical idea that first got me interested in the psychology of attraction. As an undergraduate studying psychology, I was introduced to the idea that all men are 'programmed' to be attracted to curvaceous women. Having studied this important topic at great depth, I can tell you that this is another myth of attraction. If you're interested, I've written about this research in *The Missing Arms of Vénus de Milo*.

piece of advice. Or how about this gem on 'how to make him jealous':

> Send yourself flowers with no card. They become a non-specific threat.

I'm not even sure why you'd need to make your partner feel jealous in the first place... Or what about this one on 'how to keep your boyfriend keen':

> Make sure you are always the first to end telephone conversations.

Or my favourite, this list of 'how to be a woman men love':

> You never utter the words, 'Where is this going?'
> You impose a two-drink maximum on yourself when you go out. [...]
> You watch your language.
> You say yes.

Well, no, sometimes it's not only polite, but a good idea, to say 'no'. It's easy to poke fun at trite advice that reads like it might be aimed at children rather than women,* but it does highlight why I think commonsensical ideas about attraction can sometimes be dangerous. Sending yourself flowers anonymously or hanging up before the end of a conversation may sound innocuous, but there's simply no evidence to suggest that it works. Worse still, it may actually damage a fledgling relationship, rather than strengthen it. As the advisors in *Top Tips for Girls* prove in abundance, sometimes common sense turns out to be a load of nonsense.

---

* Just in case, this book also has some excellent advice about 'how to poop at your boyfriend's house discretely'. Remember folks, 'matches and air freshener give the game away'.

RESORTING TO SELF-HELP

If commonsensical ideas about attraction don't offer much solace, what about the self-help industry? Although self-help books have been read for generations, it's only in the last several decades that the self-help industry has emerged as a multi-million dollar business. Some estimates suggest that up to a half of all Americans have purchased a self-help book, with women far out-numbering men in terms of readership. Within the genre of publications marketed to help people change or improve their lives, books about interpersonal relationships are difficult to miss. Hundreds of books have been written to provide advice about how to meet the partner of your dreams, to find love, and to have healthier and more satisfying relationships. Millions of readers have turned to such books in the search for romance. One survey found that self-help books are one of the most frequent avenues for assistance when people are looking for relationship advice.[9]

So what's so bad about a little self-help? We could start by asking what self-help books actually suggest. Someone who might know is the sociologist Arlie Hochschild, who conducted an analysis of bestselling books for women published between 1970 and 1990. She concluded that self-help relationship books, while cloaked in rhetoric about egalitarianism and gender equality, actually undermine any attempt at forming emotionally rich bonds. Hochschild's work showed how self-help relationship books invite women to be emotionally distant, to deny their emotional needs, to be distrustful of others, and to be self-reliant at all times rather than investing in social relationships. For Hochschild, these values brought to mind the image of a 'postmodern cowgirl': 'Her fear of being dependent on another person evokes the image of the American cowboy, alone, detached, roaming free with his horse... On the ashes of Cinderella, then, rises a postmodern cowgirl'.[10] Rather than expecting to give or receive love from other human beings, the postmodern cowgirl devotes herself to emotional control, forever distrustful of others with whom she might have relationships.

Hochschild's argument that self-help relationship books represent an 'abduction of feminism' is supported by Rebecca Hazleden's analysis of the fourteen bestselling relationship manuals published between 1981 and 2000. These self-help books, she says, encourage readers to seek fulfilment through self-sufficiency, to focus on the self and not others, and to prepare themselves to be 'utterly isolated, cast adrift in a loveless world'.[11] She characterises the advice from self-help books as prescribing relationships that lack any sort of compassion or mutuality, in which individuals are encouraged to distance themselves emotionally from others and terminate any relationship where self-sufficiency has been compromised. Far from being books about relationships with others, self-help books are really about one's relationship with oneself, prescribing a programme of 'loving the self' in order to distance the self from others.

Other researchers have argued that self-help books haven't simply abducted feminism, but are actively anti-feminist because they reproduce stereotypes of women and men and encourage readers to adopt traditional gender roles.[12] Rather than trying to understand the nature of relationships and their formation, self-help books reinforce gender-based inequality by making women responsible – and to blame – for any flaw in social interactions. But it isn't just women who are portrayed stereotypically. In the world of self-help books, men are often dismissed as being emotionally stunted, driven by biological urges, and preoccupied by sex and attractiveness above all else. But as we will see in Chapter 4, there's actually very little evidence to support any of these stereotypes.

And it isn't just self-help books that reproduce these gendered stereotypes. In their analysis of *Cosmopolitan* magazine, David Machin and Joanna Thornborrow discovered that, while the magazine promotes the idea of the 'fun fearless female', in which dating and relationship problems can be easily solved with the help of *Cosmo*'s 'hot tips', women are still presented as fundamentally alone in the world. The only way to hold their own is to use their bodies and their sexuality to attract and keep men, and to take a 'professional' or 'entrepreneurial' attitude toward attracting men, treating relationships like job interviews and the self as a product to be sold. Women are expected to subjugate their own needs, constructing themselves instead as sexualised objects and the ideal fantasy partner for eagerly awaiting men. And men don't get off lightly either – they are portrayed in women's magazines as lumbering fools, easily aroused, easily satisfied, and easily deceived into falling in love. Men, in this view, lack even basic emotional and verbal skills, and are instead driven by their animalistic sex drives and self-interest.[13]

You don't have to be a feminist to find these ideas about relationships disappointingly bleak. But the problem isn't just that self-help books and magazines reproduce the worst stereotypes of gendered behaviour. When we get down to it, the advice they offer women and men is often so banal to the point of being useless – 'if you like someone, it's a good idea to be friendly' was one ingenious piece of advice from *Glamour* magazine[14] – or, worse, based on pseudo-science. A common trope in women's magazines, for example, is the wheeling out of 'relationship experts' who make misleading, facile, or clichéd claims about attraction that may actually be detrimental to readers and their relationships. Individual 'studies' are taken out of context or misinterpreted to provide grand schemes or 'rules' of attraction that have little or no basis in fact.

What's more, given the vast array of sources to choose from, it really isn't surprising that the advice given by 'relationship experts' is often contradictory and confused. Conflicting messages can even be found within the same text. In Janice Winship's study of *Woman* magazine, she argued that women's magazines perform 'ideological juggling acts' in which a kaleidoscopic array of contradictory elements co-exist.[15] Take, for example, the notion – frequently peddled by 'love gurus' and 'relationship doctors' – that a woman's appearance doesn't matter so long as she is happy and confident with her body. A great-sounding idea, except that it's misleading – as we'll see in Chapter 3 – and, worse, often presented side-by-side with articles and adverts for the latest fad diet, cosmetic surgery, celebrity weight loss, and the paramount importance of appearance.

Maybe I'm being overly critical of self-help relationship advice. But it's hard not to feel as if the possibility of populating the world with more caring people and helping people to form mutually benefiting relationships just doesn't figure in the schemes offered by self-help relationship books and women's magazines. Instead, imagine a world of lonely cowgirls and cowboys, trusting no one, depending on no one but the self. A world in which you detach yourself from any sort of emotional connection, in which the most heroic act you could perform would be to face the world on your own. A world in which you craft a space for yourself by evicting everyone else – and particularly anyone who might care for you or who might need care themselves. It would be a very sad world indeed.

HOW TO GET BEAUTIFUL WOMEN INTO BED

Clicking on the link took me to a page that promised to teach me 'the art of meeting and attracting beautiful women'. This wasn't some hoax or gimmick! No, this was 'cutting-edge psychology' combined with years of experience 'in the field'. A video starts to play: a professional-looking young man tells me he was never able to attract women, but his life changed when he found the 'system'. The promises kept coming. For a small sum of money, I too would be taught how to overcome my geekiness (wait a minute... who said I was geeky to begin with?), I would learn the secrets of approaching women without being rejected, I could go to classes and boot-camps where 'game-changing' laws of attraction would be revealed. Best of all, I would learn 'STEALTH ATTRACTION skills' to get women into bed 'IMMEDIATELY (WARNING: THIS STUFF REALLY WORKS)'. Welcome to the world of the pick-up artist.

Pick-up artistry has its origins in the 1980s, and particularly in Ross Jeffries' dubious speed seduction theories based on neuro-linguistic programming,[16] but rose to prominence with Neil Strauss' 2005 bestseller exposé *The Game: Penetrating the Secret Society of Pickup Artists*. Strauss spent two years within the seduction community and, having learned the tricks of the trade from various 'masters of seduction', describes his transformation from lonely journalist to womaniser and master pick-up artist (he gave himself the moniker 'Style', which seems to be the thing to do among pick-up artists). One of the masters of seduction he discusses is the pick-up artist Erik James Horvat-Markovic, who calls himself Mystery and whose book *The Mystery Method: How to Get Beautiful Women into Bed* is one of the most prominent texts circulating in the pick-up artist community.

Mystery provides a complex 'seduction script' – the 'structured game' – that teaches men how to establish trust with women, with a focus on the importance of communication and communicative tools, the ultimate goal of which is getting laid. Other pick-up artists have taken issue with the way in which Mystery's structured approach results in 'social robots', merely parroting the seduction script regardless of the context. This has led to a new movement of pick-up artistry, known as the 'natural game', which involves a more free-flowing, improvisational approach to seduction, focused more on authentic communication. Even with the 'natural game', pre-tested routines are common and the underlying idea is still to get 'average frustrated chumps' – or AFCs – who feel inadequate enough to cough up money to learn a conglomerate of seduction techniques and accept some over-arching methodological narrative.

There has been a great deal of discussion and debate about pick-up artists, particularly the extent to which they perpetuate patterns of misogyny and propagate practices that encourage the objectification, subjugation, and ill-treatment of women.[17] These discussions are appropriate and necessary, but here I want to ask a different question: is pick-up artistry scientifically valid? This is an important question, given that pick-up artists themselves claim that their techniques are based on psychological evidence. Mystery, for example, explicitly frames his book within a scientific context, explaining that he studies the 'science of social dynamics' and offering readers an 'advanced algorithm thirteen years in the making'.[18] Readers are encouraged to go out into the field to 'improve their calibration', advised to adopt a 'decimal rating scale' to rank women's appearances, and taught how to trigger a woman's 'hard-wired attraction switches'. So is there any truth to the claim that pick-up artistry is based on scientific evidence?

The short answer is, no, not much. For example, in her textual analysis of *The Mystery Method*, Amanda Denes describes how pick-up artists like Mystery have misappropriated scientific evidence to further their own ends.[19] She argues that pick-up artists rely on faulty, armchair interpretations of psychology, biology, and physiology to make pronouncements that dehumanise and degrade women. Take, for instance, Mystery's 'Cat Theory', in which he dubiously explains that women are like cats because they do not take orders, like shiny new things, and 'rub against you and purr when they like you'. Metaphors such as these are a common trope in the world of pick-up artistry, with men being urged to 'train' women by rewarding positive behaviour and punishing negative behaviour. This dehumanises women, presenting them as biological animals in thrall to their genetic programming, lacking any sort of personal agency, their bodies all responding in the same way to seduction techniques.

It's not just that the theory underlying pick-up artistry is dubious, it's also that they don't appear to have a grasp of the scientific studies that they rely on. Pick-up artists place a great deal of importance on physiological responses to touch – or what Mystery refers to as 'kinaesthetics' – when seducing women. But as Denes shows, pick-up artists have misappropriated scientific studies to make grand claims about human behaviour that are not supported by any actual evidence. Worse, she argues, the implication of methods of seduction that are claimed to be flawless is the perpetuation of false beliefs and myths about interpersonal interactions, behaviours, and sexuality. In misappropriating the language of science, Mystery and other pick-up artists reduce interpersonal relationships to unfounded biological imperatives and show little or no awareness of the social and cultural contexts in which relationships are formed.

Similarly, in her interviews with British pick-up artists, Anna Arrowsmith discusses how they frequently resort to pseudo-scientific references and beliefs that have very little basis in fact.[20] A good example of this is the belief in extreme gender differences, that women and men represent different species that behave in very different ways. But, as we'll see over the course of these books, gender differences in attraction and relationship formation have been greatly exaggerated. Arrowsmith concludes her analysis of pick-up artistry by saying that, although pick-up artists want to portray themselves as being respectful of women and their needs, their reliance on pseudo-science and their desire to control women's behaviour means they remain trapped in their own misogyny. In her view, the techniques being taught by pick-up artists like those she interviewed in her study were unrealistic and unhelpful.

Even if we conclude that the theory underlying pick-up artistry is faulty, do the techniques actually work? The trouble is that there isn't actually any real evidence that it does. Claims of GUARANTEED SUCCESS are based on anecdotes, but anecdotes don't make for good science. And anyway, anecdotes of failures are just as easy to find as claims of success.[21] Moreover, many of the techniques preferred by pick-up artists, such as 'negging' – making negative statements, backhanded compliments, or 'accidental' insults to make women question their own value while increasing the man's value – seem to fly in the face of evidence from science (as we'll see in Chapter 5). Even if evidence of its success is scant, one might argue that helping men who suffer from social anxiety or shyness to be more confident must be a good thing. And I'd agree, except I'm not convinced that pick-up artists are the best people to help.

But there's a deeper rot here. Even if you buy into the stereotypes of behaviour and the pseudo-science, even if you're motivated not by empathy but by the promise of countless blowjobs, even if you've been lured in by guarantees of beautiful women and sex – even then it is difficult to get away from the feeling that something isn't quite right with pick-up artistry. This isn't to suggest that all pick-up artists are nefarious and perverse. But as a community, pick-up artists are morally, ethically, and – importantly – scientifically bankrupt. Pick-up artists use pseudo-science to sell an ideology about women, an approach to relationships that views women as objects to be debugged and conquered. The willingness to manipulate and deceive that permeates pick-up artistry doesn't bode well for healthy relationships. When looking for healthy relationships, we can do better than rely on pseudo-science and misogyny.

THERE ARE NO LAWS OF ATTRACTION

If common sense is frequently nonsense and if self-help 'experts' and pick-up artists have sold us a pseudo-scientific view of attraction, what are we left with? In this book, I want to offer a different perspective on attraction and relationship formation, one that is based on decades of research and scientific evidence. I'll be asking what a real science of attraction looks like and what it has to tell us about the factors involved in forming relationships with others. And I'll show that a science of attraction, based on real research by psychologists and sociologists, has much to offer in terms of a valid and evidence-based approach to relationship formation. Rather than relying on common sense, pseudo-science, or personal anecdotes about what works, I'll suggest we should instead look to the evidence provided by scientists.

At the core of this book is an idea that I'd like to try to sell you. The idea is a very simple one: there are no 'laws of attraction'. There are no guarantees of success, no fool-proof methods or strategies for getting someone to date you, let alone jump into bed with you. If that's what you're after, then I'm sorry to disappoint so soon. But if my own research has convinced me of one thing, it's that promises of guaranteed methods for attracting and keeping a partner are always hollow and empty. Human psychology is incredibly complex, and trying to reduce the processes involved in relationship formation to rules or laws is an exercise in futility. But while I will show why I believe there are no laws of attraction, this isn't the same as arguing that there is nothing to be gained from studying the processes involved in attraction.

In this book, I'll reveal the four key factors that shape the formation of most relationships. First, I'll discuss the surprising and powerful effects that physical proximity has on relationship formation. It may seem obvious, but decades of research have shown that one of the strongest predictors of whether any two people will form a relationship is sheer physical proximity. Proximity facilitates relationship formation because it reduces the 'functional distance' between two people, increasing the likelihood that they'll interact and perceive themselves as part of the same 'social unit'. But, as I'll show in Chapter 2, proximity also exerts an influence on relationship formation through some not-so-obvious ways. And I'll also present the results of my own study into how our perceptions of our surroundings have an impact on who we find attractive.

Second, I'll show that appearance matters. No surprise there. Compared to less attractive people, physically attractive folk get treated better, and that includes getting asked out on dates more frequently and even having sex more often. The sad truth is that, as much as we might protest otherwise, we judge books by their covers all the time. But what about the old stereotype that men care more about a partner's appearance than do women? In Chapter 3, I'll argue that rumours of men's shallowness may have been greatly exaggerated. For first impressions, and particularly for interactions in real life, it seems that physical appearance matters to both women and men.

But, in Chapter 4, I'll show that, aside from physical attractiveness, there's a wide range of other characteristics that matter when it comes to relationship formation. In fact, characteristics like kindness and warmth are valued in prospective partners and the strange thing is that possessing these traits can even make an individual *appear* more physically attractive. And as for the stereotype that nice guys finish last, I will show that it's just that – a stereotype. Finally, in Chapter 4, I'll show how situational and individual factors can affect how we perceive another person. I'll tell you why crossing a wobbly bridge could alter perceptions of attractiveness and I'll present the findings of my 'love-is-blind' bias studies that show how our perceptions of romantic partners are biased.

Third, in Chapter 5, I will reveal that liking is mutual. One person's liking for another usually predicts the other person's liking in return. But what's more, experimental evidence suggests that one person's liking another actually causes the other to return the appreciation. Conversely, psychologists have shown that even the slightest hint of criticism can be damaging. This is why playing hard-to-get doesn't work: years of research shows that being vague and stand-offish doesn't get you very far. You might think, then, that flattery will get you everywhere. But be warned: if praise clearly violates what we know is true, we lose respect for the flatterer and wonder whether the compliment springs from ulterior motives.

Lastly, I'll suggest that one of the strongest predictors of relationship formation is the degree of similarity between two people. Two people who share common attitudes, beliefs, demographics, and values are much more likely to form relationships than those who are dissimilar. Experiments have even shown that people often approach and form relationships with others whose attractiveness roughly matches their own – what psychologists call 'assortative mating'. But psychologists have also shown that dissimilarity breeds dislike: we assume that others share our attitudes, and when we discover that they don't, we usually dislike the person. So do opposites ever attract? Some dating 'experts' would have you believe that the best relationships are those in which two people complement each other, but as we'll see in Chapter 6, the tendency of opposites to form relationships has very little evidence in its favour.

While the focus of this book is on romantic attraction, most of the evidence I'll present also helps to explain the formation of any sort of relationship, whether it's friendships, short-term sexual relationships, or long-term romantic relationships.* We'll also see just how far these factors still matter in new forms of relationship formation, particularly in online dating. And while I'll highlight group differences where there are any, I'll also reveal how the four factors of attraction I've mentioned above exert very similar effects across groups of people, including those that differ in gender and sexual orientation. But does this mean that all

---

* In fact, the evidence I present may also help to explain relationships between humans and artificial intelligence, as in Spike Jonze's film *Her*. In the film, a man in the near future develops a relationship with an intelligent computer operating system, but many of the processes involved in that hypothetical relationship are similar to what scientists know about relationship formation between humans.

the mystery of attraction can be explained away? Not necessarily. Scientists can explain the general processes involved in attraction very well, but ultimately some aspects of attraction will remain beyond the realms of explanation (this is why relationship advice and dating tips are so difficult to put into practice). As we'll see in Chapter 7, outside the experimenter's laboratory, the sneaky hand of chance – what psychologists refer to as 'serendipity' – remains a powerful influence on the formation of relationships.

To conclude, in this book I'll explore how four factors – proximity, physical attractiveness, similarity, and reciprocity – affect the formation of relationships. But to repeat the point I made a short moment ago: these factors do not constitute laws of attraction. To put it more bluntly, this isn't a self-help book. Nor is it a manual to help you or anyone else get laid. This book doesn't come with guarantees of success in romance or the promise of immediate success in dating. But, even if the four factors we'll look at do not constitute laws of attraction, a better understanding of their effects may be useful in our everyday lives. The science of attraction and relationship formation can't guarantee you a date tonight, but it can point the way towards forming mutually benefitting relationships with other people.

2

GETTING UP CLOSE AND PERSONAL

OR, WHY GEOGRAPHY MATTERS, HOW THE INTERNET IS (AND ISN'T) CHANGING HOW WE FORM RELATIONSHIPS, AND A BEAUTY-MAP OF LONDON

Despite her mysterious persona, there are a few things we know about Ramona Flowers. We know that she works for amazon.ca and that she's capable of travelling through Subspace. We also know that she frequently changes her hair colour, that she can be quite sarcastic, and that she has seven evil exes who Scott Pilgrim has to overcome if he is to win Ramona's affection. And, lastly, we know that Ramona has recently moved to Toronto from New York. This last fact may not seem particularly important when we think about any potential relationship between Ramona and Scott, but it actually points to the hidden power that proximity exerts on the formation of relationships.

It might seem obvious, trivial even, but an important predictor of whether any two people will form a relationship with each other is physical proximity. Scientists studying this topic have come up with all sorts of names for this phenomenon – 'propinquity' is one of my favourites – but the simple fact is that most people form relationships with others who sit in the same class at school, take the same course at university, live in the same neighbourhood, or work at the same place. In fact, the chances of Ramona and Scott forming any sort of relationship would have remained very low had she stayed in New York. Conversely, her move to Toronto actually made it much more likely that the two of them would meet and initiate a relationship.

If you've never given much thought to the power of proximity, don't worry – you're not alone. When psychologist Susan Sprecher gave participants in one study a list of predictors of attraction and asked them to rate the extent to which these factors applied to the initial attraction they felt toward someone else, environmental factors including proximity were rated the least important.[1] Proximity also doesn't figure prominently, if at all, in the schemes of most self-help texts. In fact, it hasn't always appeared on the radar of attraction researchers either. That changed in the 1930s when James Bossard, then a professor of sociology at the University of Pennsylvania, forced us to think again about how relationships are formed.

THE CURIOUS CASE OF RESIDENTIAL PROPINQUITY

James Bossard wanted to know the answer to a seemingly simple question: 'To what extent do the constant and repeated contacts of the neighbourhood, in the drug stores, the shopping places, the churches, the street corners, etc., lead to more romantic relationships?' His attempt to answer the question began with him examining five thousand marriage licences that were registered in Philadelphia between January and May 1931. By tabulating the addresses of residences declared by both applicants at the time of the application for the marriage licence, Bossard was able to calculate the 'residential propinquity' – or the geographical distance – of each pair of spouses.

He found that about 12 per cent of the couples lived at the same address – in other words, they were probably cohabiting before deciding to get married. More interesting was the fact that just over 4 per cent lived at the same block but not the same address, about 23 per cent lived within two blocks of each other and about a third of all couples lived within five blocks of each other. Only about 17 per cent of marriages took place between individuals who lived in different cities. Bossard had discovered the seemingly curious finding that, as the geographical distance between couples increased, the number of marriages decreased. 'Cupid may have wings,' he concluded, 'but apparently they are not adapted for long flights'.[2]

Other researchers came to surprisingly similar conclusions. One study of marriage licenses issued in 1931 in New Haven, Connecticut, found that just over half of couples lived within twenty blocks of each other. Another, published in 1952, showed that about a third of some 400 couples that applied for marriage licenses in Columbus, Ohio, were separated by a distance of no more than five blocks when they first started dating. Just over a half of couples in the same study lived less than seventeen blocks from each other at the time of their first date. By the end of the 1950s, at least thirteen further studies had been published in support of Bossard's ground-breaking conclusion that the chances of a relationship increases when two people live near each other, with data coming from places as far removed as Duluth (Minnesota), Warren (Ohio), and Genesee County (New York).[3]

British researchers arrived on the scene slightly later, but came to very similar conclusions. In 1969, the geographer P. J. Perry published a paper that examined the marriage distance of working-class residents in twenty-seven West Dorset parishes between 1837 and 1936. Ostensibly, at least, the study was about the ending of isolation in the English countryside. West Dorset was, at the time, almost wholly rural and the twenty-seven parishes that Perry investigated formed two distinct agricultural regions, the Blackmore Vale in the north – what Thomas Hardy had called the 'Vale of Little Dairies' in *Tess of the d'Urbervilles* – and the chalk downs in the south.

In examining the marriage registers of these parishes, Perry found that the vast majority of marriages – just over 80 per cent – took place among inhabitants of the same parish. That equated to a distance of, at most, a few miles. This pattern of mainly intra-parochial marriages remained the norm until the mid-1880s. But then began steady decline, until only 32 per cent of marriages took place between people who lived in the same parish between 1927 and 1936. But even then, 75 per cent of marriages still took place between people who lived no further than 12 miles from each other. Although a number of different factors account for this change (higher wages and better education, for example), the most intriguing must be the possibility that the Licensing Bill of 1872, which closed pubs at an earlier hour, 'made the village inn generally less attractive as a social centre, forcing the countryman to look elsewhere for his recreation, and generally to become less parochial and introspective'.[4]

Some of the best work in Britain was conducted by the demographer David Coleman in the 1980s. In a survey of newlyweds in Reading, Coleman found that about a quarter were born less than six miles apart and half lived about three miles from each other when they met. Another, much larger study of over a thousand marriages that were celebrated in England and Wales in 1979 showed that just over a half of these took place between partners who lived about three miles from each other. As Coleman and a colleague noted, that's 'an hour's walk, 15 minutes' cycle ride, or 5 minutes travelling by car or motorbike'.[5] What's more, about a third lived no more than 1.5 miles from each other and a fifth lived hardly a few streets apart when they got married. Most people, it seemed, found their spouses quite close to home.

You'd be wrong to think that things have changed since then. The best contemporary research is being done in the Netherlands by Karen Haandrikman and her colleagues. In one study, these researchers used the Dutch population register to examine about 144,000 couples that began living together in 2004.[6] They found that, at birth, the average distance between future cohabiters was about thirty miles. Five years before cohabitation, the average distance dropped to seventeen miles – about a half of couples were living within a five-mile radius – and, just before cohabitation, the average distance dropped even further, to fourteen miles. In fact, half of all new cohabiters in 2004 found their partners within a four-mile radius and the most common distance between partners was about half a mile. What Haandrikman and her colleagues call 'distance-decay' is highly important in decisions about relationship formation. Most partners are found at very short distances and the further away two people live, the less likely they are to form a relationship. In short, geography matters.

PICKING THE RIGHT RANDOM NUMBER

Beginning in the 1950s, social psychologists took an interest in the way physical proximity influences who we become friends and lovers with. Perhaps the most famous, and certainly the most influential, of the studies that emerged from this period were conducted by Leon Festinger and two of his colleagues, Stanley Schachter and Kurt Back. The three social psychologists wanted to know what happens when strangers live in close proximity to each other.[7] They figured that the best way to study this without being intrusive was to focus on social relationships in student housing, where strangers are randomly assigned to live together.

Festinger and his colleagues chose a small community known as the Westgate Housing Project, part of the campus of the Massachusetts Institute of Technology. The buildings of the Westgate complex were built in a U-shape, with the exteriors facing the street and the interiors facing a central courtyard. Each apartment block had ten single-family units divided over two floors, with a married couple living in each unit. So far, so good. What the researchers wanted to know was how physical closeness affected each resident's attraction to other residents in the complex.

They were actually studying two types of proximity. The first related to the location of apartment, or what they called 'functional distance'. Festinger and his colleagues noticed that the buildings of the Westgate complex were constructed in such a way that some apartments offered more opportunities for social interaction between residents. An apartment at the bottom of a staircase would have to be passed by anyone wanting to get to the second floor. The residents of this well-placed apartment would, therefore, have better opportunities to interact with others, get to know them, and form friendships. The same was true of residents of apartments near mailboxes. In contrast, people living in apartments facing the street had no next-door neighbours and, as a consequence, had fewer friends from the complex than did residents who lived in apartments facing the courtyard.*

---

* There's another possible explanation for these findings. Psychologist Frances Cherry argues that Festinger and his colleagues missed the fact that there were many women with children living in the Westgate Housing Project. For these women, it made sense to rely on others nearby, whether it was next door or in the same building, because having children meant that participants in the study were less likely to stray too far. In her reinterpretation of the Westgate studies, Cherry concludes that relationship formation in that context was shaped by the physical circumstances of having to care for young children. More than this, she cautions against forgetting the lived experience of women in the Westgate studies: 'One man's social psychology is another woman's social history'.

Just as important as functional distance was the 'physical distance' between apartments. The researchers found that, the closer residents lived to each other, the more likely they were to become friends. In fact, residents were twice as likely to become friends with their next-door neighbours (who lived about 20 feet away) than with residents who lived two doors away (about 40 feet away). And only 10 per cent of those who lived on opposite ends of the building said they were close friends. Similarly, people who lived in the same building were more likely to be friends with others from the same building compared with residents from adjacent buildings. When the researchers asked people in Westgate to choose their three closest friends from the whole complex, 65 per cent of the friends that were mentioned lived in the same building.

What was remarkable about the Westgate studies was that Festinger and his colleagues didn't just find evidence that people are more likely to form close relationships with others who live nearby, they were also able to quantify the effect. Moreover, they demonstrated an intriguing 'architecture of friendship', where simple features of the environment like where a staircase is placed can affect who you form a relationship with. There's simply no doubting the lasting impact of the Westgate studies – they remain some of the best field studies conducted in social psychology. It's no surprise that Stanley Schachter later recalled this period working with Festinger as one of the high points of his scientific career.*

---

* More than half a century later, the Westgate studies began to infiltrate contemporary approaches to office design. When Steve Jobs famously redesigned the offices at Pixar, he noticed that their offices housed computer scientists, animators, and editors in separate buildings, which discouraged them from sharing ideas. To change this, he designed a single cavernous office that housed the entire Pixar team and a central

In the years following the publication of the Westgate studies, other researchers confirmed the basic finding that proximity is a powerful predictor of attraction, at least among university students. One study followed students who had moved into a newly-constructed college dorm. After eight months, the students were asked to name who they were friends with from the building. Roommates were named as friends twice as often as floormates and floormates twice as often as students on other floors of the building. Similarly, studies have shown that students living in high-rise dormitories report fewer opportunities for friendship formation compared to students living in smaller, low-rise dormitories. In high-rise dorms, those who live on lower, more accessible floors report a greater number of friends in the building than those living on higher floors. Evidence from Dartmouth College in New Hampshire indicates that students living in dorms even send far more emails to those who live near them than those who live in more distant rooms.[8] You might think they're being lazy, but in reality it highlights the importance of proximity in the formation of relationships.

Despite the impact of these studies, it's difficult not to wonder about the relevance of the Westgate studies to non-student populations. For example, a commonly-held stereotype suggests that city living fosters anonymity, that many people do not even know their own neighbours, let alone people who live down the road. As it turns out, studies of non-student housing reiterate the importance of proximity in the formation of relationships. In one study, Lucille Nahemow and M. Powell Lawton interviewed residents in three fourteen-storey buildings that comprised the Dyckman Houses in New York. Residents were asked who their best friends were in the housing project. Like the work of

---

atrium that facilitates interactions between co-workers and promotes 'unplanned collaborations'.

Festinger and his colleagues, this study showed how both physical and functional distance affected relationship formation. Of the residents who were interviewed, 88 per cent said that their closest friend in the project lived in the same building and about half said their closest friend lived on the same floor. And more than half said they had met their friends in 'the hallways, elevators, and entrance areas' of their own buildings.[9]

The effect of proximity on the formation of relationships isn't limited to social housing. One researcher assigned trainees at the Maryland State Police Academy to seats in alphabetical order. At the end of the term, she asked the trainees to name their three closest friends. Most named a recruit whose last name started with the same letter as theirs. In other words, two recruits sitting next to each other at the start of the term were more likely to become close friends than recruits sitting further apart. Another study of five public schools found that teachers who took breaks at the same time or who had classrooms on the same floor felt more emotionally attached to each other. And when scientists have similar research interests, they are about four times more likely to co-author research publications if their offices are in the same corridor and not on different floors in the same building.[10]

In one of my favourite experimental studies of this effect, Mitja Back and his colleagues randomly assigned first-year university students studying psychology a seat at the beginning of an introductory class. The students were then asked to come up to the front of the class individually, beginning on the right-hand side of each row, and introduce themselves. Immediately after each introduction, the other students rated how likeable the person was and how much they would like to get to know her or him. After the evaluation, the students in that row all moved one seat to the right, with the evaluated student taking the seat at the far left of the row. The procedure was then repeated row by row until all students had been evaluated. One year later, students were presented with photographs of their fellow students and were asked to rate the intensity of their friendship to each.

When the researchers examined the initial attraction ratings, they found that participants rated students who sat in neighbouring seats as the most attractive, followed by other students who sat in the same row. Least attractive were students who had no discernible physical seating relation. But proximity didn't just affect initial attraction. One year later, students who had sat next to each other in that very first introductory class were more likely to be close friends than those who sat in the same row, who in turn were closer friends than those who sat further away. 'In a nutshell,' Back and his colleagues wrote, 'people may become friends simply because they drew the right random number'.[11]

PUBLIC, CLOSED, AND PRIVATE PLACES... AND THE INTERNET

So we're more likely to form relationships with people who are nearby. But this doesn't tell us very much about where exactly these meetings take place. Fortunately, scientists have asked and answered this question. The most important studies in this context are those of French sociologists Michel Bozon and François Héran, who studied meeting places of couples in twentieth-century France.[12] In their work, they distinguished between three types of places where we meet potential partners. The first are 'public' meeting places, like bars and parks, which are open to anyone. The second are 'closed' or 'select' meeting places, such as workplaces and universities, where admission is granted only to people who fulfil certain criteria. And the last are 'private' places, such as your circle of family members or friends.

Bozon and Héran were mainly interested in class differences in where people met their future romantic partners. They suggested that higher class individuals were more likely to meet partners in closed or private places, whereas working class individuals were more likely to meet partners in public places. Just as interesting are historical trends in where people meet their partners. More than a century ago, for example, future partners tended to meet very close to home, typically through the family, church, or friends. But since the 1960s, Bozon and Héran noted that there had been a shift towards more meetings in public places – particularly nightclubs, parties, and on holiday – and among friends, while the number of people meeting through family gatherings had fallen.

Nor are the French unique in this respect. Up until the end of the twentieth century, at least, about a fifth of Britons and Americans met their future partners through their families, friends, or acquaintances, and about two-fifths met in public places like nightclubs and bars. However, by far the most common places to have met a partner in Britain and the United States were closed places, mainly work and university, but also through clubs or associations (sports clubs, political parties, and so on).[13] The most likely reason for the trends toward relationship formation in closed places is that the percentage of the population with a higher qualification increased in the second half of the twentieth century and this group are more likely to meet their partners in work settings. In the twentieth century, it seems that universities and workplaces replaced the fairs and balls of many decades ago.

But one problem with these studies is that they predate the Internet era, with more recent evidence suggesting that public, closed, and private places are all being eclipsed by the number of people meeting online. To examine just how far the Internet has changed the way people meet their romantic partners, sociologists Michael Rosenfeld and Reuben Thomas launched the How Couples Meet and Stay Together survey in 2009. The survey asked 4,002 American adults (including 3,009 with a spouse or romantic partner) open- and closed-ended questions about how they met their current partner, which allows for one of the most accurate pictures of how couples met than has previously been available.[14]

The results of the survey are illuminating. They suggest that traditional ways of meeting a future partner – through the family or friends, meeting in the neighbourhood, or at school – have been in steep decline since the start of the 2000s. For example, while the percentage of heterosexual couples whose first meeting was arranged by friends almost doubled between 1940 and 1990 (from about 20 to 40 per cent), it has been in decline ever since, dipping below 30 per cent for the most recently formed couples. Moreover, while about a fifth of heterosexual couples still meet at work or university, these figures have also been in decline since the mid-1990s. By contrast, the percentage of couples meeting online has risen dramatically since the mid-1990s, now accounting for about a fifth of all heterosexual couplings in the United States. So dramatic has been this rise that Rosenfeld and Thomas believe the Internet will soon eclipse friends as the most influential way Americans meet their romantic partners.

The figures are even more dramatic among same-sex couples in the How Couples Meet and Stay Together survey. While lesbians and gay men have always been less likely than heterosexuals to meet their partners via family members and more likely to do so at bars and restaurants, it is notable that same-sex couplings that began through friends has suffered a steep decline since the mid-1990s. By contrast, more than 60 per cent of same-sex couples that met after 2008 met online. Meeting online has not only become the dominant way that same-sex couples in the United States meet, it is now more common among same-sex couples than any way of meeting has ever been for couples, heterosexual or same-sex. To an even greater extent than for heterosexual couples, meeting online seems to be eclipsing all other ways of meeting for same-sex couples.* Another much larger study of lesbian, gay, bisexual, transgender, and queer adolescents in the United States also found that they were much more likely to initiate romantic relationships online than heterosexual adolescents.[15]

What, then, should we make of the findings of James Bossard in an age when dating can occur in a way that shatters most, if not all, geographic boundaries? It turns out that geography may still matter, even among online daters. The sociologist Andrea Baker notes that, because the intention of online dating is to eventually meet with someone, geographic location continues to exert an effect on daters.[16] In her studies of Internet couples, she found that online daters were much less likely to interact with others who lived far away from them in geographical terms compared with those who lived nearby. Or, as one respondent who was interviewed in another study put it, 'Geography is important. Thirty minute drive is enough for me; 21 sets of traffic lights max. I used to see someone who lived in Frankston – 35–40 minute drive – too far. If it's interstate, then all you have is a funtime buddy, that's no relationship...'.[17]

This isn't particularly surprising when you consider that online dating sites give users the option of pre-limiting the distance they search for potential partners in. It's even more apparent on location-aware mobile dating apps like Grindr and Tinder, where shared location is the underlying mechanism for initiating interactions with known contacts and strangers. Indeed, Baker believes that geographical proximity remains one of the most important factors determining whether any two online daters will meet offline. When users encounter others who live outside their own prespecified geographical area – the

---

* The main reason for this, Rosenfeld and Thomas suggest, is that gay men and lesbians inhabit a thin dating market and that the Internet facilitates searching for something uncommon.

maximum distance they are willing to travel to meet someone – they're much more likely to reject that person outright. And when online daters themselves are asked about the criteria they are looking for in other daters' profiles, proximity appears as an important factor for both women and men. For online daters, like their offline counterparts, it would seem that distance is a turn-off.

BUMPING INTO EACH OTHER

So far, we've seen that the likelihood of attraction, becoming friends, or forming a romantic relationship increases as the physical distance between two people decreases. Students who sit next to each other in class, residents on the same floor of a building, employees who work in the same office, commuters who get the same bus every morning, regular visitors to the same art gallery – they're all more likely to be attracted to each other and form relationships because of the power of proximity. But why exactly?

The obvious answer is that proximity matters because it increases the likelihood of unplanned encounters between strangers and acquaintances. Beyond initial contact and knowing that the other person exists, these chance meetings can determine whether two people will continue seeing each other. Imagine you meet someone interesting at a party. A few days later, you bump into each other at a gig your friends are playing at. You say hello, make small talk for a short while – it turns out, you don't live very far from each other. The week after that you bump into each other again, this time at a bus stop. You have a longer conversation this time and the conversation flows more easily. A few days later, you bump into each other again, this time at your local pub. By now, you recognise each other easily and you have lots to talk about.

The experience is a surprisingly common one. In fact, it helps to explain the attraction that Scott Pilgrim feels toward Ramona.

Having seen her at the library, he bumps into her at a party before finally orchestrating to meet her again. Like Scott and Ramona, we're much more likely to get to know someone who attends the same university or lives in the same area simply because there are more opportunities to do so. What's more, people who live near each other often shop in the same stores, attend the same schools, go for walks in the same parks, all of which provide opportunities to meet and interact. It's all about availability.

Proximity is the lubricant that facilitates liking, and with each encounter – whether by chance or not – there is a greater likelihood of mutual attraction being sparked. As Richard Moreland noted in his 'social integration theory', individuals who frequently interact with each other are more likely to feel part of the same 'social unit'.[18] Repeated interaction fosters a sense of 'groupness': the more strangers interact, the more they come to feel part of the same group and the more others treat them as part of a group. One researcher watched twelve women who worked at separate desks organised in three rows. The women did not have to work together very much, but that didn't stop them from frequently interacting. Every fifteen minutes, the researcher noted who was interacting with whom, and over the course of several weeks recorded over 1,500 conversations. The interactions took place mainly between women who sat at neighbouring desks, and the frequency of interactions also predicted the formation of cliques within the larger group of women.[19]

So proximity facilitates interaction, which in turn gives individuals the sense that they share something in common. There's also some evidence that our social circles are geographically limited. Social networking sites notwithstanding, our social environments tend to be centred on what geographers call our 'activity space'. This refers to all the locations with which we have regular, almost day-to-day contact. We might also call this our 'comfort zones'. I go to work, I meet my friends in the same places, I walk my dogs along the same routes, and only very rarely do I venture further afield. In fact, when people are asked to report their recent social interactions, they say that the majority of interactions take place nearby and only very occasionally do they take place over greater distances.[20] So, if we were to rely on our own activity spaces, it would probably mean finding a potential partner from a limited geographical area.

But that's not all. Bridging distance usually means investing a good deal of time, money, or effort. Given the choice of identical first dates in the restaurant down the road or one located on the other side of town, we're much more likely to go local. It's not that we're lazy, but rather that staying local is easier, less time-consuming, and less costly. I once heard a student of mine talk about a potential date as being 'geographically undesirable' – though she thought the two of them would make a great couple, her potential date simply lived too far away to be considered seriously. It's certainly true that distance matters much less now than it did, say, a century or two ago, but that doesn't mean that distance doesn't still exert an effect on our romantic choices.

There's one other reason why proximity matters, which we'll encounter in more detail in Chapter 6, and this is that we like people who are similar to us, and similar people live nearby. Most neighbourhoods tend to be populated by individuals who are similar along socioeconomic, ethnic, cultural, religious, occupational, or educational lines. This is sometimes referred to as 'differential association' or 'spatial homogamy' – it simply means that people tend to live among others who are similar to themselves. So, if we like people who are similar to us (and, as we'll see, we do), then it makes sense to find a partner from the pool of people living nearby. In fact, in one early study of the effects of proximity on marital choice in New Haven, Connecticut, the researchers concluded that, 'Practically no intermarriages... occurred between areas far removed in social, economic, and cultural traits'.[21]

ROBERT ZAJONC AND THE CURIOUS CASE OF MERE EXPOSURE

There's more to proximity than simply facilitating interaction. But before we find out why, here's a little experiment you can do. From the alphabet below, simply select your two favourite letters. Don't take too long to think about it. Just go with your gut feeling.

A B C D E F G H I J K L M
N O P Q R S T U V W X Y Z

Now let me try a bit of mind-reading. Am I right in thinking that your two favourite letters appear in your own name? If I'm right, then I've just demonstrated what's known as the 'name-letter effect', the outcome of one of my favourite psychological tests because of its sheer simplicity. First reported by Belgian psychologist Jozef Nuttin in the mid-1980s, the 'name-letter effect' refers to finding that most people prefer letters appearing in their own name, especially their first and last initials, over other letters in the alphabet.[22] My favourite letters are 'V' and 'S', which probably wouldn't have surprised Nuttin very much.

In fact, studies show that people of different nationalities, who speak different languages, and of different age groups all prefer letters appearing in their own name. There's even some evidence of a birthday-number effect – a similar preference for numbers appearing in your birthday – and a preference for jobs, cities, and romantic partners with similar names to us, although some of these findings are more controversial. Weirder still are studies suggesting that people prefer careers that are related to their names. In the United States, for example, people named Dennis or Denise are over-represented among dentists, while people named George or Geoffrey are over-represented among geologists.[23]

So, anyway, I like letters appearing in my own name – but what's that got to do with proximity and attraction? The answer is simple: although the name-letter effect reflects, on the one hand, the fact that we like things that are associated with ourselves, it's also a reflection of how often we see letters in our own name. Over the course of our lives, we write and see our own name countless times and so it's not surprising that we show a preference for letters in our own name. In fact, the theory of 'mere exposure' suggests just this: we show a stronger preference for stimuli (letters, faces, strange shapes, and so on) that we see more frequently. Its relevance to attraction? The theory of mere exposure predicts that attraction can be sparked by seeing someone more frequently. It may sound too good to be true, but decades of research attest to the strength of the mere exposure effect.

One of the earliest examples of the mere exposure effect was documented by the British psychologist Edward Titchener in 1910, who described the 'glow of warmth' we feel in the presence of something that's familiar.[24] But when Titchener tested the idea, he found that preferences for objects were unrelated to people's impressions of how familiar the objects were and so the idea of mere exposure remained in psychology's blind spot for the best part of about fifty years. The scholar who's best known for reviving and developing interest in the mere exposure effect is the Polish-born American social psychologist Robert Zajonc. In the 1960s, Zajonc became interested in the way in which living creatures react to new stimuli in their environment. When presented with some new object, most organisms usually react with fear. When I first brought home a new bicycle, my dog (then a puppy) Brick initially avoided going near it. I suppose I would've done the same had I stumbled across an object more than triple my size. But with increasing exposure to the bicycle, Brick began to approach and observe the new stimulus, sniffing and licking it. Now, he reacts with a crazy sort of happiness whenever I walk through the front door with my bike.

It was an observation like this one about Brick that led Zajonc to his ground-breaking work on the mere exposure effect. In a series of ingenious lab experiments, he showed that simply exposing people to a familiar stimulus led them to rate it more positively than other similar stimuli that hadn't been presented. In one experiment, Zajonc showed his participants Chinese calligraphy characters and nonsense syllables, with some characters being presented more frequently than others. The participants were then told that the symbols were adjectives and were asked to rate whether the symbols held positive or negative connotations. The symbols that had been seen more frequently were consistently rated more positively than those that were presented less frequently.

In other words, the more times the participants in Zajonc's study had seen a Chinese ideograph or nonsense syllable, the more likely they were to say it meant something good. In another study, he showed participants twelve photographs of Michigan State University seniors taken from a yearbook. Each photograph was displayed for a couple of seconds, but some pictures were shown only once, while others were shown up to twenty-five times. When Zajonc asked his participants to rate how much they liked each of the men in the photographs, he found a clear relationship between frequency of exposure and liking. The more times participants saw a man's face, the more they liked him.[25]

The mere exposure effect may seem trivial, but to fully appreciate its implications, have a read of this excerpt from a short article circulated by Associated Press in 1967:

A mysterious student has been attending a class at Oregon State University for the past two months enveloped in a big black bag. Only his bare feet show. Each Monday, Wednesday, and Friday at 11AM, the Black Bag sits on a small table near the back of the classroom. The class is Speech 113 – basic persuasion. The Black Bag seldom speaks or moves. But a newsman who attended the class says his presence becomes overwhelming. Charles Goetzinger, professor of the class, knows the identity of the person inside. None of the 20 students in the class do.

So, a student came to class in a large, black bag with only his feet visible and sat on a table at the back of the classroom. Curiously, Goetzinger found exactly what Zajonc might have predicted: the students in the class initially treated the black bag with hostility, but over time, their hostility gave way to curiosity, and eventually to friendship. The experiment showed that simply presenting the student-in-the-black-bag to students repeatedly over the course of a semester was enough to change their attitudes toward it.

When I first read the article, I thought about repeating Goetzinger's cheeky experiment with my own students, but finding a volunteer to sit through classes for an hour a week in a black bag proved more difficult that I'd expected. So, instead, I got myself a mannequin and dressed him in a pair of jeans, a t-shirt, and some dark sunglasses. The morning before the first class of term, I turned up early and seated the mannequin – who I'd taken to calling 'Hugh', because he had a passing resemblance to Hugh Laurie – at the back of the room. When my students arrived for class, I briefly introduced Hugh, but then said nothing more about him. At the end of the class, I asked all my students to rate how much they liked Hugh, as well as how interesting and 'cool' they thought he was.

Over the course of twelve weeks, I did the same thing every Monday (I sometimes wondered whether my students had thought that I'd gone mad, but none of them ever said anything). At the end of the twelve weeks, I looked at the data I'd collected and it was just as Zajonc might've predicted: Hugh became more likeable over the semester. Not only that, my students also thought he was more interesting and 'cooler' at the end of twelve weeks than after the first time they'd met Hugh. My little experiment wasn't as robust as it could've been – it's possible, for example, that my psychology students had figured out what I was up to and changed their ratings to keep me happy – but it does highlight the power of mere exposure in a small way.

Here's better proof of the mere exposure effect in the classroom. In this study, Richard Moreland and Scott Beach selected four women who looked like typical students to act as 'confederates' – a psychologist's way of saying they were 'in' on the experiment. All four had their pictures taken, then attended class in different frequencies. One never went to class, another attended five classes, the third attended ten, and the fourth attended class fifteen times over the semester. At the end of the semester, students in the class were presented with slides of all four women and were asked to rate them on various traits, such as popularity, honesty, intelligence, and physical attractiveness. They were also asked to record their beliefs about how much they liked the women, would enjoy spending time with them, and wanted to work with them on a mutual project. Once again, Zajonc was proved right. The more classes a confederate had attended, the more other students were attracted to her and wanted to spend time with her.[26]

What's more, there's evidence that mere exposure affects how we perceive other people. In one study, participants viewed photographs of men who were smiling slightly and were asked to rate the photographs on a number of dimensions – how far apart the eyes were set, how round the face was, and so on. Next, they were shown the same faces along with new photographs of men, also smiling slightly, and were asked to rate how happy the men's facial expressions were. Despite there being no differences in the degree to which the men in the photographs were smiling, participants consistently rated the familiar faces as happier than the new faces. But we don't just rate faces we've seen before as happier, we also smile more ourselves when we see familiar faces. Another study used the same basic methodology as before, showing participants photographs of some familiar faces along with new faces they hadn't seen before. But, in this study, while rating the faces, participants also had their facial muscle activity measured. The researchers found that faces that were viewed more frequently weren't only rated as more likeable, but also evoked more muscle activity in the cheeks. Viewing the same face with increasing frequency made participants smile.[27]

Likewise, there's evidence that we behave more positively towards stimuli we've been exposed to before. Robert Bornstein and his colleagues asked participants to take part in a decision-making task with two other 'participants' who were in fact confederates. Their task was to read a number of poems and decide, by majority vote, the sex of the poems' authors. In some of these tasks, the confederates were trained to disagree with each other, forcing the participant to cast the deciding vote. Prior to all of this, however, the participants had been surreptitiously exposed to one of the two confederates. The results of this experiment showed that participants were more likely to agree with the confederate they had been mere-exposed to previously compared to the non-exposed individual.[28]

HAVE WE MET BEFORE?

It wouldn't be much of an exaggeration to say that the theory of mere exposure is one of the most successful ideas in the history of social psychology. There are over two hundred studies supporting the general idea that the more frequently we're exposed to a stimulus – whether it's a person, sounds, drawings, words and names, objects, or even nonsense symbols – the more we like it.[29] The mere exposure effect has even been implicated in voting decisions in the Eurovision Song Contest: between 2008 and 2011, contestants did better if they had previously appeared in a semi-final that was seen by voters.[30] And the theory helps explain why we like others who are nearby. The student who comes to class in a black bag is likeable simply because she's there each week. Or, the person you see every morning on the commute to work seems happy and makes you smile more precisely because you see them every morning. But why does mere exposure have this effect?

The short answer is that increasing exposure to a stimulus makes that stimulus seem more familiar. And, in contrast to the commonsensical idea that familiarity breeds contempt, familiarity actually breeds liking. One reason why familiar stimuli tend to be liked is because our brains process them more easily – or 'fluently' in the parlance of psychologists – and this cognitive and perceptual fluency is experienced more positively. Evolutionary factors may also play a hand in shaping our reactions to familiar people. In general, novel stimuli tend to breed feelings of uncertainty and result in wary reactions. This is a common response in both humans and other animals – recall Brick and my bicycle. But, if repeated exposure shows the stimulus to be harmless, then we're more likely to respond favourably to the stimulus. Brick now knows my bike is harmless, so he can relax in its presence.

Another explanation for why familiarity breeds liking invokes classical conditioning, a theory made famous by Ivan Pavlov and his experiments with salivating dogs. The idea is that most social interactions leave favourable impressions and are mildly positive – or at least are not negative – and other people who we encounter more frequently become paired with that positive feeling. In the same way that Pavlov's dogs were conditioned to salivate upon hearing the sound of a bell, we come to believe that interactions with familiar people will be rewarding. To test this idea, Harry Reis and his colleagues asked college students to sit across a table from each other. An experimenter then held up a set of cards, each of which showed a question that had been designed to encourage disclosure of information. For example, one question read, 'If a crystal ball could tell you the truth about yourself, your life, your future, or anything else, what would you want to know?'

Some participants were only shown two cards, whereas others were shown six. But in both cases, one participant would ask the question, which the other would answer for thirty seconds. Then the question would be repeated and the first participant would give her or his answer, again for thirty seconds. This continued until all the questions had been asked and answered by both participants. The results showed that, when participants had an opportunity to become more familiar with each other (the six-card condition), their attraction to each other increased compared to when they had little opportunity to become familiar (the two-card condition). In a second study, the researchers had participants who didn't know each other chat freely by email, using anonymous screen-names, once, twice, four times, six times, or eight times in a week. When asked to rate their partners, the researchers found that ratings increased with the number of interactions participants had. Participants who chatted more frequently were also more likely to want to stay in touch with their partners.[31]

Familiarity also has some rather curious outcomes. Here's one that you could examine for yourself using any basic computer graphics programme. First, take a photograph of your face facing the camera. Next, on your computer graphics programme, flip the image horizontally (left-side-right) so you end up with two images – the original and your flipped version. Which image of yourself do you think you'd prefer? Theodore Mita and his colleagues did something similar. University students had their photos taken and were later shown the same photo along with a mirror image of it. Asked which picture they liked better, most participants preferred the mirror image. But when a close friend of the participants was asked which photo they liked more and which was more flattering for their friend, most preferred the true image. The reason? Because we're more used to seeing our mirror image, this is the view of ourselves that we prefer. Our friends, on the other hand, usually prefer our regular faces because those are the faces that *they* are used to seeing.[32]

Familiarity may also help to explain why people tend to marry individuals who are similar to themselves in terms of a range of physical features, as we will see in more detail in Chapter 6. The similarities between spouses has led some writers to suggest that a process of sexual imprinting takes place in humans, where early caregiving experiences from familiar people helps to organise the 'search images' that people develop in terms of what is desirable in a partner. Sexual imprinting was first described by ethologists who noted that geese that were reared by humans often directed their mating behaviour toward humans rather than other geese.[33] More recently, familiarity with our parents' and caregivers' faces has been implicated in our own preferences for potential partners.

Only a handful of studies have tested this idea, but it's possible that we sexually imprint onto familiar caregivers. In one investigation of this issue, researchers obtained photographs of women's spouses and their adoptive fathers. A sample of more than two hundred undergraduate students then attempted to match each woman's adoptive father with her spouse in a multiple-choice test (one photograph showed the true spouse and the other three were foils). The results showed that judges were able to match the women's adoptive father with their spouses much better than would be expected by chance, suggesting that early rearing experiences with a familiar caregiver may shape preferences in adulthood. Judges have also been shown to correctly match wives to their mothers-in-law at a higher rate than would be expected by chance.[34]

In another study, Chris Fraley and Michael Marks showed that, when college students were asked to judge photographs of strangers, the faces were rated as more sexually appealing when they were preceded by subliminally-presented photos of the student's own opposite-sex parent.[35] In other words, participants judged photographs of strangers as more appealing when the image of their mother's face (for men) or their father's face (for women) had been presented to them subconsciously. On another task, participants rated faces they hadn't seen before as more sexually attractive if those faces had been morphed with their own faces, compared with faces that were morphed with an unrelated face. Such findings raise intriguing questions about the effects of familiarity, but the findings are controversial.*

Other researchers believe that familiar-looking faces should elicit more positive effects in non-sexual contexts, but not in sexual contexts because of inbreeding's detrimental effects on offspring. To test this prediction, Lisa DeBruine transformed facial photographs of participants using composite images to create same-sex and opposite-sex faces that resembled participants' own faces. When asked to judge these self-resembling images, familiar faces were rated as more attractive when it was

---

* Controversial because it raises a discomforting question: if proximity, increased exposure, and familiarity lead to greater liking, then wouldn't that result in sexual attraction to the people who are (usually) nearest to us, our parents and siblings? One answer was provided in 1891 by the Finnish philosopher and anthropologist Edward Westermarck. In *The History of Human Marriage*, he wrote that human beings have an 'innate aversion' to having sex with people who live very closely together from early childhood. The Westermarck hypothesis, as it's now known, suggests that we have biological mechanisms shaped by evolution to prevent the harmful consequences of inbreeding – or what Westermarck politely referred to as 'injurious unions'. This innate aversion to sex with people who grew up in close proximity is what leads people to a moral disapproval of incest. If you agree with Westermarck – and many evolutionary psychologists do – then it's certainly plausible that we have been shaped by evolution to avoid sex with our close relatives. But not everyone agrees: beginning in the 1910s, Sigmund Freud and his followers rejected Westermarck's idea of 'innate aversion' and suggested that, were it not for the incest taboo, sexual attraction between members of a family would be the norm. In fact, in *Totem and Taboo*, Freud provocatively claimed that the repulsion that people express when incest is brought up is actually a reaction to cover up their repressed attraction to close kin. Later, in *A General Introduction to Psychoanalysis*, Freud went further when he claimed that, 'an incestuous love-choice is in fact the first and regular one'. The current consensus is that Freud probably went a little too far, but the debate between followers of Westermarck and Freud rages on.

the same sex but not when it was the opposite sex to participants. The own-sex bias in participants' preferences suggests that, while faces that resemble our own are attractive in non-sexual contexts, they are less attractive when they represent a potential sexual partner.[36]

Even if we set aside the studies on sexual imprinting, there's no denying that familiarity is an important factor in the formation of relationships. According to psychologists Ellen Berscheid and Pamela Regan, of all the general principles of attraction, 'the familiarity principle... is perhaps the most basic.'[37] Familiarity not only fosters interaction because we seek the positive rewards that familiar others provide, it also breeds feelings of comfort and safety with others, which contributes to liking. In addition, familiarity also helps to explain the effects of proximity more generally, because we see people who are nearby more frequently and they therefore become more familiar. But familiarity may also work its magic in a more global sense.

A BEAUTY-MAP OF LONDON

Francis Galton was one of the great Victorian polymaths. He wrote over three hundred scientific papers and books in his lifetime and, though he's sometimes reviled as the 'father of eugenics', Galton is also recognised as a pioneer in such diverse fields as meteorology (among other things, he devised the first weather map), fingerprinting, psychometrics, and statistics. Among his lesser-known endeavours was his attempt to collect data for a 'Beauty-Map' of the British Isles. In his autobiography, he wrote:

> I may here speak of some attempts by myself, made hitherto in too desultory a way, to obtain materials for a 'Beauty-Map' of the British Isles. Whenever I have occasion to classify the persons I meet into three classes, 'good, medium, and bad', I use a needle mounted as a pricker,

wherewith to prick holes, unseen, in a piece of paper, torn rudely into a cross with a long leg. I use its upper end for 'good', the cross-arm for 'medium', the lower end for 'bad'. The prick-holes keep distinct, and are easily read off at leisure. The object, place, and date are written on the paper. I used this plan for my beauty data, classifying the girls I passed in streets or elsewhere as attractive, indifferent, or repellent. Of course this was a purely individual estimate, but it was consistent, judging from the conformity of different attempts in the same population. I found London to rank highest for beauty; Aberdeen lowest.[38]

Perhaps unfair on the women of Aberdeen, but the problem with Galton's Beauty-Map – as he himself recognises – is that it is based entirely on his personal observations of women. Not exactly a scientifically rigorous method. Taking our cue from Galton, Eliana Garcia Hernandez and I decided we would put together a more empirical beauty-map. Ours, though, would be more modest: we would start with the boroughs of London. To begin with, we recruited participants from each of London's thirty-three boroughs. Each participant was asked to complete a short questionnaire in which they rated how attractive they thought women and men in each of the boroughs were.[39]

When we looked at the data we'd collected, we noticed that people in some boroughs were rated as more attractive than others – the City of Westminster and Kensington and Chelsea, for example. In general, people from richer boroughs were rated as more attractive than those from poorer boroughs (where wealth was measured in terms of annual gross pay and average house prices in each borough). So that there are no misunderstandings, let me emphasise that these were the subjective perceptions of Londoners, not objective differences in attractiveness between residents of different boroughs. Inhabitants of Bromley – who were rated the least attractive in our study – can rest easy.

More interesting was the fact that these attractiveness ratings were very strongly associated with ratings of familiarity. When participants were more familiar with a borough, they rated its residents as more physically attractive. Reanalysing the data, I also found that, the further away a borough was from a participant's place of residence, the less familiar she or he was with the borough and the less attractive she or he believed residents of that borough were. In other words, there are strong effects of both proximity and familiarity on our beliefs about the attractiveness of other people who live nearby. In this survey of Londoners, people who lived in nearby boroughs were perceived as more familiar and, therefore, more attractive.

One reason why people who live nearby are perceived as more familiar is because they are more similar to us than people who live further away. For example, researchers are discovering that personality traits are 'geographically clustered' – people with similar personalities tend to live closer together. The west coast of the United States is characterised by higher openness to experience and emotional stability compared with the rest of the country, whereas the east coast has a greater clustering of people with lower conscientiousness. Personality traits are also similarly clustered in London. Based on responses from 56,019 Londoners who completed the BBC's Big Personality Test between 2009 and 2011, researchers discovered that personality traits, particularly openness to experience and extraversion, were spatially clustered in more urban areas. This geographical clustering may improve life satisfaction: extraverts, for example, may gravitate towards specific neighbourhoods because those areas provide more opportunities for social interaction.[40]

Geographical proximity also affects our perceptions of people who live nearby in another way. To better understand why we seek partners within a relatively short distance, Karen Haandrikman and Inge Hutter interviewed thirteen residents of Vriezenveen, a village in the Netherlands, about the effects of geography on partner choice. One thing that became apparent in the course of the interviews was that both younger and older residents preferred partners from their own village. People from the same village were more familiar and had the same shared knowledge, the same background, things that come from sharing an upbringing in the same neighbourhood. In contrast, residents of villages further away were perceived as being less trustworthy, inferior, 'a different sort of people'. Even the littlest things were evidence of that difference, as one participant describes of a friend from another village who moved to Vriezenveen:

> Well eh… when she just lived here for two weeks, she thought, on a Sunday, well, my windows are really dirty, I am going to wash the windows on Sunday. But the whole neighbourhood criticised her so much, like how on earth could she think of washing her windows on a Sunday. She said 'but they do that in Geesteren as well!' 'Well, you don't live in Geesteren, do you? You live in Vriezenveen, and that is not a proper thing to do on Sundays!' Well, she moved back to Geesteren.[41]

If we've learned one thing, it's that in Vriezenveen you don't wash your windows on a Sunday. But more importantly, it looks as though we perceive our physical environments in a biased way. We think people who are nearby are attractive, trustworthy, the sorts of people who we'd want to hang out with, while people who are further away are a strange sort of creature, forever washing their windows on a Sunday afternoon. These beliefs matter because they can affect who we form relationships with. If you believe that people who live further away are somehow devious, then it would make sense to find your partner closer to home.

HOW EMBEDDED ARE YOU AND I?

So far in this chapter, I've discussed the effects of physical proximity, but a growing number of researchers have now turned their attention to 'social proximity effects'. This focus draws on the idea that the social environment – basically any and all

potential persons who could affect the formation of your relationships – can exert an influence on decisions about who we
form relationships with, either directly or indirectly. Consider
the likelihood of you and I forming any sort of relationship. The
idea proposed by social proximity theorists is that the likelihood increases dramatically if we are embedded in social networks that have linkages.[42] To illustrate this point, here are all
my friends on Facebook:

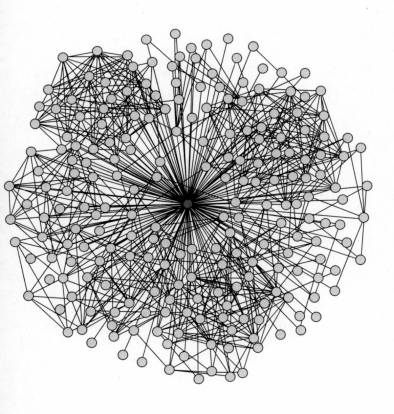

I'm the dot right in the middle and everyone's connections to me and to each other are represented by the lines. Although I don't use Facebook for much these days other than to post pictures of Brick, you can see clear clusters in this network of dots, representing the people I went to school with, my friends and colleagues, and students I work with. This is where network analysis gets interesting. Research using a variety of sources – including Facebook, emails, phone calls, instant messages – shows that the more embedded two people are, or the more they have mutual friends, the more time they spend together, and the more stable the relationship. Predicting how new relationships figure in these networks is difficult, but the evidence suggests that two people are more likely to meet and form a relationship if their social environments are embedded. In other words, the chances of you and I meeting increases as the number of social links separating us decreases.[43]

One way of testing this idea is to see whether the two people in a relationship would already have been connected to each other through their social environment prior to actually meeting one another. In one study, researchers asked students to choose one same-sex friend. For that friend, participants were also asked to list their twelve closest network members. Finally, they were asked to indicate how many of those twelve people they'd met before ever meeting the selected friend. The researchers found that two-thirds of participants knew at least one person in their friend's network prior to actually meeting their friend. Having friends in common makes it more likely that you and I will meet and interact and, the more embedded our social environment, the more stable will be our relationship.[44]

Even more intriguing is the possibility that human beings come equipped with biases that mean we positively evaluate anyone we expect to interact with in the future, particularly people in our social environments. In one clever experiment, John Darley and Ellen Berscheid invited female psychology students to take part in a departmental survey of 'acceptable sexual behaviour in dating situations'. As part of the survey, which was just a ruse, the women were given ambiguous information about two other women, one of whom they were expected to meet and discuss their sexual habits with. Asked how much they liked each one, the researchers found that participants preferred the woman they were going to meet. Other classic research has shown that, even when we anticipate that we will interact with someone we don't like, we perceive them more positively than when we don't expect any interaction. It seems that we accentuate the positives when we anticipate interaction, even with someone we don't like, so that those future encounters are tolerable, if not enjoyable.[45]

In another classic social psychological study, researchers first asked participants to watch a recording of three people having a discussion. Some participants were then led to believe they would be dating one of the people they'd seen in the recording for five weeks. Others were told they would date the same person just once, while yet others did not expect to date any of the people in the recording. The researchers found that participants who expected to date the target for five whole weeks evaluated the person most positively, with the least positive ratings given by those who did not expect a date. In other words, if circumstance forces us to be in someone else's company – for example, if we have to sit next to someone in a classroom over a semester – we focus on the positives so as to maximise the rewards we might get from the relationship.[46]

END OF THE ROAD

In this chapter, I've shown that proximity exerts an effect on relationship formation, both in its own right but also indirectly through the influence of familiarity. A useful way of thinking about proximity is that it's the factor that sets the stage for the formation of relationships. To return to the example of Scott and

Ramona at the start of this chapter, the likelihood of the two of them forming any sort of relationship increased purely as a function of Ramona's move from New York to Toronto. The intersection of their two worlds is facilitated by their geographical proximity to one another, and enhanced by being embedded or, minimally at least, linked to one another's social environments.

I'm not suggesting that the effects of proximity will guarantee anyone a date. But coming into contact with another person is facilitated by proximity, whether geographical or social, and is necessary for the initiation and development of a meaningful relationship. Familiarity, in turn, increases the likelihood of further interactions taking place. Think of it in this way: if proximity sets the stage, then familiarity is the lubricant – if you'll forgive the pun – that facilitates social interaction and the initiation of a deeper relationship. Proximity and familiarity are what bring two people together, but also what helps to ensure they'll keep seeing each other. But, by themselves, they aren't enough to explain the formation of relationships.

3

APPEARANCE MATTERS

OR, HOW WE JUDGE BOOKS BY THEIR COVERS, HOW MEN AREN'T FROM MARS AND WOMEN AREN'T FROM VENUS, AND WHY WHAT IS BEAUTIFUL IS GOOD

Despite the proverbial advice not to judge a book by its cover and that beauty is 'but skin deep',* it's undeniable that appearance matters. When Scott first sees Ramona, on that fateful day in the Toronto Public Library, it isn't her personality or her musical taste or her use of language that attracts him. No, at that moment, he's attracted to Ramona's appearance – and, more precisely, her physical attractiveness. The reason for this

---

* The phrase is usually attributed to Sir Thomas Overbury, who wrote in 1613, 'And all the carnall beauty of my wife / Is but skin-deep'. What Lady Overbury thought isn't known.

is simple: that first time he sees her, Scott simply hasn't got any information about Ramona beyond what he can see. In fact, he may not be aware of it, but Ramona's appearance is already providing Scott with a good deal of information about her – her gender and age, for a start, but also clues about her emotional state and personality. In any case, the point is that what Scott can see, he likes.

So, appearance matters – and, as we'll see in this chapter, it probably matters a great deal, particularly for romantic relationships. But saying that appearance matters actually doesn't really tell us a great deal about why it matters, or who it matters to. In this chapter, I'll argue that we're all prone to judging books by their covers, with attractive people receiving a sort of 'premium' in terms of relationship formation. More than that, I'll argue that the old stereotype that men care about a partner's appearance more than do women is, well, not the whole story. The truth turns out to be more complicated than painting men as hopelessly shallow creatures. And if appearance matters, then we should ask why – it turns out there are some good reasons why we're attracted to attractive people.

JUDGING BOOKS BY THEIR COVERS

Imagine you're walking along a street one afternoon, when all of a sudden you witness a traffic accident. There are two victims, both of whom have suffered injuries that require immediate attention. But there's one crucial difference between the victims. For some reason, you find one victim more physically attractive than the other. So, which of the victims would you help first? I'm sure you're thinking that the victims' physical appearance would have very little to do with who you help first, but let me tell you that it probably does. This hypothetical scenario is actually a simplified version of a study my colleagues and I have conducted, where we found that respondents were more likely to indicate they would help someone they perceived as being attractive compared to less attractive victims.[1]

Here's another example. Imagine the two victims of the traffic accident have been helped and you're making your way along the street again. This time, you spot what looks like a dropped envelope, stamped and addressed. Inside, there's a completed university application form with a photograph of the applicant. Would how attractive you think the applicant is determine whether or not you put the envelope in the post? Again, this is a simplified version of a study that was conducted by Peter Benson and his team in the 1970s. In the study, the researchers left what appeared to be misplaced graduate school application forms in public phone booths at an airport. The forms included a photograph of the supposed applicant, which was used to convey information about the applicant's physical attractiveness (attractive or less attractive). The researchers then waited to see what would happen. What they found was that people who'd found the forms were more likely to mail them or take them to an airport official if the person depicted in the photo was attractive.[2]

Just one more example. In a study entitled 'Beauty is talent', David Landy and Harold Sigall had participants read essays that were supposedly written by a female college student. They then evaluated the quality of the essay, as well as the ability of its writer, on several dimensions. By means of a photograph attached to the essay, some participants were led to believe that the writer was physically attractive, while others were led to believe that she was less attractive. The researchers also varied the quality of the essay, with some participants reading a version of the essay that was well-written and others reading a poorly-written version. They found that participants judged both the essay and its writer as more competent when the 'writer' was attractive than when she was less attractive. The effect was more pronounced when participants read the poor quality essay – in this case, participants were willing to overlook poor grammar and spelling mistakes if the supposed writer was attractive.[3]

I could keep going. In fact, I will. In occupational settings, attractive people are more likely to be recommended for a job and more likely to be hired, to be paid more for the same job, more likely to be promoted, and less likely to be fired. In the courtroom, attractive defendants are less likely to be perceived as guilty when they've been charged with a crime and, even when they are found guilty, attractive defendants receive more lenient sentences and have lower bails and fines imposed on them. In higher education, attractive students are more likely to be offered a place at university and are more likely to receive higher marks, while attractive lecturers receive better student evaluations. In politics, attractive candidates are evaluated more favourably by voters and are also more likely to be elected. More generally, we give attractive people more personal space, we let them win more arguments, we defer to them more frequently, and we trust them more with our secrets.[4]

But why stop there? Physical attractiveness also matters in the formation of friendships. In one study, preschool children between the ages of four and six were rated by adults on a physical attractiveness scale. The children were then shown a board that had been filled with photos of their classmates and asked to pick three photos of children they 'especially liked' and three they 'especially disliked'. Physically attractive children were not only more popular and liked, they were also perceived by other children as being self-sufficient and independent than less attractive children. Attractive adolescents tend to be those first drawn into mixed-gender interactions – such as at school dances – and groups than less attractive peers, have larger friendship circles, and are also more likely to be the target of crushes than less attractive peers.[5]

The same is also true online. In one study, Tobias Greitemeyer and Irene Kunz created Facebook profiles that contained information about a person, along with a profile photo that had been earlier rated as showing someone either attractive or less attractive. Using the fake profiles, the researchers then sent friendship requests to all Facebook users who lived in the town of Innsbruck or who studied at the University of Innsbruck and who were roughly the same age as their fictitious characters. Then they waited. After seven days, they found that friendship requests were more likely to be accepted when the request came from someone with an attractive profile photo compared to a less attractive photo. In fact, we're more likely to accept friendship requests from profiles without photos than we are from profiles with photos that we think are unattractive.[6]

There's also some evidence that we view Facebook profiles differently depending on whether the profile photograph depicts an attractive or less attractive person. One study tracked participants' eye movements for sixty seconds while they viewed Facebook profiles of strangers varying in physical attractiveness. The researchers found that participants paid more attention to the main profile photograph if the target was attractive, particularly if the profile owner was a woman. Participants also spent more time focusing on information that was irrelevant to forming an impression of the profile owner, such as advertising banners, when viewing the profiles of less attractive individuals. Simply put, attractiveness matters on Facebook as much as it does in the real world.[7]

JUDGING DATES BY THEIR FACES

It's perhaps in the realm of dating and romantic relationships that the influence of physical attractiveness is most apparent. The research that's often held up as the classic demonstration of the power of physical appearance is the 'computer dance' study conducted by Elaine Walster (now Hatfield) and her colleagues. In this study, the researchers advertised a 'computer dance' for students at the University of Minnesota. When students came to sign up for the dance, four judges secretly assessed each student's physical attractiveness. The participants were then asked to complete a lengthy questionnaire, which they were told would be inputted into a computer and used to allocate an 'ideal partner' for them on the evening of the dance. In fact, the pairing was done randomly (except that no man was assigned to a taller woman) and the dance was held two days later. During the dance, having briefly interacted with their dates, participants were asked to fill in a new questionnaire about the dance.

The results of the study showed just how important physical attractiveness was. First, physically attractive dates were liked more by their partners than less attractive students. In fact, physical attractiveness was rated as far more important than other qualities, such as a partner's intelligence and personality. Physical attractiveness was also found to be the most important factor predicting how much students enjoyed the dance and whether two dates would see each other again. The importance of physical attractiveness may have been inflated in this study because students had no choice about their dance partners,* but the computer dance study highlights just how important appearance can be.[8]

The findings of the 'computer dance' study are borne out by more recent research using speed-dating events. Originally conceived by Rabbi Yaacov Deyo in Los Angeles as a way of helping Jewish singles meet, speed-dating allows paying members of the public to have a series of brief dates with other attendees. The duration of the dates can vary – though they are usually

---

* In fact, when the computer dance study was repeated, this time with the students being allowed to meet and interact before the dance, students expressed greater liking for partners who were similar to themselves in levels of physical attractiveness, a point I return to in Chapter 6.

between three and eight minutes long – as can the total number of dates a person has in an evening. At the end of the evening, speed-daters complete a short questionnaire in which they indicate whom they'd be interested in meeting again ('yesses') and who they would rather not see again ('nos'). If there's a match, the event host provides a way for mutual 'yesses' to get in touch with each other. Because speed-dating allows psychologists to study real relationships with a potential future in controlled environments, it has emerged as an important tool for studying relationship formation.

One of the most important findings to emerge from this research is just how pervasive the effects of physical attractiveness are on relationship initiation. In one speed-dating study, 382 German singles took part in a series of speed-dates held at Humboldt University in Berlin with the aim of finding a real-life romantic or sexual partner. Each date lasted three minutes and, after each date, participants noted on a scorecard whether they wanted to see their date again (they were allowed to revise their decisions after seeing all potential partners). Each participant also had photographs of their faces and recordings of their voice taken – these were rated by an independent group of judges for attractiveness – had their body size and height measured, and completed measures of education, income, and personality.

So, what did the researchers find? Well, firstly, they noted that an individual's probability of being chosen by one of the dating partners in a session was about 35 per cent, whereas the likelihood of achieving a match with one of those partners was just over 11 per cent. Six weeks after the event, the likelihood of two daters forming a relationship was about 7 per cent, while a year later the figure stood at about 4 per cent. It's difficult to know what to do with these figures – what would be the likelihood of meeting and forming a relationship with someone at a bar or café, for example? It's quite likely that speed-dating is much less time-consuming, if nothing else, but surely the point here is that a number of Germans are no longer single thanks to science.

But what predicted whether an individual would be chosen by a speed-dating partner immediately after the event? Of the range of factors that were examined (attractiveness, education and incomes, and personality), facial attractiveness was the strongest predictor of whether or not a person received a 'yes' – that is, their partner wanted to see them again. The second most important predictor was vocal attractiveness. In fact, the choices made by men were almost entirely predicted by a woman's physical cues – her facial and vocal attractiveness, and whether or not she was slim. Women, on the other hand, also emphasised physical cues, but were more concerned by a man's height and, to a lesser extent, his personality and income. In short, speed-daters judge their dates (more or less) by their faces.[9]

So, attractive people receive a premium in terms of romantic relationships. As a result, they have more social interactions with others and get asked out and go on dates more often, and – shock, horror – have sex more frequently. Among North American undergraduate students who have had their attractiveness independently measured, attractive women and men have more sex – both sexual intercourse and sexual contact without intercourse. It's not that attractive people are more sexually liberated – attractiveness isn't related to attitudes about sex or more forgiving morals. Rather, attractive people just have more sexual opportunities. If that wasn't enough, there's even some evidence to suggest that attractive people have better sex.* Women

---

* Why attractive people have better sex is an interesting question in itself. Maybe when we have sex with attractive people, we're more psychologically and sexually excited because of what we can see, hear, and touch. Another possibility is that all that sex that attractive people are having makes them better at it, which helps to improve sexual satisfaction for both parties.

having sex with attractive men, as rated by independent judges, are more likely to have an orgasm during or after their partner's ejaculation, whereas men having sex with attractive women have better erectile function.[10]

If, like some scholars writing in the 1960s, you think that the power of attractiveness is 'undemocratic',[11] I'm afraid I have to tell you it doesn't get any better online.* If anything, things may be worse (or better, if you're particularly attractive) on online dating sites, where users may focus on physical cues displayed in photos more than they do other features conveyed in a profile. In a study of over five thousand online daters in San Diego and Boston, researchers compared the rated physical attractiveness of a dater to the rated physical attractiveness of profiles the dater browsed and subsequently sent a message to. They found that, for both women and men, the likelihood of sending a message to a browsed profile increased with the profile's physical attractiveness, regardless of the dater's own attractiveness. Far from levelling the playing field, online dating mirrors what's happening offline.[12]

MEN ARE FROM MARS, AMIRITE?

While it's true that attractive people get sent more messages on online dating sites, that isn't the whole story. As OkCupid

---

* Or, for that matter, on mobile dating apps like Grindr and Tinder, which together have over fifty million users worldwide. Both sites have a simple premise: they present users with photos of nearby potential partners. After looking at a photo, users swipe to the right to indicate interest in the person or swipe to the left if they aren't interested. On Tinder, at least, two people can only interact via app-based messages if they both show an interest in one another – they both swiped right on each other's faces. Although users can see some basic profile information, the user experience is almost entirely dependent on perceptions of appearance.

cofounder Christian Rudder puts it in *Dataclysm: Who We Are (When We Think No One's Looking)*, 'men and women experience beauty unequally'.[13] On OkCupid, while profiles of attractive people receive more messages per week than less attractive daters, beautiful women get far more messages from men than attractive men do from women. In other words, men account for the bulk of message traffic directed at attractive people on OkCupid, possibly even creating an unfortunate dynamic where some women feel overwhelmed by the messages they're receiving.

So it's all men's fault, right? This is certainly the stereotypical view presented in self-help books, which claim that women and men are from different planets, with different patterns of behaviour and feelings. These stereotypes are widespread and reproduced throughout popular culture. For instance, both women's and 'lad' magazines dismiss men as emotionally stunted creatures driven by biology to focus on a woman's appearance. In lad magazines, in particular, sexualised images of women are presented alongside content that reflects and reinforces the belief that men care about physical attractiveness and sex above all else.[14] But is it really true? Are men really the shallow creatures they're made out to be?

Well, it turns out that the answer to this question is complex. It depends on whether the situation involves hypothetical partners or real, face-to-face interactions. For hypothetical situations, there's quite a bit of data to suggest that men do in fact value physical attractiveness in a potential partner more than women do, whereas women focus more on a potential partner's earning prospects and status. One line of evidence comes from personal ads that women and men place in newspapers and magazines and, more recently, online. The idea is a simple one. If men do really care about physical attractiveness more than women, then they should mention this preference more frequently in personal ads. After all, why lie?

Perhaps unsurprisingly, studies routinely show that men's ads are more likely to mention physical attractiveness as something sought and offer financial security, while women are more likely to offer beauty and seek actual and potential financial security. And this pattern remains relatively stable even into old age. Using ads posted on Yahoo! Personals, one group of researchers found that, even among men older than 75 years, physical attractiveness was sought and status-related information offered more than women. Likewise, women – even at over 75 years of age – were more likely to seek status-related characteristics, although they were less likely to offer attractiveness as they aged.[15]

What's more, physical attractiveness and earning prospects also affect response rates to personal ads by women and men. In one study, Donald Strassberg and Brittany English first designed personal ads that were generic and typical of ads placed online. This is the female-seeking-male version:

> SWF, 27, with brown hair and brown eyes. I am confident and laid back. I love hiking and painting and people who make me laugh. For me, a great time would include movies or videos followed by a candlelight dinner. I am considerate, reliable, and sincere. I think kids are great. If you're willing to start as friends, let's get in touch. Let me know more about you.

And here is the male-seeking-female version:

> SWM, 33, with brown hair and eyes. I'm upbeat, confident, and have a good sense of humor. I love bike riding, photography, kids, and listening to all kinds of music. For me, a good time would be going out for dinner followed by a movie or some dancing. I've never been married, but only because I've not found the right person. Tell me what you're like and let's see if we could be friends and then maybe more.

The researchers then created three more ads for women and men, respectively. For the female-seeking-male ads, they created one in which the woman described herself as 'lovely... slim... and very attractive'. In a second, she described herself as 'sensual and passionate', while in a third she was 'financially independent... successful [and] ambitious'. The new male-to-female ads also included a few key words to distinguish them from the ad above. One said that 'women tell me I'm good looking', while another read, 'I'm an accomplished attorney with a large firm'. The final ad described a 'hopeless romantic looking for a woman to adore'. Each of the ads offered something different – attractiveness, passion, or success for the female-seeking-male ads, and attractiveness, success, and romance in the male-seeking-female ads.

The ads were then placed on the personal ads section of Craigslist, a free, text-only site, for two weeks each in a number of cities in the United States. When responses to the ads were tallied, the researchers found that the 'attractive' female ad received by far the most responses, far more (268 in total) than the successful (202), passionate (119), and control ads (106). For the male-seeking-female ads, the successful version received the majority of responses from women (87), followed by the control ad (24), the romantic ad (21), and the attractive ad (18). In short, men were more likely to reply to ads they thought had been placed by women advertising physical attractiveness, whereas women were more likely to reply to ads that mentioned success and earning potential.[16]

Beyond sex differences in stated preferences for hypothetical partners, there's also some evidence of differences in the importance of physical attractiveness and earning potential as a function of sexual orientation. One study presented heterosexual women and men, gay men, and lesbians with photographs of strangers accompanied by text that described the target as being either successful ('medical doctor') or less successful ('work on a conveyor belt') and wealthy ('gross salary: €7000 per month') or less wealthy ('gross salary: €1100 per month'). The researchers found that heterosexual men were most likely to be swayed by the attractiveness of the strangers, followed by gay men, heterosexual women, and finally lesbians.[17] Heterosexual women were more likely to focus on targets who were of high social status than the other three groups, although status generally had a weaker influence on dating desirability than attractiveness. Lesbians, in particular, appear to have more flexible standards of beauty than heterosexual women and men, but may also emphasise other traits in hypothetical partners. In personal ads, both butch and femme lesbians place a premium on honesty above all other traits. For lesbians, being authentic to their sense of gender or being visibly lesbian may be important aspects of identity, so finding partners who are honest may be highly important.[18]

HYPOTHETICAL VERSUS REAL PARTNERS

But there's one big problem with studies of hypothetical partners, which is that those partners almost always remain hypothetical. In these hypothetical scenarios, there may be a great deal of pressure on (heterosexual) women and men to conform to what's expected of them in terms of gendered behaviours. In societies where men have more power than women, including greater wealth and status, it may make sense for women to report a desire for status. Conversely, men are more likely to be stigmatised for desiring women who have higher status than themselves, so end up emphasising physical attractiveness instead. In other words, responses to hypothetical scenarios reflect gendered norms of behaviour, but more than that, they also remain hypothetical decisions. So what happens in real-life scenarios?

The evidence suggests that differences between women and men disappear in real-life, face-to-face scenarios. In the 'computer dance' study I mentioned earlier, for example, there was no sex difference in the importance of physical attractiveness on how dance partners were evaluated. Physical attractiveness mattered to both women and men in that study. And in speed-dating studies, there don't appear to be any major sex differences for the effects of attractiveness and earning prospects on romantic interest.[19] In another study, two opposite-sex and single participants were invited to a room where they sat around a coffee table and had a ten-minute conversation. They were told they could talk about anything they liked, but that they would have the opportunity to share their contact details with their partner after the conversation if they wanted to. After the conversation was over, participants were asked to rate how much romantic chemistry they felt with their partner, whether they were interested in getting to know the other person, and whether they would be interested in going on a date with their partner. The researchers wanted to know what factors – physical attractiveness, warmth, and status – would predict romantic interest and decisions about further contact. In this study, they found that physical attractiveness was the strongest predictor of romance for both women and men.[20]

In fact, studies and reviews are increasingly coming to the conclusion that sex differences have been greatly exaggerated. When partners meet face-to-face, appearance really does matter, but it matters to both men and women equally. Perhaps it's not so much a case of men being from Mars, but both (heterosexual) men and women being from Earth. Another point – one that I hope is obvious – to make is that not all women behave in the same way. One study examined the impact of women's sociosexuality on their partner preferences. Sociosexuality refers to the difference between preferring casual, uncommitted sex without love or commitment versus a preference for long-term, committed relationships. In the study, the researchers measured women's sociosexuality and then asked them to rate a series of profiles of men that varied in attractiveness and ambition. Not surprisingly, women who preferred casual relationships were more likely to be swayed by a profile's physical attractiveness. In fact, physical attractiveness mattered more than ambition for all women in the study when they were asked to rate the potential partner's desirability for casual sex. Ambition only emerged as an important factor when the profiles were rated for long-term suitability as a partner.[21]

Another Internet survey asked almost two thousand heterosexual women about their mate preferences as well as their financial independence – whether or not they were dependent on other people financially. This study found that women who were more financially independent showed a stronger preference for physical attractiveness over financial prospects. Likewise, another study found that, the more a woman endorses feminist attitudes, the less importance she placed on a partner's earnings. Instead, women who endorsed feminist attitudes were more likely to prioritise traits like kindness, understanding, and creativity in a potential partner.[22]

The point is that treating all women as a homogeneous group does everyone a disservice. The truth is, some women – like some men – may prefer short-term, casual relationships and, in those situations, emphasise a partner's physical attractiveness over other traits. Other women – like other men – may prefer longer-term, committed relationships and, in those situations, emphasise a partner's physical attractiveness alongside other traits. This is a point I return to in more detail in the next chapter, but the bottom line is that everything you've been told about sex differences in the importance of appearance may have been an exaggeration. In real-life scenarios, where the chance of meeting is not hypothetical, appearance matters to both women and men.

WILL YOU HAVE SEX WITH ME?

Another way of approaching the issue of sex differences is to look at responses to offers of casual sex. Unlike in speed-dating scenarios, where the focus is presumably on the desirability of dates as long-term partners, studies of casual sex are focused much more on the short term. In classic studies conducted by

Russell Clark and Elaine Hatfield between 1978 and 2003, college students were approached by a fairly attractive member of the opposite sex, who was really a confederate of the researchers. This confederate would hang around campus and, once a target had been selected, she or he would walk up to the target and say, 'I have been noticing you around campus. I find you to be very attractive'. Next, the confederate would ask one of three questions: (1) Will you go on a date with me? (2) Will you come back to my apartment? or (3) Will you have sex with me?[23]

For the first question, there was no clear sex difference – across studies, 56 per cent of women and 50 per cent of men accepted the date. But for the other questions, which could be interpreted as questions about casual sex, there were clearer sex differences. For the question about going back to the confederate's apartment, 69 per cent of men consented compared to only 6 per cent of women. And for the final, 75 per cent of men agreed to sex, while not a single woman said yes to sex. In fact, every time the study was repeated, not a single woman agreed to sex at any time. In a more recent study, fairly attractive psychology students approached a member of the opposite sex in public places in four cities in Denmark and asked: (1) Would you go on a date with men tonight or during the week/weekend? (2) Would you come over to my place tonight or during the week/weekend? or (3) Would you go to bed with me tonight or during the week/weekend? When individuals in relationships were excluded from the count, 68 per cent of men and 43 per cent of women agreed to a date, 40 per cent of men and 21 per cent of women agreed to go to the student's place, and 59 per cent of men but none of the women agreed to casual sex.[24]

These studies would seem to confirm the idea of sex differences in receptivity to sex, but let's not jump to conclusions. For one thing, there may be some obvious reasons why women turn down the offer of casual sex. As psychologist Terri Conley has argued, engaging in casual sex in patriarchal societies differentially stigmatises women. Women are perceived more negatively for engaging in the same sexual behaviours as men and are expected not to express their sexuality as freely as men. As a code of behaviour, this sexual double standard restricts women's sexual freedom and reinforces the subordination of women, but it also helps to explain why women turn down offers of casual sex. In fact, in a series of studies, Conley and her colleagues found that women anticipated more negative judgements for accepting a casual sex offer and that fear of stigmatisation influenced how likely they were to accept the offer.[25] In other words, the sexual double standard – a form of gender inequality – impedes women's sexual expressions, including whether or not they accept offers of sex.*

There are lots of other reasons why women may be more likely than men to turn down offers of casual sex. Men are perceived as being more aggressive and women may also be more concerned about the dangers of a casual sexual encounter. This isn't just about potential violence† – men are also perceived as carrying a greater risk for sexually transmitted infections. Women may also expect that they will receive less pleasure than men in casual

---

* A more radical critique of the research on sex differences goes something like this: when you focus on the content of women's and men's behavioural responses, such as their responses to offers of casual sex, you ignore the social and historical production of those responses. When we fail to acknowledge the fact that we live in a society where women and men face different expectations about appropriate sexual behaviour, we end up reinforcing sexual inequality as a supposedly 'natural' outcome of evolution or biology.

† Although this is incredibly important in itself for explaining sex differences. Patriarchal societies control women through the threat of rape, perpetuating myths that target women who show sexual agency, including accepting and engaging in casual sex. The belief that sexual women will be – and deserve to be – raped both threatens women into subordinating their sexual needs and blames them for sexual assault.

sexual encounters – men are more likely than women to reach orgasm with a casual partner, so get the most physical reward from casual encounters. There are also other reasons why men may be more likely to accept offers of casual sex from women. Men are socialised to think that their status is enhanced when they have sex with many women, and the desire to enhance their status motivates men to engage in casual sex – and also to exaggerate their number of sexual partners. Men also use sex as a way of reaffirming their heterosexuality – 'I have heterosexual sex, therefore I am a man'. All in all, Conley believes that the 'casual sexual proposal deck is stacked against heterosexual women'.[26]

In support of her ideas, Conley found, in a series of studies of hypothetical partners, that men who approached women for casual sex were uniformly perceived as cold, physically dangerous, less able to provide sexual satisfaction, and of low status. Conley then moved on to find out whether there were any situations in which women would be more likely to accept an offer of casual sex. One thing she found was that sex differences in responsiveness to casual sex disappeared when the person making the offer was familiar and physically attractive. In one study, Conley asked her participants to imagine a scenario where they were propositioned by someone famous:

> You are fortunate enough to be able to spend your entire winter vacation in Los Angeles. One day, about a week into your stay, you decide to visit a trendy café in Malibu that overlooks the ocean. As you are sipping your drink, you look over and notice that actor Johnny Depp is just a few tables away. You can hardly believe your eyes! Still more amazing, he catches your eye and then approaches you. He says, 'I have been noticing you and I find you to be very attractive. Would you go to bed with me tonight?'

Men were asked to imagine the same hypothetical scenario, with Angelina Jolie in the place of Johnny Depp. In this study, where the person making the offer of casual sex was familiar to participants, women and men were just as likely as each other to respond positively to the offer. What's more, when the hypothetical offer came from someone famous but relatively less attractive, women and men were just as likely to reject the offer. In Conley's view, feeling safe is an important consideration in offers of casual sex. This is why offers from familiar people are more likely to receive a favourable response than offers made by unfamiliar people, particularly if they are perceived as being unattractive. Of course, offers of casual sex from Johnny Depp and Angelina Jolie are improbable, but Conley also found the same basic pattern of results when the hypothetical offer came from the participant's best opposite-sex friend.

In other words, it matters who the offer of casual sex is coming from. When strange men approach women for casual sex, women are likely to be repulsed by the offer because of what it conveys about the proposer. Strange men asking for casual sex probably means risky, unsatisfying sex. If that's the case, then it's not really surprising that women are more likely to turn down offers of casual sex. What's more, gay men and lesbians are equally likely to accept offers of sex from members of their own gender. And bisexual women are much more likely to accept an offer of casual sex from a woman than from a man, suggesting that being approached by a man is not the same as being approached by a woman. On the other hand, both women and men are more likely to accept an offer of sex when the proposer is perceived as being sexually capable and warm.[27]

What does this all mean? First, sex differences in responses to casual sex may appear to be larger than they actually are. If the right person comes along, the risk is low, and there is the potential for a good night of sex, women and men are equally likely to accept the offer of casual sex. And for both women and men, physical attractiveness matters. One study found that responsiveness to offers of casual sex increased when the proposer was physically attractive – more so for women than men. In fact, when it comes to casual sex, both women and men are willing to compromise on the intelligence and status of a partner, but not on their physical attractiveness. The bottom line is that, for sexual and romantic relationships, physical appearance matters – and it matters to both women and men.[28]

WHAT IS BEAUTIFUL IS GOOD

If appearance matters to both men and women, then we really should ask why. One intriguing possibility is that seeing attractive people is rewarding in some way. When we're presented with images of attractive people while having our brains scanned, there appears to be increased activity in some parts of the brain more than others. In these studies, participants are asked to judge images of attractive and less attractive strangers while having their brains scanned in imaging machines. When we see attractive faces and bodies, the parts of the brain that are activated – regions known as the nucleus accumbens and the orbitofrontal cortex – happen to also be those regions that are involved in the processing of rewarding stimuli.[29] In the scan of my brain on the next page, the white arrow points to the approximate position of the orbitofrontal cortex – this is also the part of the brain that is activated when we anticipate or receive rewards, like drugs or money.

In other words, the brain's reward circuitry is stimulated by beautiful people. Recent neuroimaging studies also suggest that we may remember attractive faces better than neutral faces. When viewing attractive faces, there appears to be stronger connections between the reward circuitry of the brain and areas of the brain associated with memory function. In fact, researchers now think that attractive faces are special 'human stimuli' that facilitate the encoding of memory.[30]

This being the case, it's perhaps unsurprising that we express a desire to form relationships with attractive people. The first time

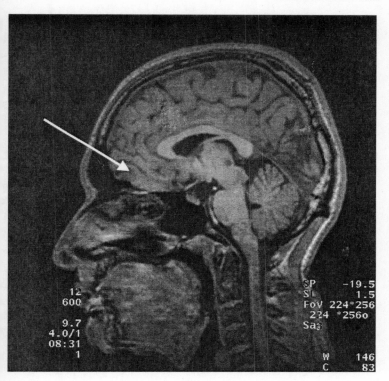

we see someone we find beautiful, we experience a positive emotional reaction that draws us toward that person. And every time we see that person again, our brains experience the same positive reaction, reinforcing our attraction. This doesn't mean that the effect is unending. But in the same way that a piece of music or chocolate is rewarding, our brains are stimulated every time we see an attractive face or body. And to ensure that that reward occurs again, we try to form relationships with those attractive people. Consistent with this idea, studies show that individuals are not only more interested in forming relationships with attractive others, but also report more care for lovers and friends who are perceived as attractive.[31]

But there's another reason that helps to explain why appearance matters so much. In a now classic study, Karen Dion, Ellen Berscheid, and Elaine Walster invited participants to take part in a study that they were told was about the accuracy of impression formation. Participants were each given three envelopes, which contained yearbook photos of 'a physically attractive stimulus person..., a person of average attractiveness, and... a relatively unattractive stimulus person'. For each photograph, participants were asked to provide a series of ratings related to personality traits, life experiences, and occupational success. When the researchers analysed the data, they found that their respondents had rated the attractive individuals, both women and men, more positively on a range of measures. Not only were attractive people judged to be more socially desirable, they were also rated as more likely to secure prestigious jobs, to have happier marriages, to be better parents, and to lead more fulfilling lives.[32]

On the basis of their study, Karen Dion and her colleagues concluded that, in people's perception of others, 'what is beautiful is good'. What's now known as the 'beautiful-is-good bias' has been found in numerous studies since then. Attractive people are judged to be, among other things, more honest, less maladjusted, happier, more sociable and popular, and generally better at everything they do compared to less attractive individuals. So here's a second reason why appearance plays such an important role in relationship formation. If we are biased in our perceptions, believing attractive people to be generally better people, then it makes perfect sense that we'd want to be in relationships with them. More generally, individuals seem more interested, sociable, and enthusiastic – according to objective judges – when they believe they're talking with someone physically attractive, which helps to facilitate relationship formation.[33]

Having said that, the term 'bias' suggests that these judgements are in some way faulty, so just how accurate are our perceptions of attractive and less attractive people? This is important because it may help to further explain why appearance matters. It's one thing to say that we're biased in our perceptions of attractive people. But if attractive people really are, say, funnier or happier, then there may be good reasons to want to form relationships with them. So, are attractive people really all that different from their less attractive counterparts?

When Alan Feingold reviewed all the evidence available up until 1992, he suggested that any difference was likely quite trivial. He did note that good-looking people were less lonely, less socially anxious, more popular, and more sexually experienced than less good-looking people, but his overall conclusion was that any difference was negligible. 'Good-looking people,' he concluded, 'are not what we think.'[34] But more recently, some psychologists have suggested that attractive people may in fact be different from less attractive people in a number of ways. Judith Langlois and her colleagues, for example, concluded that among both children and adults, attractive people were more extraverted and popular, had better social skills, and had more dating experience. They also noted differences on other dimensions, including intelligence and mental health, although here the differences between attractive and less attractive people were less pronounced.[35]

It would seem that physically attractive people may have some qualities that make them more popular partners. An interesting question is why these differences exist. One answer is that, because we perceive attractive people in a more positive way and because we may also act on these perceptions, attractive people come to internalise those beliefs and act in ways that are consistent with them. Consider this example: a physically attractive child is perceived and treated as being more extraverted simply because she's attractive. Once the child begins to conform to others' expectations of how she should behave, the cycle repeats itself indefinitely. Over time, the child comes to perceive herself as an extravert and behaves in ways that are consistent with that perception.

There's some evidence to support this idea. In one classic study, men and women were recruited for an experiment ostensibly on a telephone conversation exercise. The men were given a purported photo of the woman (either an attractive or a less attractive photograph) they were to have a conversation with, while the women didn't receive any such information. Before the conversation, men who anticipated physically attractive partners expected relatively sociable, humorous, and socially adept women, while men who anticipated less attractive partners expected unsociable, awkward, and socially inept women. Importantly, the researchers also found that women in the 'attractive' condition behaved differently from those in the 'unattractive' condition during the ten-minute phone conversation. As rated by objective raters, women in the 'attractive' condition were rated as more enthusiastic and animated during the conversation. What had initially been stereotypes about the personalities of women based on their appearance had become reality in the women's behaviours.[36]

These processes may also help to explain why attractive people receive more initial messages on online dating sites. In one study, researchers first gathered a hundred profiles and their corresponding photos, posted by men in New York and Seattle on popular online dating sites. They then asked women who didn't know the men to rate the photographs for attractiveness and, separately, to rate the profile texts for how kind, intelligent, humorous, and confident they thought the writers were. The results of the study showed that men who were rated as more physically attractive also wrote more appealing profiles. The appeal of the texts seemed to be driven mainly by the level of confidence on display. In other words, attractive men may be more confident than less attractive men and so write more appealing profile texts.[37]

FIRST (AND SECOND) IMPRESSIONS

So, appearance matters and it probably matters quite a bit. In fact, studies suggest that it takes less than a second to form first impressions about other people, including how attractive we think they are. The speed at which we form impressions of other people suggests that these judgements are made automatically, possibly outside of our consciousness. And these first impressions are heavily shaped by a person's physical appearance. Even when provided with descriptive information about a person, we still rely on physical cues when forming impressions about that person's personality and capabilities. In what are known as 'zero-acquaintance contexts' – that is, when we have no information of the person being judged beyond physical cues – it seems that we use a person's physical appearance as a shorthand way of making inferences about their personality.[38]

The intriguing thing is that these judgements may actually contain a kernel of truth. Based on 'thin slices' or short excerpts of social behaviour, we are able to draw fairly accurate inferences about a person. For example, researchers have found that a recording of a person having a conversation for just a few seconds is enough for us to make accurate judgements about that person's sexual orientation, intelligence, and personality. Other research has shown that, after viewing photos of people in a neutral position and self-chosen position, observers were fairly accurate at judging the target's extraversion, emotional stability, self-esteem, and religiosity. By combining information we glean from a person's physical characteristic and facial expression, we seem able to piece together fairly accurate images of a person's personality, which helps to explain why appearance matters so much in the absence of social interaction.[39]

There's also some evidence to suggest that the accuracy of our first impressions improves when we perceive someone as being physically attractive. In one study, university students were placed in small groups and asked to interact with every member of the group for three minutes. After each meeting, participants rated each other's personality, intelligence, and physical attractiveness, before providing self-ratings of their own personality and intelligence. After just three minutes of interaction, participants made fairly accurate judgements about others' personality and intelligence. But, for participants who were rated as being physically attractive, other participants' impressions of them were more accurate. As the researchers concluded, 'people do judge a book by its cover, but a beautiful cover prompts a closer reading, leading more physically attractive people to be seen... more accurately'.[40]

But a word of caution: things may be slightly more complicated online, where first impressions are heavily influenced by the photographs that daters use to attract partners. The trouble isn't so much that online daters lie about their appearance – men tend to intentionally lie about their height, whereas women tend to lie about their weight, although the degree of deception is small* – but rather that different images of the same person can result in different impressions. In fact, research suggests that, when participants are presented with different images of the same person, it can result in remarkably different impressions.[41] This problem of forming accurate impressions of someone based on different images is compounded on online dating sites, where daters are able to manage the information they present – at least non-verbally – in ways that blur the boundaries between deception and just wanting to present well. One common strategy that online daters use is to craft profiles that describe a future,

---

* Most online daters lie about at least one thing on their profiles, but the magnitude of the deceptions tends to be small and would be difficult to detect face-to-face. Very few online daters lie about things like relationship status and whether they have children, presumably because these things would be very easy to uncover in the early stages of the relationship.

potential version of the self, rather than describe their current or actual selves.[42] Is this deception? It's difficult to say.

In any case, these first impressions that we form of other people have a huge influence on relationship development. When we form positive first impressions of a stranger, we are much more likely to communicate intimately with that person, maintain ongoing contact, and ultimately develop richer and more meaningful relationships with that person. For example, one study found that roommates who reported more positive first impressions were more likely to get along and continue living together in the long term. But it's not just how positive those impressions are that matter. The accuracy of first impressions is also known to have influence on relationship formation. More accurate impressions of new classmates in another study predicted how often they interacted with each other over the course of a semester and whether they wanted to keep interacting in the future.[43]

Of course, the importance of appearance won't be the same for everyone. Because physical attractiveness is essentially something that is seen, we might predict that the appearance of a potential partner should matter less to individuals with visual impairments. One study tested this possibility in a sample of German adolescents. As predicted, the researchers found that, compared to sighted individuals, adolescents with visual impairments placed less importance on the physical attractiveness of a partner, and instead emphasised psychological and emotional maturity. As the authors of the study concluded, the importance of maturity to visually-impaired participants supported the popular German saying that 'what is essential is invisible to the eye'.[44]

APPEARANCE REALLY DOES MATTER

The difficult truth is that, for most people, appearance really does matter. One interesting idea is that the importance of physical attractiveness varies as the early relationship progresses. Before any kind of social interaction has taken place, physical appearance is probably very important – especially if other avenues for gathering information are closed. Think back to that first time that Scott sees Ramona at the library. At that moment, prior to any social interaction, appearance matters a great deal because Scott hasn't got much information about Ramona other than what he can see. In that scenario, Scott's first impression of Ramona is swayed by her physical appearance. And, likewise, Ramona must find Scott physically attractive if the relationship is to progress to something more romantic.

But once social interaction has occurred, other traits rapidly become important while the importance of appearance may decline slightly, only to rise again if the relationship is maintained.[45] Anyway, all this talk of appearance shouldn't obscure the fact that a person's physical attractiveness is only one trait that we consider when making decisions about relationship formation. As we'll see in the next chapter, characteristics like warmth, kindness, and honesty all matter, but the really interesting thing is that these characteristics may also make a person seem more physically attractive. The emerging picture is that physical attractiveness isn't a static quality and that it can evolve and change depending on the characteristics of the individual as well as the situation they find themselves in.

4

APPEARANCE MATTERS, PART II

OR, HOW OTHER THINGS MATTER TOO, WHY NICE GUYS DON'T ALWAYS FINISH LAST, AND HOW LOVE IS SOMETIMES BLIND

On their first date, Scott and Ramona meet at a park and go for a walk together. It's a chilly evening and Scott has on his parka, on the left sleeve of which he has a patch marked by the letter 'X'. When Ramona asks him what the 'X' represents, his reply is meant as a joke:

Scott: Oh, this? Well, obviously, one of us went to Professor Xavier's School for Gifted Youngsters, and one of us didn't.

Ramona: Obviously *one* of us is a total nerd. Did you make the patch yourself?

Scott: I don't have to answer that!

They go on to talk about other things, but this brief exchange is notable because it marks the first real point – whether they realise it or not – when characteristics other than appearance begin to shape Scott and Ramona's relationship. Scott's attempt at humour and Ramona's teasing reply both provide information about the self that wouldn't have been obvious in the absence of interaction. It's this sort of initial interaction that allows us to form a fuller picture of another person, a picture built on multiple characteristics that go far beyond appearance. Appearance does still matter, but other things now matter, too. But what things exactly?

A LIST OF CHARACTERISTICS

The most straightforward way of figuring out the qualities that people value in a potential romantic partner is to ask them. In fact, you could do it, too, if you wanted. The task is an easy one: simply build up a mental image of your ideal partner, someone you would like to date or even marry. Once you have an image of this ideal person, make a list of that person's key or important characteristics. Are they caring? Do they like children? Are they hot? Romantic? Simply list all the characteristics that make up your ideal partner. Once you have your list, start ranking all the different characteristics by importance. Which is the most important trait, the one thing you couldn't do without in a potential partner? Which traits are less important to you?

In a classic study, Garth Fletcher and his colleagues asked undergraduates at the University of Canterbury in New Zealand to complete the task above, creating lists of characteristics desired in a long-term, romantic partner. They came up with forty-nine characteristics, which a second set of undergraduates then rated in terms of how important each item was in describing an ideal partner.[1] This is the list, with characteristics ranked in order of importance:

Rank	Characteristic	Importance rating	Rank	Characteristic	Importance rating
1	Trustworthy	6.45	26	Adventurous	5.31
2	Honest	6.36	27	Deals well with criticism	5.29
3	Interesting	6.11	28	Romantic	5.26
4	Communicative	6.08	29	Active lifestyle	5.25
5	Good fun	6.00	30	Sexy	5.21
6	Understanding	5.99	31	Attractive	5.20
7	Supportive	5.95	32	Spontaneous	5.17
8	Good sense of humour	5.94	33	Outgoing	5.15
9=	Considerate	5.93	34	Does not smoke	5.08
9=	Affectionate	5.93	35	Generous	5.04
11=	Kind	5.87	36	Assertive	4.88
11=	Friendly	5.87	37	Ambitious	4.83
13	Reliable	5.81	38	Nice body	4.82
14	Broad-minded	5.77	39	Creative	4.65
15	Sensitive	5.75	40	Likes children	4.43
16	Good listener	5.74	41	Sporty and athletic	4.34

(Continued)

Rank	Characteristic	Importance rating	Rank	Characteristic	Importance rating
17	Warm	5.66	42	Successful	4.31
18	Easygoing	5.57	43	Dresses well	4.25
19	Intelligent	5.54	44	Financially secure	3.89
20	Independent	5.50	45	Good job	3.85
21	Good lover	5.48	46	Appropriate age	3.83
22=	Mature	5.47	47	Nice house or apartment	2.79
22=	Stable	5.47	48	Appropriate ethnicity	2.56
24	Self-aware	5.43	49	Religious beliefs	2.44
25	Confident	5.39			

Using a statistical technique called factor analysis, the research-ers were able to condense this list of characteristics into three broad groups: how warm, intimate, and loyal a potential partner is, how attractive and energetic a partner is, and the social status and resources the person possesses. For both women and men, personal characteristics linked to warmth, intimacy, and loyalty were rated the most important traits in a potential partner, while those related to status and resources were rated the least impor-tant. It would seem that, when we ask people what they desire in a potential partner, it's characteristics like warmth, kindness, honesty, and loyalty that come top of the list.

Before we pop champagne and rejoice in the fact that the human race isn't so shallow after all, I'm afraid I need to warn you that people's stated preferences may not be all that reliable. This might sound counterintuitive. After all, if someone expresses a desire for someone warm and kind, wouldn't we expect them to end up with just such a partner? Or what about someone who expresses a strong preference for redheads? Wouldn't we expect that person to end up dating a redhead? In fact, there's some research suggesting just the opposite – that our stated preferences do not actually predict who we end up in a relationship with.

In one speed-dating study, Paul Eastwick and Eli Finkel asked participants to complete a questionnaire in which they rated the importance of a potential romantic partner's physical attractive-ness, earning potential, and personality. These participants then attended a speed-dating event, where they had an opportu-nity to interact with between nine and thirteen members of the opposite sex for four minutes each. After each date, participants rated each person on physical attractiveness, earning potential, and personability, and at the end of the evening they indicated which of those dates they'd like to see again.

The researchers tested the simple idea that people who before the event expressed a desire for a particular characteristic – physical attractiveness, say – should want to date other event participants who they rated highly on that quality. But this wasn't what they found. In fact, there was no relationship between people's stated desires before the event and who they wanted to see again after the event. Someone who said they desired a physically attractive partner was not more likely to want to date someone who they themselves had rated as attractive. Or, for that matter, someone who stated a desire for a friendly partner was not more likely to want to date someone they had rated as being friendly.[2]

In another study, single participants viewed a profile of a potential partner – who was in fact a confederate of the researchers – that contained three characteristics, such as those listed in the earlier table. Participants were told that the potential partner had selected these characteristics as the three that best described her or him. In actual fact, the participants had reported, several weeks earlier, which traits they desired the most in a potential partner. The profiles they were viewing actually contained two of the three traits that the participant had rated as important (the ideal condition) or two of the three traits the participant had rated as least important (the non-ideal condition). After viewing the profile, participants reported how much they desired the potential partner and, not surprisingly, participants reported a strong desire toward the person in the ideal condition compared to the non-ideal condition.

But that's only part of the story. Next, the participants had an opportunity to have a five-minute interaction with the confederate. During the interaction, the participant and the confederate took turns to describe a series of pictures to one another. This was done to ensure that interaction was constrained. The confederate's responses had been scripted beforehand and participants weren't able to learn anything new about the confederate that would allow them to confirm or contradict what they had read in the profile. After this brief interaction, participants were asked to rate how much they desired the person they'd been interacting with. Now, there was no difference between participants in the ideal and non-ideal conditions. In other words, participants' desire for a potential partner was related to the extent to which the partner matched ideal characteristics before any interaction had taken place, but not after face-to-face interaction.[3]

Does this mean that people's stated preferences are meaningless? When some people say they're looking for a partner who's 'tall, dark, and handsome', does it actually matter in terms of who they end up in a relationship with? Well, there's some evidence that ideals matter in the long term. When dating participants are asked to state their ideal partner preferences and rate the extent to which their partners possessed those traits, the degree of similarity is associated with better relationship quality and a lower likelihood of breaking-up.[4] But, in the much shorter term, particularly for first interactions, stated preferences may not reliably predict whether two people will form a lasting relationship. Partner ideals may help us determine the extent to which a partner is a good fit, but they may not determine who we get together with in the first place.

Some psychologists think that stated preferences don't exert much of an effect on initial interactions because, well, people are complex. In a face-to-face interaction, the meaning of 'warm' might shift depending on all sorts of contextual and individual issues, and so a comparison between an individual's ideals and a partner's traits may not be as easy as when the comparison is made with characteristics listed on a profile. Determining how friendly or warm someone is may not be very easy in initial interactions and, in these encounters, people may be more likely to rely on emotional or gut responses. It's maybe easier to see gut responses at work in online dating. Once contact has been made with another dater online, meeting offline is the next crucial stage – and it is here that perceptions of 'chemistry' between two people can determine whether the two daters will meet again.[5]

Another way of looking at this is to say that the things we think matter in initial interactions actually may not matter very much. In January 2013, OkCupid launched a mobile app called Crazy Blind Date, which paired daters together and helped them arrange to meet locally. The two daters had no way of communicating before the date and the only information they had about each other was a first name and a scrambled profile photo. After the date, the app asked how it went. Most people said they'd had a good time – 75 per cent of women and 85 per cent of men, in fact – but the surprising thing was that attractiveness just didn't matter. It didn't seem to matter which person was more attractive or even by how much, the people on these blind dates just seemed to have a good time.[6]

In fact, there's some data to suggest that physical attractiveness may not matter when it comes to predicting the longevity of a relationship formed online. In a study of online daters in the United States, researchers found that impressions formed of a person through online profiles and through the exchange of messages didn't change very much after a face-to-face meeting. In other words, impressions of physical attractiveness formed online seem to be largely confirmed when partners actually go on a date. It's likely that, by the time online daters meet in person, the importance of appearance has gradually declined and daters were measuring up other characteristics. In fact, the same study found that the best predictor of whether two online daters would meet again after their first date was not physical attractiveness, but how well the daters felt they had gotten to know their partners. When online daters feel like they've got to know their partners well after the first date, they're more likely to meet again and form a longer-term relationship.[7]

I HEART YOU BECAUSE YOU SEEM NICE AND THEREFORE HOT

Why were so many people on OkCupid's Crazy Blind Dates having fun, regardless of how attractive they were and how attractive their blind dates were? One answer is that it had to do with personality. Let's unpack that a little. Imagine you turn up to a blind date and you realise your date is maybe not as attractive as you'd hoped. It doesn't really matter what you'd imagined your date would be like, but she or he just doesn't live up to what you'd dreamed of before the date. Even so, you decide you're going to give her or him a chance. So the two of you sit down and have a drink. You talk. Your date cracks a few jokes. You laugh. It turns out, she or he is nice – warm, friendly, funny. At the end of the evening, as you're saying goodbye to each other, you realise that your date is a lot more attractive than you thought she or he was when you first met.

Is it even possible that a person's personality can affect how physically attractive we find them? One way of examining this issue is to see what happens to perceptions of hypothetical partners when you provide observers with information about the target's personality. This is what my colleagues and I did in one study with more than two thousand men at universities in London. We asked these participants to rate a series of images of women that varied in their body sizes from emaciated to obese. Some participants rated the women's physical attractiveness in the absence of any other information. Others were given fictitious information about the women's personalities. Sometimes the personality information was positive and sometimes it was less positive. An example would be a woman who was described as friendly, cheerful, and spontaneous, versus a woman with a similar body size but who was described as quiet, thoughtful, and private.

When we looked at who the men had rated as the most physically attractive, we found that there were no differences whether or not participants had been given personality information. Most men rated a relatively slim woman as highly attractive and being given personality information about the women didn't seem to change this. But in the same study, we also asked participants to rate the thinnest and largest women they found attractive. It was for these ratings that personality information made a differ-ence. Overall, when participants were given positive personal-ity information, the range of figures they found attractive was wider than when they received no information. And when the images were paired with negative personality information, the range of attractive figures was constricted. One way of looking at these results is to say that positive personality information makes figures that would otherwise seem less attractive appear more appealing.[8]

In another study, participants were seated in front of a com-puter and shown photographs of women and men taken from a university yearbook. They were first asked to rate how physically attractive they found each person in the photographs. Next, they were asked to start counting down from a large number – 9,748 for example. After two minutes, they were told to stop and, using the number they were at, to begin counting forward by thirteens for another two minutes. This was a distraction task, used so that participants would find it harder to remember their earlier ratings.

In the final part of the experiment, participants viewed the same photos again, but this time they were paired with person-ality information, either desirable characteristics like honesty and intelligence, or undesirable traits like abusive and rude. In addition to making ratings of physical attractiveness again, participants were also asked to rate the photos based on how much they would like to be friends with and date the persons in the photograph. Compared to when the photos were paired with undesirable traits, photos paired with desirable personal-ity characteristics were rated more positively in terms of dating and friendship potential. But the really interesting thing was that personality information also changed participants' attractiveness ratings. When the photos were paired with positive information, the photos were rated as more attractive than earlier when there had been no such information.[9]

THE SLACKER VERSUS THE OLYMPIAN

All of the studies I mentioned above involved hypothetical people, but there's also good evidence showing that personality shapes the way we perceive the attractiveness of real people. Kevin Kniffin and David Wilson asked participants in one study to rate the attractiveness of their high school classmates based on photographs from a yearbook. They did this by placing a removable sticker next to each photograph and giving each classmate a rating of physical attractiveness based on participants' own feelings, rather than what might be deemed attractive by wider society. Next, the photos were also rated for familiarity ('How well did you know the individual?'), liking ('How much did you like the individual?'), and respect ('How much did you respect the individual for his or her actions, attitudes, etc.?').

What the researchers found was that the perception of physical attractiveness was not based purely on physical cues. Rather, the perception of physical attractiveness of classmates appeared to be influenced by knowing those people and their non-physical traits. In particular, the more classmates were liked, the more physically attractive they were perceived. To illustrate this point, the researchers looked at the photograph that one woman rated as the least physically attractive. 'To us (and to the stranger who rated the photographs),' the researchers wrote, 'he did not seem ugly at all but rather quite average in physical attractiveness.' When they showed the participant the photograph and asked why she had rated him as so unattractive, 'her face became contorted with disgust as she related what a horrible person he was, what a foul mouth he had, and so on. She was physically disgusted by his image, even though the unfavourable qualities she described had nothing to do with his physical characteristics.' Even though thirty years had passed since the two had last interacted, she was still so disgusted by him and that continued to colour her judgement of attractiveness.

The researchers found the same thing in a second study with members of a university rowing team who'd spent a year training together. The rowers were asked to rate not only the attractiveness of the other team members, but also their talent and effort, and how much they were respected and liked. Strangers who didn't know any of the team also rated the same people by looking at a team photograph. Just as in the first study, a team member was rated as more physically attractive by his fellow rowers the more she or he was liked and respected, and the more talented or hard-working she or he was. One rower who was considered a slacker by the rest of the team was uniformly rated as unattractive by his team members. Another rower was so hard-working that he was considered a contender for the country's Olympic team. He, unlike the slacker, was uniformly rated as attractive by his team members. But when strangers rated the two rowers, there was no difference in how attractive they rated the slacker and the potential Olympian.

In a third and final study, the researchers followed a group of archaeology students attending a six-week summer course where they would be working together on a dig site five days per week and up to eight hours per day. On the first day of the course, Kevin Kniffin visited the class and administered a questionnaire that asked the students to rate each other for familiarity, intelligence, effort, liking, and physical attractiveness. Since the students had only just met that day, some of the questions would have been difficult to answer, but the students were told to provide a vague impression if they could. The same questionnaire was also completed by the class on the last day of working together, six weeks later. As in their earlier two studies, non-physical traits – particularly liking – predicted the ratings of physical attractiveness at the end of the course.

One woman in the group was rated as below average (3.25 out of a possible score of 9.0) on the first day of class. But this particular woman turned out to be very hard-working and as a result became more popular and was well-liked. On the final day of class, when her attractiveness was rated by her colleagues, she'd ended up with a mean score of 7.0. Another student was rated as roughly average in terms of her physical attractiveness on the very first day of class, but – as observed by her instructors and one of the researchers – she was lazy and uncooperative. Not only was she disliked by her classmates, but also her mean attractiveness rating fell from a high of 5.07 to a 4.14 by the end of the study. She probably hadn't done anything to alter her appearance throughout the course, but because she was disliked by the group, she came to be perceived as less physically attractive.

At the very least, these studies suggest that our first impressions of a person's physical attractiveness can be overwritten by personality information gleaned over the course of social interactions. Characteristics like warmth, kindness, and basic decency are valued by both women and men, and to the extent that individuals possess these qualities they become more desirable partners, but also appear more physically attractive. Or as Kevin Kniffin and David Wilson concluded at the end of their research paper, 'If you want to enhance your *physical* attractiveness, become a valuable social partner'.[10] But it's not just a person's personality that can make the difference.

A good sense of humour is another trait that, like personality, can affect how desirable a person is judged as a partner. Broadly speaking, both women and men value a good sense of humour in a potential partner, possibly because it signals warmth.[11] Someone with a good sense of humour is likely to be warm, cheerful, and optimistic – all traits that are desired in a potential partner. In fact, studies show that, when we're attracted to someone, we're more likely to initiate humour and to laugh at that person's jokes. What's more, research by Norman Li and his colleagues showed that a sense of humour affected attraction toward people who were rated as physically unattractive. In their study, a humorous introduction – 'I am a fun-loving, caring person who is unique...

just like everyone else' – increased participants' attraction for targets who had earlier been rated as the least attractive, possibly because humour affected perceptions of warmth.[12] In other words, a good sense of humour may possibly make up for a lack of physical attractiveness. And on that note: why are pirates called pirates?*

DON'T NICE GUYS FINISH LAST?

All this talk of warmth and kindness actually flies in the face of a common stereotype that, far from desiring niceness, women actually end up dating 'bad boys'. In other words, nice guys finish last. Fleshed out, the stereotype goes something like this: women claim they want 'nice' characteristics because they believe this is what's expected of them. But, in reality, what they want is the 'challenge' that comes with dating a not-so-nice guy. Or worse, that women don't care about a man's personality either way and are really only after his money, social status, or power. It's difficult not to see the mind of the misogynist at work in these claims,† but is there any truth to the stereotype? This is crucial because, if nice guys really do finish last, then it would seem to contradict the research I presented earlier.

One way to find out is to present women with descriptions of hypothetical men with different personality types and see which ones they prefer. In one study, participants were given a script in which a woman named Susan is taking part in a game show, not unlike *Blind Date*. Susan is given the opportunity to go on a date with one of two male contestants, Todd or Michael, and must choose between them based on answers to her questions. In the

---

*   Because they arrr.

†   The stereotype is almost always presented in this gendered way. You never hear of nice ~~gals~~ women finishing last.

experiment, participants were randomly assigned to one of three groups, where they encountered different versions of Todd. 'Nice Todd' always gave responses that we'd associate with a nice guy. For example, when Susan asks for his definition of a 'real man' and whether he is one himself, 'Nice Todd' answers:

> A real man is someone who is in touch with his feelings and those of his partner. Someone who is kind and attentive and doesn't go for all that macho stuff. He's also great in the bedroom and puts his partner's pleasure first. I'd definitely say I'm a real man.

'Middle Todd' on the other hand always gave more neutral, middle-of-the-road responses:

> A real man knows what he wants and he knows how to get it. Someone who works hard and plays hard, and who is good to the woman he loves. He's also great in the bedroom. I'd definitely say I'm a real man.

Finally, 'Jerk Todd' was an insensitive tool:

> A real man knows what he wants and he knows how to get it. Someone who knows who he is, but keeps other people guessing and on their toes – he doesn't go in for all that touchy-feely stuff. He's also great in the bedroom and can tell his partner what he likes. I'd definitely say I'm a real man.[13]

Michael, like 'Middle Todd', also always gave neutral responses. After reading the script, participants were asked which of the dates, Todd or Michael, Susan should go on a date with and also which date the participants would prefer to date themselves. So what did the researchers find? Contrary to the stereotype that nice guys finish last, it was actually Nice Todd that was chosen most frequently both for Susan and for participants themselves. When participants rated the different versions of Todd on a number of different dimensions, 'Nice Todd' was found to be rated as no less exciting or interesting than 'Jerk Todd', but he was certainly perceived as nicer, kinder, and more intelligent. In another similar study, participants who read dating ads in which people described themselves as altruistic ('I enjoy helping people' and 'I volunteer at a food bank') were rated as more attractive short-term dates and long-term partners than those that didn' mention altruistic characteristics.[14]

So far, so good. Except that we still haven't gotten around the possibility that women may say one thing, but do something altogether different. In other words, women may say that they prefer 'Nice Todd' and even select him on paper when given the choice, but may actually end up dating 'Jerk Todd' in real life. Part of the problem with continuing down this path is that saying someone is 'nice' – or, for that matter, a 'jerk' – is actually quite banal. What do these terms actually mean? To try to untangle this issue, Jerry Burger and Mica Cosby asked participants to read descriptions of a fictitious character they called John. In one condition, participants read some basic information about John – his hobbies, what he was studying at university – and then learned that a personality test had found that John's five most prominent traits were aggressive, assertive, confident, demanding, and dominant. In another condition, participants read the same basic information about John but then learned that his most prominent characteristics were easy-going, quiet, sensitive, shy, and submissive. A third group of participants read the same paragraph about John but didn't learn anything about his personality.

Participants reading both versions where personality information was presented rated John as a less desirable date and romantic partner than did women who weren't presented with any personality information. To get to the bottom of things, the researchers asked participants to indicate which of the terms used to describe John were ideal for a date and for a romantic partner. The winning characteristics were sensitive, confident, and easy-going. Not one woman in the study wanted a date who was demanding – or, for that matter, submissive. Being aggressive, shy, and quiet were all also selected by very few women.[15]

The picture that emerges is less complicated than it might seem. When rating hypothetical partners, women seem to prefer men who are easy-going, warm, sensitive – read 'nice' – but also confident. Appearance matters, too, but positive personality traits and confidence seem to matter just as much, if not more. To test this idea, Gorkan Ahmetoglu and I asked female undergraduates to view one of three one-minute video recordings. In all three videos, participants saw a man enter a room, choose a chair, and then begin a conversation with two people who were just out of frame. In the first recording, the man performed what we called 'closed-body' movements – he kept his arms folded across his chest and his legs close to the chair. Two other recordings showed the man with 'open-body' movements that demonstrated confidence – he kept his arms stretched across the sofa and his legs partially open. In one of these two open-body recordings, the man could also be seen gesticulating and touching the out-of-frame partner in a sexually suggestive manner. When women rated the man in each of the three conditions for attractiveness, we found he was more attractive to the extent that he engaged in 'open-body' movements.[16]

The conclusion to be drawn from these studies is that women want both 'niceness' and confidence in a potential partner. And why not? After all, both traits are desirable and can exist in the same person. Of course, this isn't an attempt to say all women (or men) are identical in their choices. In the study I mentioned at the start of this section, where Susan was faced with a choice between Michael and Todd, a small minority of women chose 'Jerk Todd' for themselves while suggesting that Susan should go for 'Nice Todd'. So, there may be some women who go for jerks – just as there may be some men who go for jerks – or there may be some occasions when jerks seem more attractive, but the general picture that emerges is that kindness and confidence are both desirable qualities in a potential date.[17]

One final point about the nice-guys stereotype, which is that it can be very damaging for relationship formation. For one thing, it feeds directly into the misogynist's wet dream of deceitful women and earnest 'nice' men, baffled by their lack of dating success. The plea is a common one: 'Why do women always fall for these jerks? And why do guys like me who care about them always finish last and usually never have a girlfriend?'[18] It allows (some) men to blame women, to engage in woman-hating as a means of deflecting attention away from their own problematic or idiotic behaviour. Incidentally, it seems to me that if someone has to highlight their own niceness, then perhaps they aren't so nice after all.

But women don't get off so lightly either. To the extent that women endorse stereotypical constructions of 'nice guys' and 'bad guys', it may actually compromise the possibility of forming meaningful relationships. In her study of college women, for example, Kristie Ford discusses the incompatibility of some traits desired in an ideal partner, particularly that ideal partners should be 'thug'-like in appearance but 'nice' in their behaviour.[19] In short, stereotypes are often damaging, not only because they aren't based on fact, but because acting in accordance with a stereotype can create unrealistic expectations that damage relationships. And even if you think jerks are sometimes attractive, be warned: they don't make very good long-term partners.[20]

FANCY CROSSING A WOBBLY BRIDGE?

It's not just a person's personality, sense of humour, or warmth that can affect perceptions of physical attractiveness – the situation and our emotional states often matter, too. To illustrate this point, let me tell you about three studies conducted by Arthur Aron. In the 1960s, a number of psychologists became convinced at there was a connection between sexuality and aggression. t Yale University, Andrew Barclay and Ralph Haber had shown at having a lecturer berate his students for having done poorly n a test not only increased the students' anger, it also made them el more sexually aroused.[21] While the results of this study were ken as support of an aggression-sexuality link, Aron disagreed. e believed it was only a special case of a more general relationnip between any sort of emotional arousal and sexual attraction. ut how do you go about testing this idea?

His solution was to use fear. For his doctoral dissertation Aron esigned a simulation in which participants played the role of a oldier taken prisoner. Participants were 'tortured' by an interroator – really a female confederate – who dripped acid onto the articipants' forehead until he revealed all his military secrets. he 'acid' was in fact just water, but Aron encouraged the paricipant to cry out whenever he felt the 'acid' on his forehead, o imagine he felt an unbearable pain, and that if the interroation continued the acid would eventually burn through to his rain. Aron would later recall, 'At the time, simulations were still fairly new idea and I thought it would be hard to create emotion hrough role playing. I was wrong. The subjects' hands shook, hey perspired, and when asked later, they all said yes, they felt *ery* strong fear'.[22] Even the assistant who'd played the role of the nterrogator had to be comforted and calmed after 'torturing' articipants all day.

In a control condition, the confederate and participants layed the same roles, except this time the fluid really was supposed to be water, which wouldn't bother the participants too much. What did Aron find? The participants who went through he harrowing experience of being tortured were more attracted o the confederate. They had a greater desire to kiss the confederate and, when asked to write stories later, they included more romantic and sexual themes. In short, the results of Aron's doctoral dissertation had shown that a fearful situation was enough

to generate romantic attraction.[23] But Aron wasn't done scari
people yet.

Having graduated, Aron travelled to Vancouver, where he a
fellow social psychologist Donald Dutton decided to see if fe
could spark attraction in a more naturalistic setting. To do th
they relied on the fear caused by crossing the Capilano Cany
Suspension Bridge. This bridge was specifically chosen becau
of its fear-inducing properties: it had a tendency to wobble ar
sway, it had very low handrails, and it had a 230-foot drop dov
to rock and shallow rapids. Another, 'control' bridge was fu
ther up river, but this one was constructed from solid wood, w
firmer and didn't sway, and only ten feet above a shallow rivule
Bridges selected, Aron had a female experimenter lay in wa
Whenever a single man crossed either one of the bridges, th
experimenter would go up to him and explain that she was doir
a project for her psychology class on 'the effects of exposure t
scenic attractions on creative expression'. She then asked the me
if they would complete a short questionnaire.*

The first page of the questionnaire contained a few question
about prior visits to the bridge and so on, to throw the men o
the scent. On the second page, participants were shown a pictur
of a young woman covering her face with one hand and reachin
out with the other. Their task was to simply write a brief stor
based on the picture. When they'd finished writing the story, th
female experimenter thanked the men and offered to explain th
experiment in more detail when she had more time. She the
tore off a bit of paper, wrote down her name and phone number

---

* Writing in *Love and the Expansion of Self*, Aron recalled the boredom o
having to drive the confederate to the bridge every day and stand by
watching to make sure everything went well. 'About the only excitemen
to this part was the day the assistant came running to announce that a
man was about to jump off the bridge. The park ranger and I talked him
out of it'.

nd asked the men to call if they wanted to talk further. To help
he researcher identify which bridge had been crossed, the exper-
menter told men who'd crossed the suspension bridge that her
ame was Gloria, whereas if they'd crossed the stable bridge her
ame was Donna.

Back in the lab, the stories that the men had written were
cored based on the amount of sexual imagery they'd included –
mention of sexual intercourse received five points, for example,
vhile kissing got a score of three. Results showed that the men
vho had crossed the wobbly bridge were more likely to include
exual imagery in the stories they'd written compared to the men
vho'd crossed the stable bridge. Even more interesting was the
act that men who'd crossed the wobbly bridge were more likely
o later give 'Gloria' a call. That they were more attracted to the
xperimenter is suggested by the fact that very few of the men
vho'd crossed the stable bridge called to speak to 'Donna'. Sadly,
ve aren't told what happened when the men called and, I presume,
vere informed that Gloria/Donna wasn't even her real name.*

The third of Aron's studies was conducted in a laboratory set-
ing. Male undergraduates at the University of British Columbia
vere invited into a room full of electrical equipment and were
old that, as part of the experiment, they would receive an electrical shock. Some of the participants were told that the shock
would be painful, while others were told it would be a 'mere
tingle', possibly even 'enjoyable'. In both cases, there was a second 'participant' in the lab at the same time – this other 'participant', an attractive young woman, was in fact a confederate of the
experimenter.

---

* Most accounts of this study fail to mention the fact that, when a male
experimenter approached women who'd crossed the same bridges, the
women in the wobbly bridge condition were no more likely than the
women who'd crossed the stable bridge to write stories that included
sexual imagery or to call up the male experimenter.

Once everything was in place, the experimenter said it wou[ld] take a few minutes to get the equipment set up and asked t[he] men and the confederate to complete a brief questionnaire wh[ile] they waited. The questionnaire included a few questions abo[ut] anxiety – not surprisingly, the men who thought they wou[ld] get the painful shock felt more anxious than those who thoug[ht] they'd get a mild shock – but also asked how much they wou[ld] like to date and kiss the confederate. As in the bridge study, pa[r]ticipants were also asked to write a short story based on the pi[c]ture of the woman covering her face. The results of this stu[dy] showed that men in the strong shock condition wrote stori[es] with more sexual imagery, and also expressed a stronger desi[re] to date and kiss the confederate.[24]

MISATTRIBUTION OF AROUSAL

So, what was going on in these studies? The first thing to no[te] is that physiological arousal is the same for most strong emo[-] tions – whether you're experiencing anger or joy or fear, you[r] heart beats more rapidly, your breathing quickens, your muscle[s] tense up, you sweat more profusely, and you feel more awak[e] and vigilant. We learn the appropriate labels – fear, anger, jo[y] and so on – for these different states of arousal in childhood an[d] through our personal experiences. We learn, for example, tha[t] we are supposed to feel anxious before giving a public talk to [a] bunch of strangers, but fear when those strangers chase you ou[t] of the building. In both cases, the physiological response is th[e] same, but the label we have learned to associate with these differ[-] ent events determines the emotion we feel.*

---

* This is known as the Schachter-Singer two-factor theory of arousal[,] named after Stanley Schachter and Jerome Singer, who proposed th[e] idea in 1962. In their classic study, these researchers showed that, in th[e] absence of an 'appropriate explanation' for their arousal, participants

Aron believed that there are some occasions when we aren't so great at recognising the source of our arousal. Take the men who'd crossed the wobbly bridge. In all likelihood, these men were feeling physiologically aroused – their hearts were probably beating faster, they would have been feeling tense, and they would probably have been sweating more. Then along comes an attractive woman, wanting to talk about her psychology project. Talking to her at that moment, the men may have assumed they were feeling aroused by the woman and not because they had just crossed the swaying bridge. The men on the stable bridge, not feeling the same physiological arousal, were less likely to make this error. Psychologists call this a 'misattribution of arousal' and it helps to explain the findings of Aron's studies.

The misattribution of arousal doesn't always have to be based on fear. The physiological arousal from exercising makes other people, particularly attractive people, seem more appealing. Sexual arousal works, too. In one study, male students who had volunteered to take part in a study on dating were given a story to read while waiting for a date. Half the participants read an erotic story, while the other half read a story about seagulls. When the participants were given a description of the prospective female date, the men who were sexually aroused rated her as more attractive and sexier than the men who read about seagulls. In another study, men were told their heartbeats would be amplified while they looked at slides of half-naked *Playboy* bunnies. In fact, the heartbeats were not their own, but had been pre-recorded and beat faster at random occasions when the participants viewed the slides. Later, the researchers asked the men to rate the bunnies

---

could be manipulated into experiencing an emotion, such as fear or euphoria. More specifically, they demonstrated that the arousal induced by epinephrine injections could be attributed to immediate situational cues, resulting in feelings of either anger or euphoria depending on the nature of situational cues and information given to participants.

for attractiveness. Result showed that the men rated the women who supposedly made their hearts beat faster as more attractive than those who didn't make their hearts beat as fast. After the experiment was over, participants were offered a poster of a *Playboy* bunny as a token of appreciation for taking part in the experiment. Consistent with their ratings, the men were more likely to choose a poster of a bunny who had made their hearts beat faster.[25]

For anyone thinking of using the misattribution of arousal idea to give their love-lives a jump-start, there's one major problem. Not everyone lives near a wobbly bridge or has access to a room full of electrical equipment,* so getting others to a state of physiological arousal can be difficult. Thankfully, there are readily available substitutes. In one study, researchers approached individuals at amusement parks as they were waiting to go on a roller coaster ride or just after they'd gotten off the ride. The individuals were shown a photo of an opposite-sex person and asked to rate that person on attractiveness and desirability as a date. Consistent with the theory of misattribution of arousal, single women and men who'd gone on the roller coaster ride rated the person in the photo as more attractive and more desirable as a date than those who were waiting their turn.[26]

If amusement parks are not your thing, the right movie could have the same effects. For example, when asked about movies seen on a date, the vast majority of respondents in one survey recalled at least one instance of seeing a scary movie. Given that dating relationships are usually characterised by affection rather than terror and fear, scary movies would seem like an odd choice for dating couples. One reason why scary movies may be such a

---

* As it happens, I do have access to a room full of electrical equipment, but – trust me – it's not a great venue for a first date. Third date, maybe.

popular choice is that it provides opportunities for heightened arousal that helps to cement attraction. One study, in which couples were recorded as they entered and exited a cinema, found that couples who'd watched an arousing movie expressed more affection towards one another – in terms of both words and physical gestures – after the movie than before seeing it. The same wasn't true of couples who'd watched a movie that wasn't arousing.[27]

There's another, more serious problem with applying this research in the real world, which is that it may not actually work. In the 1970s, for example, Richard Dienstbier conducted a number of studies into the misattribution of arousal, including several where he found that, even when blindfolded participants were told they would be startled by the tilting of a dentist's chair, they still misattributed their arousal to an experimenter who happened to be in the room. Despite the findings of his own research, Dienstbier believed that 'it may be seldom that such arousal is a major component in the feeling of romantic attraction in normal settings... The romantically inclined reader is therefore cautioned that investment in dental equipment may not be warranted'.[28]

The bottom line is that physiological arousal does not guarantee attraction, let alone falling in love. Beyond arousal, other characteristics still matter. People need to feel that their companion, the person sitting next to them on a roller coaster or in the cinema when watching a scary movie, is suitable in terms of other desired qualities. If, for whatever reason, you are watching a scary movie with someone you already perceive as unattractive, the arousal caused during the show will actually decrease further the attraction you feel toward your date. On the other hand, if your companion is someone you like or think is desirable, then watching a scary movie or venturing into a room full of electrical equipment together may actually be a good idea and help to spur attraction.[29]

BEAUTY IS IN THE EYE OF THE BEER-HOLDER

Situational effects on attraction don't depend on the misattribution of arousal alone. Consider what happens in pubs and clubs as it gets closer to closing time. According to folk psychology, people who we would in daylight find unattractive gradually become more and more attractive as the night wears on. Folk psychology has a name for this phenomenon: the closing time effect. But is there any truth to this idea? In a very early study, research teams visited three bars at different times of the evening. The bars all closed at 12.30 in the morning. At 9PM, 10.30PM, and 12AM, researchers approached bar patrons and asked them to provide a global assessment of the attractiveness of all other members of the opposite sex who were in the bar. Results showed that, for both women and men, perceptions of attractiveness increased as the night went on.[30]

The closing time effect has been attributed to reactance. This is the idea that the threat of having something taken away or prohibited makes us want that thing even more.[31] In bars and clubs, as the opportunity for meeting potential partners and the number of available options is removed – people are going home or pairing up with someone else – nearer closing time, the remaining people become more desirable. But we can't be completely confident that the closing time effect is due solely to reactance. One reason is that neuropsychological studies have shown that even moderate alcohol consumption stimulates the reward centres of the brain, which in turn triggers the release of sex hormones.[32] If alcohol consumption increases sexual desire, then other people may become more attractive as the night wears on simply because more alcohol has been consumed. It's because we wear 'beer goggles', and not because of reactance, that other people become more attractive as the pub or club is about to close.

To test this idea, Michael Lyvers and his colleagues recruited female and male students from a campus pub and from campus parties in Australia's Gold Coast. The participants were all recruited between 9PM and 12AM, so ensuring that different amounts of alcohol would have been consumed. If a participant agreed to take part in the study, she or he took a breathalyser test to measure their levels of blood alcohol consumption. Next, they were asked to rate a number of photos of unfamiliar faces for attractiveness. The results of this study showed that, the more alcohol participants had consumed, the more attractive they rated the unfamiliar faces, confirming the beer goggles phenomenon.[33] In other words, it was the effects of alcohol that made other people seem more attractive, rather than the threat of having no one to go home with at closing time.

In another study, researchers asked patrons at a beachside pub in Sydney to provide breathalyser samples at different points in the evening, starting at 9PM and ending at the closing time of 12AM. Each time they provided blood alcohol samples, they also rated the attractiveness of all other participants in the study, as well as the two female and two male bartenders. Results of this study showed that attractiveness ratings increased as the evening wore on, but only for opposite-sex patrons. Interestingly, this closing time effect was found for both participants who were single as well as those in relationships. Reactance wouldn't seem to be the right explanation here. Those in a relationship shouldn't have been threatened by the approach of closing time. On the other hand, alcohol consumption increased as the evening wore on. As blood alcohol consumption increased, so did ratings of the attractiveness of other, opposite-sex patrons and bartenders.[34]

The beer goggles effect is interesting, not simply because it demonstrates how our perceptions of attractiveness are affected by alcohol, but also because it may sometimes lead us to make really dumb decisions. If consuming alcohol makes strangers seem more attractive, it may increase the likelihood of risky sexual behaviour. In other words, consuming alcohol not only impairs our decision-making abilities directly, it may also lead us to make poor decisions indirectly, by affecting how attractive we think potential partners are.[35] There is another, more troubling outcome of the beer goggles effect, which is the way some men try to subvert it. Summed up in the phrase 'go ugly early', the idea is that

> since it's inevitable that a guy's gonna get drunk and make a poor judgment about who to take home to fuck, he might as well get drunk quickly and choose the ugly girl early – make that poor judgment sooner rather than later... I think it says to men, 'Fuck anything you can... any hole is a good hole,' that's what I think this message says. Ideally, you would not want to fuck something that you don't want to face in the morning, but, you know, if you have to...

In her ethnographic research, Annette Markham spent time with men who live out the 'go ugly early' ideal. For these men, sex with an unattractive woman is preferable to no sex and the primary goal is to have sex with as many women as possible, using whatever means possible. As she spends time with these men, Markham comes to see how the 'go ugly ideal' both illustrates and perpetuates a tolerance of acts that violate and demean women. It is indicative of a lack of respect for women, a view of the world in which men are deserving of sex and women are nothing more than sexual objects. 'Beer goggling', far from being something that naturally occurs over the course of an evening, becomes a tactic practised in the misguided belief it guarantees sex. A small consolation appears at the end of Markham's account, when she's talking to one of the men she's been hanging out with:

Phil:	So I'm officially asking you out for a date, it's on record.
[Markham]:	Where are you taking me?
Phil:	Anywhere you want to go.
[Markham]:	No place is where I want to go with you. On or off the record.[36]

LOVE IS BLIND

I want to end this chapter on a more positive note, so let me start by telling you the story of William Steig. Best known to children as the creator of Shrek, Steig was an incredibly prolific cartoonist – so prolific in fact that *Newsweek* once dubbed him the 'King of Cartoons'. The son of Polish immigrants in New York, Steig began selling his drawings to magazines during the Great Depression to support his parents and younger siblings. He was twenty-three when he sold his first cartoon to the *New Yorker* in 1930 (a drawing that featured a convict telling another convict, 'My youngest is a terror. We can't do a thing with 'im.'), the first of some 1,600 drawings and 117 covers that he would draw for the magazine.

Steig's early drawings and cartoons captured the mood of the period between the two world wars: domestic disputes of rich folk dressing for dinner, Jewish immigrant life in the tenements, and children shrewdly observing the world around them. Later, during the Second World War, Steig began exploring more abstract, psychological states: the drawings in *The Lonely Ones*, for example, deal with alienated members of an alienating society, whose private obsessions – 'Mother loved me but she died' or 'People are no damn good' – many of us will have experienced during times of loneliness.*

---

* A decade later, and perhaps still reeling from an overwhelming sense of isolation, Steig began visiting Freud's former disciple, Wilhelm Reich. Reich's rather peculiar view was that our "primordial cosmic energy" – what he called the "orgone" – was being thwarted by physically damaging neurosis. The cure was his "orgone accumulator", a box composed of alternating layers of ferrous metals and organic insulators, large enough for adults to sit in and absorb "concentrated orgone energy". Dismissed by most psychoanalysts as a form of quackery, orgone therapy nevertheless gained some notable devotees, including Steig, who is said to have sat in an orgone accumulator every day for the rest of his life.

Steig's despair and loneliness found a more resonant expression, curiously enough, in a series of children's books he began producing in the mid-1960s. Most have become classics and deal with grown-up ethical and philosophical dilemmas through the eyes of farm animals. As a child, I remember reading *Sylvester and the Magic Pebble*, in which a donkey is saved from a lion by his unthinking wish that a magical pebble turn him into a rock. The magic pebble falls off the rock, poor Sylvester is unable to revert to his donkey form, and the rest of the story deals with Sylvester's attempt to change back into his true self.*

And then, of course, there is the fairy tale picture book *Shrek!*, first published in 1990 and later made into an award-winning animated comedy, bringing Steig's work to a worldwide audience. In Steig's book, Shrek is a green-headed ogre so hideous that 'any snake dumb enough to bite him instantly [gets] convulsions and dies'. Kicked out of his home by his parents, Shrek happens to meet a witch, who (after recovering from the sight of him) prophesies his marriage to a princess even uglier than he is. Shrek sets off in search of his beastly princess, 'slogging along the road, giving off his awful fumes'. He eventually finds her, though not before scaring half the countryside, and the two ogres are united in marriage... with the bride carrying a cactus for a bouquet.

So, what's the relevance of Shrek to our discussions of relationships? Well, for psychologists, Steig's irreverent tale is a curious example of blind attraction. Despite her monstrosity, Shrek sees in the ogre-princess such beauty that only he can comprehend. To objective observers, and possibly even to herself, the princess may appear as nothing more than a hideous ogre, but to Shrek she is the epitome of beauty. There must surely be something

---

* In case you're wondering, all ends well. *Sylvester and the Magic Pebble* even netted Steig the prestigious Caldecott medal.

wrong with Shrek, right? How can we explain his attraction to this monstrosity of a princess?

In 2007, I stumbled across an example of blind attraction in my own research. Based on an idea from studies of self-assessed intelligence, my colleagues and I asked participants to provide ratings of their own attractiveness as well as ratings of their romantic partners. Try it for yourself: based on the figure below, which shows the typical distribution of attractiveness scores in any given population, first rate your own overall physical attractiveness and the attractiveness of your various body parts. You can choose any value represented in the figure that you feel best reflects your own attractiveness. Once you've done this for yourself, do the same for your current romantic partner. If you're not currently in a relationship, I'm afraid you'll have to sit this one out.

When we asked participants from London to complete an extended version of this questionnaire, we found that both women and men rated their opposite-sex partners as being more physically attractive than themselves. The effect was most pronounced

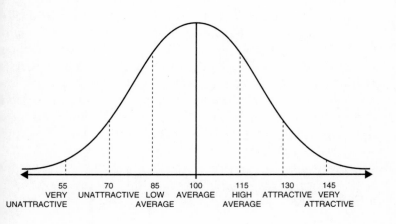

	You	Your Partner
Overall physical attractiveness		
Eyes		
Nose		
Skin		
Stomach		
Hair		

for ratings of overall physical attractiveness, but also extended to ratings of specific body parts including the mouth, nose, and even hands. An obvious objection to these findings is that the comparison is an unfair one: our respondents were all involved in heterosexual relationships and may simply have believed that individuals of the opposite gender are more attractive than their own gender. But, in a follow-up study, I found that gay men and lesbians in romantic relationships also rated their same-sex partners as more physically attractive than themselves.[37]

Another example of this effect was provided in a study of facial attractiveness. Fourteen heterosexual couples were invited to a laboratory, where they had their photographs taken individually and also completed measures assessing their attitudes toward their relationships and their partners. The photographs were then manipulated to either increase or decrease facial attractiveness, resulting in a set of seven images for each individual. One was the original image, three were less attractive than the original, and three were more attractive than the original. Several weeks after the photographs had been taken, the participants were asked to select the original images from the seven-image array. Participants who rated their relationships and partners positively were more likely to select images of their partners that had been made artificially more attractive than the original images.[38]

In fact, the finding that we perceive our romantic partners through rose-tinted glasses is very robust. The same pattern of results has been found in different countries and using different methods. The really curious thing is that it's even found among couples in new romantic relationships, with the effect being stronger for individuals who believe that their attraction was a case of love at first sight.[39] It seems that romantically involved couples, including those at the very earliest stages of a relationship, are biased in their perceptions of their partners. So robust are these findings that Adrian Furnham and I termed it the 'love-is-blind bias',[40] in reference to a line from *The Merchant of Venice* spoken by Jessica:

> Here, catch this casket; it is worth the pains.
> I am glad 'tis night, you do not look on me,
> For I am much ashamed of my exchange:
> But love is blind and lovers cannot see
> The pretty follies that themselves commit;
> For if they could, Cupid himself would blush
> To see me thus transformed to a boy.[41]

As it turns out, biased perceptions of our romantic partners are incredibly common. In reality, our everyday experiences of social worlds and interactions are based, in part at least, on perceptions that deviate from reality, or what have been called 'cognitive biases'. These biases are not exactly 'errors' in our thinking, but are more accurately described as misconceptions or misunderstandings in the way in which we perceive and understand the world.* One particular type of cognitive bias is positive illusions,

---

* The notion of cognitive biases stems from work first conducted in the early 1970s by Amos Tversky and Daniel Kahneman. Here's a simple example, first used by Tversky and Kahneman in their 1973 paper: in the English

which refers to biases that are self-enhancing in some way – such as when I take credit for my successes but deny responsibility for my failures – and are protective in that they buffer an individual's self-esteem in the face of threats posed by negative information.

So, the love-is-blind bias is a positive illusion that leads us to believe that our romantic partners are more attractive than they actually are. Far from reflecting faulty or erroneous ways of thinking, the love-is-blind bias may actually be an integral part of any developing relationship. Consider the difficulties that any couple might face during the early stages of a relationship – they are still getting to know each other and there may be competing interests from other individuals. Early on in the romance, the love-is-blind bias may help to focus attention on newly-chosen partners, creating feelings of hope and security, and helping us feel that we've made the right choice. Given the importance that most people place on appearance in a potential partner, the love-is-blind bias may help to placate doubts and cement the growing relationship. Like Shrek, most of us wear rose-tinted glasses in the early stages of a romantic relationship.

APPEARANCE AND OTHER CHARACTERISTICS

There's no getting around the fact that appearance matters, but in this chapter I've tried to show that other characteristics matter, too. Kindness, warmth, understanding, honesty, and a good

---

language, do you think there are more words beginning with the letter 'R' or that have 'R' in the third position? Most English-speaking people believe that words beginning with 'R' are more common, simply because they are easier to think of (roar, rhyme, rank). In actual fact, words that have the letter 'R' in third position are more common (street, care, borrow), but they don't come as easily to our minds. This is an example of an availability heuristic, where people overestimate the frequency of an event based on how easily examples can be brought to mind.

sense of humour are all desirable traits in a potential partner and can even make an individual seem more physically attractive. The point is that perceptions of physical attractiveness aren't fixed, they aren't static. There are many different ways in which judgements of attractiveness can change, depending on the individual and the situation. The essential point is not to get too hung up on looks. And if all else fails, just be nice (and confident). And don't forget to smile.*

And once a relationship has been initiated, the good news is that perceptions of attractiveness may be biased, particularly if the two people in the relationship like each other. Of course, all relationships involve a fine balancing act between reality and illusion, wanting to believe and knowing the truth. For couples in relationships without a strong foundation, positive illusions that are proven empty will eventually cause disappointment and conflict. But, particularly in the early stages of a relationship, we can probably take heart in knowing that, although love is often blind, that may not be such a bad thing after all.

---

* A smile increases perceptions of physical attractiveness and is also associated with more positive attributes.

5

LIKING THOSE WHO LIKE US

OR, HOW I LIKE YOU BECAUSE YOU LIKE ME, THIRTY-SIX QUESTIONS THAT MAY (OR MAY NOT) CHANGE YOUR LIFE, AND WHY PLAYING HARD-TO-GET IS... HARD

Someone should've checked the weather forecast. While walking through the park on their first date, Scott and Ramona become engulfed in a heavy snowstorm. It's snowing so hard that, eventually, Ramona uses Subspace to transport Scott and herself back to her apartment. Both before and after their date was halted by the snowstorm, Scott and Ramona exchange a good deal of information about each other – about their past lives, their living arrangements, even Ramona's penchant for tea.* Later, back at

---

* In her cupboard she has sixteen types of tea: blueberry, raspberry, ginseng, green tea, green tea with lemon, green tea with lemon and honey,

her apartment, Scott stumbles in on Ramona, who had gone into her bedroom to change out of her wet clothes. A moment passes, and then another, and then the two embrace in a kiss.

Underlying their move from conversation in a park to first kiss is what scientists call the principle of reciprocity. In its most basic form, this principle proposes that we like people who express a liking for us. This might sound like an incredibly simplistic idea, but some scientists believe the principle of reciprocity is the single most powerful determinant of whether one person will like another. Consider the growing relationship between Scott and Ramona. If at first Ramona didn't seem particularly interested in Scott, that has surely changed by the time they arrive back at her apartment. The most obvious explanation is that Scott's liking for Ramona – his obsession for her, as she puts it – is now being reciprocated.

Although the principle of reciprocity might seem straightforward, in this chapter I'll show that there are some limits to its effects. And perhaps more importantly, I'll argue that an appreciation of the principle of reciprocity calls into question a number of popular dating strategies, including playing hard-to-get. In this chapter, I'll also consider how liking can be facilitated through reciprocal self-disclosure, or the sharing of self-relevant information. This has important implications for our understanding not only of how relationships develop, but also for the use of chat-up lines. Yes, I will be discussing the science of chat-up lines. Finally, in this chapter, I'll ask whether you should be a chameleon.

I LIKE YOU BECAUSE YOU LIKE ME

In a classic study, sociologists Carl Backman and Paul Secord set out to test whether liking is reciprocal – if Scott expresses liking

---

liver disaster, ginger with honey, ginger without honey, vanilla almond, white truffle coconut, chamomile, vanilla walnut, constant comment, earl grey, and something called sleepytime.

for Ramona, does this cause Ramona to like Scott in return? They had groups of same-sex strangers take part in a series of weekly group discussions over a six-week period. Before the first meeting, the participants were told that, based on personality information they'd provided earlier, the researchers would be able to predict which group members would like each other. In actual fact, the names of the group members were randomly selected, but the participants didn't know that. After the first discussion, the researchers found that participants expressed more liking for the other group members who they believed liked them.[1]

Another way of assessing the impact of reciprocity is to make use of what's known as the 'bogus stranger paradigm'. In this method, participants don't meet face-to-face, but are instead presented with information about a bogus stranger who either likes or dislikes the participant. In one study, psychologists Andrew Lehr and Glenn Geher invited university students to a lab, where they were asked to complete a brief character evaluation of themselves. They were asked to write down things about their university degree, interests, and so on, and also completed a questionnaire about their attitudes toward current issues. Two weeks later, the participants returned to the lab and were told that other participants in the study had read their character evaluations. In some cases, the participants were told that the person reading their evaluations rated the participant as 'very likeable', whereas in other cases the participant was judged as 'not very likeable'. The participants were then given the character evaluations of the person who had supposedly judged them as likeable or not likeable. In fact, these evaluations had been written by the experimenters themselves. Here's an example:

> I am a 21-year-old female who is a psychology major. I am also a student of [State University of New York at] New Paltz. I come from Rockland County but I eventually want to live in New York City. I'm taking part in this study in order to earn credits toward the class that I am taking

this semester. I enjoy psychology very much and would like to go on to pursue a career in the field, once I graduate. However, I might want to take time off before graduate school. I'm not sure.

After reading this evaluation of the bogus stranger, participants were asked to rate how likeable they found the person and how desirable they were as short- and long-term romantic partners. As expected, the bogus stranger was rated as more likeable and more desirable as a short- and long-term partner when participants believed the stranger liked them. In short, liking was mutual.[2]

While acknowledging the usefulness of the principle of reciprocity in explaining attraction, psychologist David Kenny argued that there's an inherent problem with the sorts of studies I've described above. These studies aren't actually manipulating the actual liking of one person for another. Rather, they're only measuring the appearance of liking. The distinction is important, Kenny argued, because the effects of actual and perceived liking could be very different. For one thing, people often assume reciprocity. If you like someone, chances are you think that liking will be reciprocated. But that complicates studies of reciprocity, especially if those studies only measure the appearance of liking and not actual liking.[3]

There's quite a bit of evidence to support this thinking. For example, in his classic study of the acquaintance process, Theodore Newcomb obtained attraction ratings repeatedly from groups of students in university accommodation over a 15-week period. He found that actual reciprocity became stronger as students got to know each other over the course of the study, but even after fifteen weeks the degree of actual reciprocity remained fairly modest. Another study of dating behaviour found almost no relationship between how much a person liked his date and how much the date liked him in return. There was also no relationship between whether a man wanted to date his partner again and whether she wanted to see him again.[4]

To explain the discrepancy between the strong effects of reciprocity in bogus stranger studies and its weaker effects in real-life scenarios, Kenny argued that there are actually two types of reciprocity. The first is what he called 'generalised' reciprocity. This refers to an individual's tendency to like and be liked. The key question here is whether people who have a tendency to like are liked in return. Studies that have tried to answer this question have generally shown that 'likers' are themselves liked by others. In one study in which targets expressed liking for many other individuals and objects – political figures, cafeteria workers, cities, movies, and university courses – participants tended to like those targets more than the targets who expressed liking for few others or few objects.[5]

The other type of reciprocity is 'dyadic' reciprocity, which refers to a specific reciprocal relationship between two individuals. Take Scott: one the one hand, he could like everyone and everything he comes across – this is what is being measured in 'generalised' reciprocity. But he also specifically likes Ramona. The relevant question here is whether Scott's specific liking for Ramona – over and above his tendency to like everyone – causes Ramona to like him in return. This is what is being referred to in 'dyadic' reciprocity. When David Kenny and William Nasby measured these two types of reciprocity separately, they found weak effects of generalised reciprocity and stronger effects of dyadic reciprocity. In other words, likers are generally well-liked, but the effects are probably weak. On the other hand, a person's unique and specific liking for another tends to be reciprocated. It's dyadic reciprocity that matters when it comes to mutual liking.[6]

To really appreciate the difference between generalised and dyadic reciprocity, we have to consider its impact on romantic relationships. In non-romantic interactions, expressing a platonic liking for lots of other people should result in reciprocal liking. But in romantic relationships, demonstrating liking for everyone you come across may not be such a good idea, as it could suggest a lack of discernment or, worse, desperation. To test this possibility, Paul Eastwick and his colleagues examined the impact of selectivity in a speed-dating scenario. In their study, participants had four-minute speed-dates and then completed 'interaction records' after each date and said whether they wanted to see any date again. On each interaction record, participants rated how attracted they were to their partners and how much chemistry they felt with each one. They were also asked to assess their dates' selectivity by guessing what percentage of other people their date would want to see again.

As expected, if a partner uniquely desired a particular date, then attraction tended to be reciprocal. In other words, a participant's unique and selective desire for a date predicted the partner's experience of unique attraction and chemistry with the participant. In contrast to these effects of dyadic reciprocity, participants who desired lots of other dates tended not to be desired in return. In fact, a tendency to like everyone resulted in lower reports of attraction and chemistry toward that participant. These negative effects of generalised reciprocity remained even after the researchers took into account participants' physical attractiveness. It wasn't simply the case that less attractive people were liking everyone and being disliked in return. The results of this suggest that there's a clear difference between dyadic and generalised reciprocity, at least for romantic relationships. In the early stages of a relationship, being made to feel special generates greater liking.[7]

I LIKE YOU, BUT...

There are lots of good reasons why we like people who like us. For one thing, when we think someone likes us, we behave more positively towards that person. In one experiment, researchers brought pairs of same-sex students to a laboratory, where they had a five-minute conversation with each other. The researchers then told one member of each pair that she or he was liked or disliked by their partner. Finally, the students were reunited for a ten-minute conversation, during which they were asked to talk about current events, such as medical costs and the proliferation of nuclear weapons. Two independent raters watched this conversation from behind a one-way mirror and rated the eye gaze, body language, and movements of the participants. When the researchers looked at their data, they found that participants who believed they were liked not only reciprocated that liking, but were warmer, disagreed less, had a more pleasant tone of voice and general attitude, and disclosed more information.[8]

These sorts of positive interactions are rewarding and so it's no surprise that reciprocity facilitates further social interactions. In fact, the simple fact of being liked by someone else is rewarding because it validates the self. Knowing that I'm liked makes me believe that I must have some likeable qualities. In this sense, reciprocal liking is an important tool that helps to maintain a person's self-esteem. In addition, when people like us, they often want to continue interacting with us in the future, even if it comes at a cost. For example, people are more willing to help people they like, because they assume that support will be reciprocated in the future. And when someone signals that they're willing to provide care and support for us, we not only come to perceive those people more favourably, we're also more likely to reciprocate their affection.

The bad news is that the effects of reciprocity aren't always straightforward. Simply saying to someone that you like them is no guarantee that your liking will be reciprocated. There are lots of factors that facilitate and, more often, limit the effects of reciprocity. For example, in his book *Ingratiation*, the social psychologist Ed Jones pointed out that the reciprocity effect is affected by the perceived motives of the target.[9] Before we begin interacting with someone, we try to work out whether that person will behave benevolently or try to exploit the interaction. If we believe the person is motivated by genuine liking, we're more likely to believe the interaction will be successful and so attraction is reciprocated. But if the other person is judged to have an ulterior motive or is insincere in their liking, attraction won't be reciprocated.

Take Scott and Ramona. Scott says he likes Ramona because that's the truth. But Ramona might have her doubts. She might believe, for example, that Scott is only saying he likes her because he wants a quicker delivery service from Amazon. In that scenario, Ramona is unlikely to reciprocate Scott's liking, despite all the conditions being in place for reciprocal liking. One reason why ulterior motives might reduce attraction is because we experience psychological reactance – the same explanation that has been used to explain the closing time effect we saw in the previous chapter. In the 1960s, Jack Brehm developed his ideas around reactance and conducted a study that sheds light on the effects of an ulterior motive on reciprocity.[10]

In the study, participants were instructed to form an impression of another individual, the target. In one condition – the high-importance condition – participants were told the accuracy of the impressions was absolutely critical. The study's goal was to predict the target's future success in life, and participants' predictions were crucial to that goal. In another condition – the low-importance condition – participants were simply told that the study was being conducted as part of a student's project. Next, the target either brought the participants a soda or nothing at all. After the participants rated the target, they were also given an opportunity to help her or him. The results of the study showed that participants in the high-importance condition were less likely to help the target after being brought a soda. The explanation? According to the theory of reactance, being brought a soda threatened participants' freedom to make an independent judgement of the target in the high-importance condition. Only by restoring the perception of freedom and not reciprocating the help received could the participants evaluate the target freely.[11]

It isn't just the presence of an ulterior motive that affects the reciprocity of liking. Ed Jones also believed that size of the sacrifice made by someone could affect liking. If someone makes a sacrifice as part of an interaction, we're more likely to believe that the person is sincere and trustworthy. On the other hand, if something is done to demonstrate liking without any personal cost, we believe the display is unreliable because it could be repeated elsewhere and with other people. Of course, the 'display' in this case doesn't have to be tangible. If just saying you like someone comes at a risk – you might be rejected, for example – then we still perceive that display as being honest and reliable.

To test the effects of sacrifice on reciprocity, Dean Pruitt had participants interact with a confederate who had either $1 or $4. The participants, meanwhile, had $2. During the interaction, the confederate gave the participant either 20 per cent or 80 per cent of their money. Participants who received 80 per cent of the confederate's $1 gave back more money to the confederate than those who got 20 per cent of $4. Although the amount of money was the same in both conditions – 80¢ – attraction was greater when the confederate made a bigger sacrifice. One reason for this is that participants believed the confederate who'd made the larger sacrifice was more likely to behave in a similar way in the future and it was that belief that sparked attraction.[12]

All of these different studies might suggest that there are lots of different underlying factors affecting reciprocal liking. The psychologist Matthew Montoya believes it might be possible to bring everything together if we focus on trust. His view is that expressing liking for someone is a symbolic act of investment in the relationship. Saying 'I like you' or even 'I love you' – or demonstrating these feelings by bringing someone a cold drink or even just blushing or swooning – conveys a willingness to continue investing in the relationship. In turn, these expressions of attraction lead to trust, which generates even more attraction. What's more, when we believe someone is trustworthy, we're much more likely to want to interact with that person in the future, simply because we believe those interactions are going to be beneficial in some way. In short, expressing liking leads to attraction and feelings of trust, which in turn leads to greater attraction.[13]

A FLEETING SMILE

How do I know that you like me? In the very early stages of a relationship, this seemingly simple question is actually incredibly important, but also difficult to answer. Imagine you've spotted someone you think is attractive across a crowded room or in a bar. How do you decide whether you'll approach that person? Rejection in these situations can be painful, so to minimise the chances of a negative response, we make use of a number of different 'approach tactics'. But I should really clarify what I mean by 'we'. You see, gendered dating scripts – the ideas and beliefs we have about dating – for heterosexual couples allow for approach behaviour by men, whereas women are socialised to engage in behaviours that signal interest. This isn't to say that women don't ever approach men, just that women are more likely to be perceived as transgressing gendered norms of behaviour when they do so.*

---

* Of course, and to repeat a point I've made several times already, not all men are the same. Nevertheless, ideas of "paternalistic chivalry" – the notion that men should initiate and take control of approach behaviours and dating decisions – continue to dominate how heterosexual couples interact. The most obvious reason for this is that we live in societies where women have less power than men. But gender-stereotypical dating scripts also provide couples with a familiar and mutually-agreed framework of behaviour that reduces anxiety, particularly in the early stages

Bearing this in mind, what are some of the behaviours that people engage in to signal liking? Albert Scheflen, a psychiatrist, provided one of the earliest descriptions of signalling behaviour in his paper about client-therapist interactions during psychotherapy sessions. He noted that both therapists and clients engaged in behaviours that were reminiscent of courtship, but because it occurred in an inappropriate context – psychotherapy sessions – he called them 'quasi-courtship' behaviours. Among the behaviours he identified were less 'belly sag', hair stroking, adjusting one's clothing, leaning forward, and 'palming' or displaying the open wrist and palm of the hand. Despite his description of these behaviours as 'quasi-courtship' signals, Scheflen also believed they shouldn't be taken as serious signals of romantic interest.[14]

A better way of figuring out the things that people do to signal interest is simply to ask them. In the 1970s, a team of researchers stopped college students while they were out and about and asked them to list the types of behaviours they thought were used by women in heterosexual social interactions. Based on the list generated, the researchers categorised 'cold' and 'warm' behaviours. Warm behaviours included things like smiling a lot, using expressive hand gestures, licking one's lips, and playing with an object, such as a pencil or a ring. In a follow-up study, the same researchers asked an actress to display some of these warm behaviours or some cold behaviours. As expected, she was

---

of interaction. Even if these scripts facilitate smooth interactions in the short term, they may make authentic communication between women and men difficult, especially if they limit what a person can and can't express or do. Online dating websites get around this to a degree by allowing potential partners to easily indicate liking at the click of a button. Once a 'like' (or a wink or a flirt, depending on the site) is received, the receiver can decide whether to respond in kind or more fully by sending a message.

rated as more attractive by men when she displayed the warm behaviours.[15]

An even better method is to observe what happens in real-world settings. This is exactly what Monica Moore did. She observed women at a range of different venues and compiled a catalogue of 52 types of different behaviours that she believed were courtship behaviours that signalled interest. The list included what sex researcher Timothy Perper calls 'proceptive' behaviours – things like smiling, leaning forward, laughing, glancing, and nodding.[16] But how do we know these behaviours signalled interest? In a second study, Moore observed the frequency of her catalogue of behaviours at four locations – a singles bar, a university snack bar, a university library, and a women's centre. She found that women were far more likely to do the things in her catalogue when they were at a singles bar compared to all other venues. In fact, in a later study, Moore and a colleague found that these behaviours were so striking that a trained observer could use their frequency to predict the outcome of interactions with men.[17]

Other researchers have found that men are much more likely to approach a woman if she first makes repeated eye contact, followed by smiling. In fact, mutual gaze seems to be important before any formal interaction has taken place. In another study, pairs of high school students were filmed while meeting for a brief interaction in a lab that had been set up to look like a living room. In this research, a participant's liking for a partner was associated mainly with mutual gaze. The more two people looked into each other's eyes, the more they were attracted to each other. But more important than the actual behaviour is the frequency of a woman's signalling behaviour. In fact, Moore found in her research that the frequency of signalling was even more important than a woman's physical attractiveness. When women, regardless of how attractive they are, increase the frequency of their signalling behaviour, they are more likely to be approached by men.[18]

The point of any signalling behaviour is to make social interaction more likely, but this relies on accurate perceptions of a partner's behaviours. The trouble is that men seem to have trouble with this and often end up misinterpreting women's behaviours. In one piece of research, women and men were asked to take part in a five-minute conversation, while another pair of participants secretly observed the interaction. Men, regardless of whether they were participating in the conversation or just observing, rated the woman in the conversation as more promiscuous and seductive than did the women in the study. In other words, men seemed to be misinterpreting a woman's friendliness as romantic attraction – or more. Men are especially likely to misinterpret a woman's behaviours when those behaviours are ambiguous or when men have been consuming alcohol.[19]

These issues are far from trivial. On the one hand, if individuals are misinterpreting each other's signals, it might mean that otherwise satisfying relationships fail to develop. One of the biggest impediments to relationship formation is fear of rejection. Individuals often don't ask to see someone on a date or on a second date because of fears their liking won't be reciprocated. The curious thing is that, when participants are asked what might motivate a partner's inaction – why the other person didn't ask for a date – individuals usually interpret it, not in terms of fear, but in terms of pessimism.[20] When I don't ask someone out on a date, it's because I'm afraid of rejection. When someone doesn't ask me out, I think it's because they don't like me. It's sad to ponder how many relationships have floundered because of such misperceptions of liking.

If individuals misinterpret other people's behaviours, it can also have more serious consequences. In fact, surveys consistently show that women are more likely than men to experience misperceptions of their friendliness as sexual or romantic interest. Although most such interactions are resolved amicably, some women report how such misperceptions escalate to involve a degree of sexual coercion. Some researchers believe that the issue is about 'thresholds' – men, the argument goes, have different thresholds for interpreting interest in a potential partner.[21] The trouble with this explanation is that there's a big difference between misinterpreting a behaviour and carrying on despite misinterpreting a behaviour. The former can be passed off as an error of judgement; the latter can't.

WHAT'S YOUR FAVOURITE PIZZA TOPPING?

A woman signals her interest. A man approaches. Next comes the opening gambit, better known as the dreaded chat-up line. You might be surprised to know that scientists actually spend their time analysing chat-up lines, but there are good reasons for this. Chat-up lines can be seen as a form of courtship display. Men might use chat-up lines to display their wealth – 'I'm one of the owners of this bar; would you like to dance?' – or their knowledge of high culture, as depicted in this exchange in which a man turns to a woman and points out the large piano in the corner of a room:

Man: It's a fine instrument, wouldn't you say? A Steinway concert grand if I'm not mistaken.

Woman: Oh really... do you play then?

Man: Just a little myself. I'm not really good enough to perform... unless, that is, you would like me to...

Woman: Well, I wouldn't want to force you into it... But I've always loved Beethoven's Moonlight Sonata...

Man: Ah... yes, the Moonlight Sonata, or to give it its true name, Sonata Quasi Una Fantasia. A fittingly beautiful piece for a beautiful lady. I will try, but I can only hope that my attempt will do you justice.[22]

But beyond signalling potentially desirable traits, chat-up lines also serve a different purpose. On the part of the man, they signal interest. Whatever the content of the chat-up line, its use is one way in which a man can display to a potential partner that he's interested. It could also be used as a quick way of screening women who might or might not be interested. And on the part of the recipient, a positive response could likewise signal interest. A woman who responds positively to a chat-up line might signal that she's interested in having a conversation with the man, whereas a woman who responds negatively is clearly uninterested. This was in fact what was found in one observational study of women and men at a bar. Women who laughed at a man's sexual jokes seemed more interested in him than women who chose not to laugh.[23]

So, chat-up lines may be a way for women and men to gauge the potential for reciprocal liking. More than that, chat-up lines may also be a useful way to facilitate reciprocal exchange of information during an interaction. In *Quirkology*, his book about 'the science of everyday lives', Richard Wiseman describes the results of a mass speed-dating study that took place at the Edinburgh International Science Festival. A hundred people went on three-minute dates before being asked who they would like to see again. Wiseman and his team of researchers then compared the conversations of participants who were rated as very desirable or undesirable by their dates. One thing they found was that men were much more likely than women to use closed questions or statements. These were typically one-liners that required a yes or no answer or just made interaction awkward – 'My best friend's a helicopter pilot'.

Not only did these sorts of questions stifle conversation, they also resulted in the suitor being perceived as less desirable as a date. In contrast, the most effective chat-up lines were those that were impossible to answer with a simple 'yes' or 'no'. 'What's your favourite pizza topping?' is an example of a light-hearted, open-ended question that doesn't just facilitate interaction, but allows for creative responses. Another, used by the most desirable man in the study, was 'If you were in *Stars in Your Eyes*, who would you be?' The results of this speed-dating study suggest that the best opening gambits are those that facilitate reciprocal exchange of information that might give glimpses of a date's personality or character. In case you're wondering, my favourite pizza topping is pepperoni.[24]

Of course, just because a chat-up line was successful at the Edinburgh International Science Festival doesn't mean it's going to be effective in every social situation. Context matters – walking up to someone in a library, for example, and asking them about pizza toppings is unlikely to lead anywhere. And subcultures may develop unique forms of initiating a conversation. For example, among Goths who have a penchant for elaborate footwear, 'Nice boots!' has become a standard chat-up line.[25] As for women using chat-up lines, the evidence suggests that opening gambits in which the woman directly signals liking are the most effective. Giving a man her phone number, asking whether the man is single, or asking directly for a date may be effective for women because they make it easier for a man to understand that she's interested in him.[26]

The science of chat-up lines might sound like a bit of fun, but it shouldn't obscure the way in which opening gambits are increasingly used by some men as a demonstration of misogyny. Demands for sex, abusive responses to rejection, and dick pics – unsolicited photos of genitals – are all common forms of woman-hating in contemporary dating. In one study, researchers who were interested in men's perceptions of speed-dating placed ads calling for participation on online dating and social networking sites. When the ad was placed by a male researcher, there was almost no response. But when the ad was placed by a female researcher, not only did it bring more interest in the study, men also began sending the researcher dick pics, invitations to meet, requests for a relationship, and demands for sex. When the same researcher interviewed the men about their speed-dating experiences, she quickly found that men steered the conversations in a predatory manner. During one online interview, for example this happened:

Zoe:	Is there anything else you would like to tell me? Anything you thin I've missed out?
Ryan:	No hun so how about us meeting then or do u know anyone that wud like to meet me tomorrw in town
Zoe:	Well as I said I'm already in a relationship so I can't meet you, bu I really do appreciate your help with my research.
Ryan:	Thank u hun we kud meet just don't say owt to yor partner.[27]

These sorts of interactions occurred repeatedly, both in online and face-to-face interviews, despite the researcher making it absolutely clear she was not interested in dating any of the men and that she was only interested in the academic research she was conducting. These men were using sexual innuendo, propositions of sex, and claims about their sexual prowess to regain some of the power from the interviewer. When that failed, they objectified her body, pointing at her breasts and using her figure in their narratives. Even among men who weren't behaving in a predatory manner, a form of benevolent sexism was common: the poor female researcher, forever needing to be protected like all women, should beware of other predatory men. Understanding when and why men engage in these sorts of behaviours might be interesting from an academic point of view, but the same can't be said for women on the receiving end of this misogynist crap.

WOT RU DOING 2NITE?

Of course, the scenarios I've used above assume that people are still initiating romance in bars and clubs, but as we saw in Chapter 2, that's not really the case anymore. In fact, surveys now show that young people in particular are much more likely to ask someone out on a first date by text message, rather than face-to-face or with a phone call.[28] But it's not just young people who are living their romantic lives through text messages. Even among adults, texting – or sending messages via free apps like WhatsApp – is emerging as an important form of approach behaviour. The most obvious advantage of a text is that an approach can be made without having the courage needed to make the same approach face-to-face or via a phone call. In fact, in *Alone Together*, the social psychologist Sherry Turkle argues that young people in particular are so used to text-based communications that their skills in spontaneous conversation are declining. For these young people, texting allows users to avoid awkward silences.[29]

Texting at the start of a relationship raises some new – and some old – questions about approach behaviour. Among teen-agers, it is now common to exchange a series of texts before becoming romantically involved. This exchange of texts is a means for both girls and boys to gauge the other person's interest before actually asking the other person out. It also enables girls to express romantic interest without actually asking the boy out herself, and so preserves a masculinist fiction of the boy being in control. Likewise, boys can avoid the embarrassment of rejection by working out via text if a girl is interested before actually ask-ing her out. In fact, some researchers believe that the ability to connect with a potential romantic interest, while keeping them at physical distance, is empowering for girls and boys negotiating new relationships.[30]

But texting also brings with it a whole new set of problems. Because texting occurs in the absence of the sorts of cues that are common in face-to-face conversations, like tone of voice and facial cues, getting across humour or sarcasm can be difficult. It can also encourage people to behave differently to how they'd behave in person or on the phone. Sometimes, this can be a good thing – like when it allows someone who is otherwise shy to ask a potential partner out on a date. Other times, it results in the sorts of obnoxious, sexually aggressive behaviour that is chronicled on Straight White Boys Texting. The tumblr is full of texts where men open a conversation with a woman with inept sexual advances, like 'I need an opinion on my penis size' or 'Mmmmmmm baby what are you wearing baby?' The misogyny that drips from texts like these make any sort of further interaction unlikely.

But even when texts don't reflect and enact such blatant misogyny, interactions via text can have a huge effect on budding relationships. Grammatical or spelling errors can be off-putting for some people, while for others the use of text-speak – OMG amirite? – could change a person's impression of you instantaneously. In person or on the phone, there is the opportunity to correct or rephrase something, but in the world of texting, such opportunities are difficult to come by. Moreover, the anxiety caused by waiting for a reply can sometimes make people behave in stupid ways. The Bye Felipe tumblr is a good example of this it's full of messages from men who, while polite initially, turn hostile when ignored or rejected.

In fact, the anxiety of waiting for a reply appears to be a common theme among people using text messages for romantic purposes. Some people seem to have developed strategies for dealing with replies – not texting back immediately appears to be a common strategy, although the advised delay can vary from a few minutes to days – but sadly, empirical research on this all-important matter is lacking. What we do know is that texters use their replies to manage impressions, and paramount above all else is the wish to avoid seeming too desperate. By not texting back immediately, texters are also able to manage power in the budding relationship. And in using replies as a reward, individuals are also able to gain a sense of control in the relationship and so manage how the relationship progresses. In this way, text exchanges are similar to non-text romantic interactions.[31]

AFFINITY TESTS AND SECRET TESTS

If a relationship survives the chat-up line and the initial social interaction – or the initial texts – then individuals begin to use other strategies to determine whether liking is reciprocal. The trouble with these early stages of a relationship is that they are often characterised by uncertainty – why did he say that? how should I respond? does she like me? how will he behave in the future? These sorts of questions are common in initial relationships because we have such little information about the other person. And when individuals feel uncertain, they evaluate their partners more negatively and feel as though the relationship is more turbulent.[32] To lessen feelings of uncertainty, we try to acquire information about the other person and the state of the relationship.

In the 1970s, Charles Berger and Richard Calabrese proposed the 'uncertainty reduction theory' to account for the impact of uncertainty on initial interactions between strangers. According to this theory, in the early stages of interaction, individuals use three different strategies to gather information about their partners and so reduce uncertainty. Before any social interaction has occurred, they begin by simply observing the other person. This is known as 'passive' information-seeking, but the 'data' it provides is of a relatively poor quality – there's only so much you can learn about a person just by observing their behaviour. Better yet is to observe the target as they interact with others, particularly in informal social settings where there's no reason to constrain one's behaviour, or to ask a third party about the target. This sort of 'active' information-seeking brings better 'data' – it provides a glimpse into the 'real' nature of the target beyond what can be inferred when she or he is silent or isolated.[33]

Once interaction has begun, individuals engage in what Berger and Calabrese called 'interactive' information-seeking. In the first few minutes of an interaction, individuals try to find out basic information about their partner by asking lots of questions. In fact, studies show that the first few minutes of interactions between strangers can involve up to twenty-two questions, mostly about a partner's biographic and demographic characteristics. Where are you from, how old are you, what are you doing here, do you have any pets, what's your favourite pizza topping.... These sorts of questions can provide us with very useful information about the other person, and some scientists believe that we use this information to make quick assessments of relationship 'fit'. In other words, we seem to use these first few minutes of interrogating another person to gather information about whether she or he is someone worth forming a relationship with.[34]

Asking questions might be a very efficient way of seeking information and reducing uncertainty, but the problem with asking too many questions is that it can be very obtrusive. Do you really need to know what my favourite pizza topping is? Really? Not surprisingly, people switch to other information-seeking strategies a few minutes into the interaction. One such strategy is to make the target feel relaxed and comfortable, the idea being that a relaxed partner is more likely to offer personal or vulnerable information about themselves. In fact, there's some evidence that target relaxation efforts – learning forward, supportive language, head nods – are more frequently used by people who are interested in their partners. But the trouble with this technique is that it may not provide the information we want or find useful in determining whether to pursue the relationship.[35]

One final strategy that Berger and Calabrese identified is known as 'self-disclosure' and relies specifically on the norm of reciprocity. The premise of self-disclosure goes something like this: I offer you some personal information about myself, which puts pressure on you to reveal the same information about yourself in return. By telling you that my favourite pizza topping is pepperoni, I've put pressure on you to reciprocate. Talk about pizza toppings might seem trivial, but the same principle is at work when we disclose more personal information or even secrets to a partner. Self-disclosure is one of the most important building blocks for intimacy and relationship formation, so I return to it more fully later in the next section of this chapter.

For now, it's important to note that the three strategies above – passive, active, and interactive information-seeking – occur in the initial stages of all relationships. Things might be slightly more complicated when we're trying to figure out whether our liking for a person is reciprocal. In a classic study, William Douglas found that, when individuals want to know whether attraction and liking is mutual, they employ a range of different information-seeking tactics in initial interactions. In fact, he found eight different strategies of what he called 'affinity-testing'. These are described in the table below along with examples from interviews that Douglas conducted with heterosexual women and men:

Confronting	Actions that put pressure on a partner to provide immediate and (usually) public evidence of her or his liking	'I asked her if she liked me'
Withdrawing	Actions that require a partner to make an effort to sustain the interaction	'I would be silent sometimes to see if he would start the conversation again'
Sustaining	Actions that are designed to maintain the interaction without affecting levels of intimacy	'I tried to keep him talking. I asked him questions. I told him about me'

HAZING	Actions that require the partner to do or provide something at a cost to her or himself	'I told him I live 16 mile... away... I wanted to see if he would try and back out'
DIMINISHING SELF	Actions that make the self look bad, either through self-deprecation or by identifying potential alternative partners	'There were these other guys there. I kept pointing them out to her'
APPROACHING	Actions that imply greater liking to which the partner has to respond	'I would touch his shoulder or move closer to see if he would react by staying where he was or moving closer'
OFFERING	Actions that facilitate intimacy	'I waited for him to come out of the restroom. Everyone else had left by that time. If he wanted to ask me out, he could'
NETWORKING	Actions that involve third parties, either to get more information or to transmit information to the partner	'I went over and asked his friends about him'

In his research, Douglas found that 'confronting' and 'approaching' were generally perceived as the most efficient strategies for finding out whether attraction was mutual. 'Withdrawing', 'hazing', and 'diminishing self' were not only seen as the least efficient strategies, they were also rated as the least socially appropriate.

The participants in this research also rated 'sustaining' as the most socially appropriate strategy.[36] This seems to fit with the interrogation strategy that Berger and Calabrese identified. So what works best? Putting together these two bodies of research, it would seem that the best strategy in initial interactions is to ask lots of biographic and demographic questions. This is seen as socially acceptable by most people, but it's also a fairly efficient way of working out whether romantic attraction is reciprocal. Asking a person directly whether or not liking is mutual may be more efficient, but it's also less socially acceptable.

Many of the strategies that Douglas identified are also used to work out how a romantic relationship is progressing over time. For example, Leslie Baxter and William Wilmot found that, when trying to work out the state of a romantic relationship, individuals engage in what they called 'secret tests'. These included things like testing the lengths a person would go to for the sake of the relationship, seeing how a partner responded to a particular public introduction ('this is my girlfriend...'), and not seeing each other to see how committed a partner is. One specific type of strategy used once a romantic relationship had been initiated was 'triangular tests'. These involved introducing third parties into the mix – for example, flirting with someone else to see how a partner responds.[37]

In their research, Baxter and Wilmot found that couples tended to use these indirect strategies to acquire information about the state of the relationship. The use of indirect strategies was particularly rampant if the relationship had potential, but hadn't yet been formally defined as exclusive – relationships where the couple were 'more than friends' but not yet romantically involved. In fact, other research has shown that the use of secret tests is commonplace in romantic relationships – one study found that young adults averaged 4.5 secret tests in their current relationships. The use of these secret tests generally decreases as the relationship progresses, when direct questioning becomes more common. As a romantic relationship progresses, we begin to use fewer secret tests and more direct questioning to work out whether attraction is mutual.[38]

So far, I've highlighted the negative impact of uncertainty on relationship formation. I've shown you that uncertainty decreases liking for a partner, increases relationship turmoil and negative emotions, and makes communication between partners more difficult. But some researchers believe that uncertainty can be also rewarding. Too much certainty might make a relationship too predictable and therefore monotonous, whereas uncertainty can sometimes lead to deeper processing of information, which in turn sparks interest.[39] And there may be some situations where we would prefer to maintain uncertainty, rather than decrease it. For example, some people may use uncertainty as a way of piquing a partner's interest, while others avoid seeking information if they know that information isn't what they want to hear. In the early stages of a relationship, for instance, we might avoid asking about a partner's relationship status if we like them but would rather not know that they aren't single.[40] Uncertainty may be bad for a relationship, but we're not always motivated to reduce uncertainty.

I WANT TO LIVE FOR ANOTHER THOUSAND YEARS

On my left forearm, I have a tattoo that reads, 'I want to live for a thousand more years'. It's a line from a poem called 'Aku', meaning 'Me', by the Indonesian poet Chairil Anwar. The poem says something about the nature of individuality and freedom, and I think it's that which made me want to have the line tattooed on my arm. Anyway, I mention this because tattoos, particularly visible tattoos, can be interpreted as a form of self-disclosure – a deliberate act of revealing information, thoughts, or feelings to someone else during the course of an interaction. Tattoos, like wedding rings and even the clothes we wear, are a form of non-verbal self-disclosure.

In fact, anything that conveys a message or communicates information to another person is a form of self-disclosure, but most of the time when scientists refer to self-disclosure they mean its verbal variety. This occurs when one individual – the 'discloser' – verbally communicates some information to a listener. Self-disclosure comes in many different forms, but it can also vary in content. If I said to you, 'I like tattoos', that tells you something descriptive about me. But if I said, 'I want to live for a thousand years more', that would tell you something about my subjective feelings or emotions. Or I could say, 'I like people who have tattoos,' and that would tell you something about my relationships with other people.

In the 1970s, Irwin Altman and Dalmas Taylor developed their rude-sounding 'theory of social penetration', which places self-disclosure at the heart of relationship formation. According to their theory, individuals will increase the range of activities they share with one another if a relationship progresses in a positive direction. This, ahem, social penetration can include non-verbal gestures (smiling or kissing, for example), but the theory emphasises the important role played by self-disclosure. Social penetration theory identifies a number of different dimensions of self-disclosure. These include how many different topics are being disclosed, or topic breadth, and how intimate the level of disclosure is, or topic depth. According to Altman and Taylor, self-disclosure occurs gradually, progressing from superficial to more intimate topics.[41]

To see self-disclosure in action, Dalmas Taylor followed freshmen who were assigned as dormitory roommates at the beginning of an academic semester at the University of Delaware. The roommates were all initially strangers to each other and, several times over the course of the semester, they completed questionnaires measuring how much information they shared with one another. Taylor found, as the semester progressed, participants exchanged information about a greater number of topics. Most of the time, they discussed superficial topics, but later into the semester they were more likely to talk about intimate issues. In other words, at the start of a relationship, roommates were cautious about revealing too much personal information about themselves, but as they got to know one another, they were more willing to discuss intimate topics.[42]

While social penetration theory predicts a gradual process of self-disclosure, this isn't always what happens. There are times when we 'click' with someone else. At the start of a relationship, we make quick assessments about how well someone fits our ideas of a friend or partner.* If the fit is good, it can sometimes accelerate the process of self-disclosure, leading us to communicate intimate details about ourselves very early on in the relationship, spending lots of time with that person, and quickly identifying them as a 'partner' or 'close friend'. This is called the 'clicking model' of relationship development and, as the name suggests, high levels of self-disclosure can sometimes occur very quickly.[4] In fact, when it comes to friendships, it seems that we make our minds up about the other person within the first ten minutes of a conversation. These initial impressions, in turn, are associated with how much information we exchange with the other person and how intimate the relationship becomes over time.

Self-disclosure could accelerate very quickly, as the clicking model suggests, or it could occur more gradually. In reality, we probably use different patterns of self-disclosure with different people. Negotiating the early stages of a relationship can be tricky, as individuals decide how open they're going to be with the partners. At every stage of a relationship, we have to make decisions

---

* Or, alternatively, we might determine to what extent that person resembles a mental representation we have for someone positive, such as a parent, close friend, or previous partner. If the resemblance is high, then it's possible that we 'transfer' some of that liking onto the stranger and, as a result, both like that person more and self-disclose more to them.

about how much information we want to share with a partner and how intimate (or not) that information is going to be. Sometimes, the exchange of intimate information will nurture the relationship, drawing the two people involved closer together. Other times, we might worry that disclosing too much information will mean we'll be ridiculed or stigmatised.* Or maybe the other person will end up getting hurt. Balancing all of these different concerns means that patterns of self-disclosure will change over time depending on the nature of the relationship.[44]

The big question: women self-disclose more than men, right? Well, yes and no. When we take into account the range of relationships we form – friendships, romantic relationships, and so on – then, yes, women generally self-disclose more than men.[45] Self-disclosure is seen as more gender-appropriate for women than for men, particularly among new acquaintances. The one possible exception to this general rule is in the early stages of a romantic relationship. In the first stages of a romantic relationship, men seem to use self-disclosure strategically. In other words, they use self-disclosure to try to accelerate the 'getting to know you' stage of a relationship. This might be particularly true when men can fulfil gender stereotypes about being the 'initiator' at the beginning of a relationship.

As a test of these ideas, researchers had women and men who were strangers to each other take part in group conversations

---

* For example, the decision to come out among lesbian, gay, bisexual, transgender, and queer individuals can be difficult if they believe they will be stigmatised. Concealment of sexual orientation is a common coping strategy among this group of individuals, but it comes at a cost. Individuals who conceal their sexual orientation report lower satisfaction with their friendships and work relationships, and have poorer mental health. On the other hand, coming out is generally viewed as a positive part of developing a stable identity and sense of self, and brings with it an array of mental and physical health benefits.

to get to know one another. Once that was over, participants were assigned to a partner, either a woman or a man, for a second phase of the study. This partner didn't in fact exist, but the participants didn't know that. Instead, they were told that the partner was interested in getting to know the participant better based on the group conversation. To facilitate the second phase, a research assistant was tasked with preparing a self-description of participants for their bogus partners. The results showed that, when men thought their partner was a woman, they self-disclosed more to the assistant than women paired with a man. In other words, when men occupy the role of initiator, they are more likely to self-disclose, which also increases their liking for a partner.[46]

One place where things might be slightly different is on social networking sites like Facebook. Aside from the fact that users have profiles that usually include their profile photo and basic identifying information, the nature of communication on sites like Facebook means that self-disclosure occurs between large groups of people – so-called 'masspersonal communication'.[47] Consider a status update: even with strict privacy settings, updates are still usually shared with a group of people. In fact, studies show that most Facebook users disclose a large amount of personal information through their status updates, although most of it isn't intimate. The interesting thing is that reading status updates of our friends on Facebook has a similar effect as offline interactions. One study of German students found that reading self-disclosing status updates, even if those updates were entertaining rather than intimate, enhanced feelings of closeness.[48]

In fact, people seem to think there is a lower risk to self-disclosure on Facebook, which allows them to express themselves more freely through status updates. This might be particularly beneficial for people with low self-esteem, who are normally less willing to self-disclose and who have difficulty maintaining satisfying relationships. Unfortunately, when researchers have examined the Facebook posts of people with low self-esteem, they've found those posts to be highly negative. One study asked participants to log in to their Facebook accounts and provide researchers with their ten most recent status updates. The researchers then categorised the updates based on how negative or positive they were, and asked a new set of participants to rate how much they liked the persons who'd posted the updates. They found that participants with low self-esteem tended to post very negative updates and, as a result, were liked less than participants with high self-esteem. The authors of this study end by advising people with low self-esteem to share more of the positive things that happen to them and to be selective about the negative things they post.[49]

THIRTY-SIX QUESTIONS

So far, I've mainly discussed self-disclosure as a one-way process – one person discloses something to another. But self-disclosure is often a reciprocal transaction. When I tell you that I love tattoos or my favourite pizza topping is pepperoni, you infer that I must like and trust you. I'm not about to share my deepest secrets with anyone and everyone, so when I self-disclose to you, it gives the impression that I am invested in you. In turn, you are more likely to self-disclose something about yourself. Over the course of an interaction, this self-disclosure reciprocity builds mutual trust and liking. In fact, we seem to be biased to remember these sorts of positive reciprocal interactions.[50] Or, we can also look at it from the opposite point of view. Say I've just told you about my love of tattoos. The norms of conversation suggest you should reciprocate, either by telling me about something you love or – better yet – by agreeing that tattoos are awesome. If you don't, well, then the conversation just gets awkward. We want to avoid feeling uncomfortable in social interactions, so there's an impetus to reciprocate my self-disclosure.

In fact, how a person responds to self-disclosure in the course of an interaction has a huge impact on how the relationship will develop. In one study, Deborah Davis and William Perkowitz set up an experiment about the 'acquaintance process'. A participant and a confederate took turns answering a series of questions. Most of the questions were about a superficial topic – 'What would you do if you suddenly inherited a million dollars?' for example. In some cases, the participant and the confederate answered the same questions 80 per cent of the time, while in others they did so only 20 per cent of the time. Despite the superficiality of the questions, Davis and Perkowitz found that, when participants and the confederate answered more questions in common, the participants felt more acquainted with the confederate. In fact, they concluded that conversational reciprocity 'affected something more basic than attraction, namely the perception of a "bond"' between the two people in the study.[51]

Instead of responding to my self-disclosure with the same content, you could just listen, nod your head, and choose to reciprocate much later in the conversation or even the next time we meet. But this might not be such a good idea. Susan Sprecher and her colleagues had unacquainted individuals engage in a conversation over Skype for a few minutes. In one condition, a participant would ask a question – for example, 'What is your happiest childhood memory?' – which her or his partner would answer. That partner would then ask the same question, which the first participant would then answer immediately. In a second condition, one participant asked the questions while the other answered. After all the questions had been asked, the two switched roles. Despite reciprocal self-disclosure occurring in both conditions, the researchers found that only participants in the first condition reported greater liking and closeness for their partners. In other words, turn-taking in self-disclosure seems to be the key to building intimacy.[52]

However, the type of information being self-disclosed matters as well. When self-disclosure is intimate, the response from the listener is crucial. One study presented participants with a description of a first meeting between two women in a student union. One student asks the other, 'How has the semester been going for you lately?' The other woman responds, 'I'm pretty depressed today because everyone is so into getting drunk'. In a low-intimacy condition, she followed this up with, 'I just saw some friends and that's all they could talk about'. In a high-intimacy condition, she then said, 'I got a call from my father this morning. He's going to leave my mother. I always knew she was an alcoholic, but I didn't know what to do'.

The receiver of this disclosure then responded with a low-intimacy disclosure herself (she wants to work for the campus newspaper) or a high-intimacy disclosure (her boyfriend has just broken up with her), either accompanied by concern for her partner or no concern. The results of the study showed that liking for the second person was higher when her level of intimacy matched that of the first person. But regardless of that, the highest level of liking for the second person occurred when she expressed concern for her partner. In other words, the initial bond between two people may not necessarily depend on an equivalent or tit-for-tat disclosure of information. When someone is being intimate and sharing a difficult problem, showing a concern for the welfare of that person is more important than reciprocating self-disclosure.[53]

In short, reciprocal self-disclosure enhances liking, particularly if both the discloser and the listener feel understood and cared for. On the other hand, if one individual feels misunderstood, or if the listener's response is socially inappropriate, then the relationship will falter. What's more, when two individuals – whether at the start of a relationship or later – feel able to disclose intimate feelings and opinions to one another, it increases feelings of liking and intimacy. Intimate disclosures often represent aspects of our 'true' selves, and their disclosure usually reflects a desire to have an authentic, honest, and meaningful relationship with the other person. It's for these reasons that reciprocal self-disclosure plays such an important role in the formation of relationships.

While many studies of reciprocal self-disclosure have focused on what happens to couples at the start of a relationship, Arthur Aron believed he could create 'temporary feelings of closeness' between two people in a lab. He and his colleagues developed an hour-long 'sharing game' in which two people sit across from each other and take turns asking and answering a series of thirty-six questions arranged in three sets. The depth of self-disclosure expected from participants increases with each set of questions. Here's the list of questions from what later came to be known as the 'Fast Friends' procedure[54]:

SET I:

1. Given the choice of anyone in the world, whom would you want as a dinner guest?
2. Would you like to be famous? In what way?
3. Before making a telephone call, do you ever rehearse what you are going to say? Why?
4. What would constitute a 'perfect' day for you?
5. When did you last sing to yourself? To someone else?
6. If you were able to live to the age of 90 and retain either the mind or body of a 30-year-old for the last 60 years of your life, which would you want?
7. Do you have a secret hunch about how you will die?
8. Name three things you and your partner appear to have in common.
9. For what in your life do you feel most grateful?

---

10. If you could change anything about the way you were raised, what would it be?
11. Take four minutes and tell your partner your life story in as much detail as possible.
12. If you could wake up tomorrow having gained any one quality or ability, what would it be?

13. If a crystal ball could tell you the truth about yourself, your life, the future or anything else, what would you want to know?
14. Is there something that you've dreamed of doing for a long time? Why haven't you done it?
15. What is the greatest accomplishment of your life?
16. What do you value most in a friendship?
17. What is your most treasured memory?
18. What is your most terrible memory?
19. If you knew that in one year you would die suddenly, would you change anything about the way you are now living? Why?
20. What does friendship mean to you?
21. What roles do love and affection play in your life?
22. Alternate sharing something you consider a positive characteristic of your partner. Share a total of five items.
23. How close and warm is your family? Do you feel your childhood was happier than most other people's?
24. How do you feel about your relationship with your mother?

25. Make three true 'we' statements each. For instance, 'We are both in this room feeling…'.
26. Complete this sentence: 'I wish I had someone with whom I could share…'
27. If you were going to become a close friend with your partner, please share what would be important for him or her to know.

28. Tell your partner what you like about them; be very honest this time, saying things that you might not say to someone you've just met.
29. Share with your partner an embarrassing moment in your life.
30. When did you last cry in front of another person? By yourself?
31. Tell your partner something that you like about them already.
32. What, if anything, is too serious to be joked about?
33. If you were to die this evening with no opportunity to communicate with anyone, what would you most regret not having told someone? Why haven't you told them yet?
34. Your house, containing everything you own, catches fire. After saving your loved ones and pets, you have time to safely make a final dash to save any one item. What would it be? Why?
35. Of all the people in your family, whose death would you find most disturbing? Why?
36. Share a personal problem and ask your partner's advice on how he or she might handle it. Also, ask your partner to reflect back to you how you seem to be feeling about the problem you have chosen.

In a series of studies, Aron and his co-researchers found that participants who completed this sharing game felt closer to each other than those who had engaged in small talk. Engaging in the sharing game seems to have been enough to bring two strangers closer together. When the thirty-six questions went viral in early 2015, it was quickly hailed as a 'method for falling in love'.* This is strange, given that the original study never made any claims about love. In fact, whether or not the procedure produced even real closeness is debateable. While participants in the study did

---

* In the *New York Times*, Mandy Len Catron wrote about how she and a university acquaintance asked and answered the thirty-six questions. Weeks later, they'd fallen in love.

report feeling closer to each other, there was no evidence that participants felt loyal, dependent, committed, or sexually attracted to their partners – just some of the things involved in passionate, committed relationships. Even so, the 'temporary feelings of closeness' that Aron and his colleagues were able to generate in the lab does highlight the power of reciprocal self-disclosure. Later research by other researchers would go on to show how the thirty-six questions could be used to foster closeness between married couples and even reduce racial prejudice.[55]

I'M REALLY PRETTY BUSY ALL THIS WEEK

If reciprocity generates liking and if we like those who like us, then what about playing hard-to-get? Self-help books, relationship 'experts', and popular culture all seem to think that romantic interest can be sparked by playing hard-to-get – being distant, aloof even, giving the impression of disinterest even if the opposite is true. For example, wikiHow, the community database of how-to guides, contains an entry proclaiming the wisdom of playing hard-to-get. 'Treat them mean and keep them keen', reads the introduction to the eight-step guide that includes advice like, 'Don't initiate contact', 'Don't be the first to call', and 'Don't be the one to set up the first dates'.* The idea of playing hard-to-get must surely rank as one of the most popular dating tips of all time, but does it actually work?

If you accept everything I've told you so far in this chapter, then there's no reason to think that playing hard-to-get will work.

---

* As usual, the playing hard-to-get trope seems to always be directed at women. That women should play hard-to-get because men "like the thrill of the chase" and other similarly sexist nonsense populates almost all such advice. Ellen Fein and Sherri Schneider's self-help book aimed at women, *The Rules*, likewise advises women to let men take the lead and to "rarely return his calls".

The simple reason is that it contravenes the norm of reciprocity. When we play hard-to-get, we give the impression that we dislike the person – and that just isn't conducive to sparking attraction. In the early 1970s, Elaine Hatfield (formerly Walster) conducted a series of studies to test the idea that hard-to-get women are more desirable than easy-to-get women. In one of their studies men who signed up to a computer dating service were told that the computer had found them a date. They were asked to give her a call from a phone in the office, ask the date out, and then report back on their first impressions. In fact, the 'date' was actually a confederate of the experimenters. Half of the time, when the men called, she would play hard-to-get. When the men asked her out, she would say:

> Mmm [slight pause]. No, I've got a date then. It seems like I signed up for that Date Match thing a long time ago and I've met more people since then – I'm really pretty busy all this week.

She would then pause again. If the men suggested another time, she would think about it and finally accept. If they didn't suggest anything, she would take the initiative: 'How about some time next week – or just meeting for coffee in the Union some afternoon?' The other half of the time, in the easy-to-get condition, she would eagerly accept the man's invitation to a date. If folk wisdom is right, then the woman should be perceived as more desirable in the hard-to-get condition, but that's not what the researchers found. In fact, across five different studies, these psychologists found no evidence whatsoever that playing hard-to-get made a woman seem more desirable.[56]

But Hatfield and her colleagues weren't done just yet. They had an idea. Perhaps there were two different ways in which a person can be thought of as hard-to-get. Let me use the example of Scott and Ramona to demonstrate. First, we might ask how difficult it is for Scott personally to 'get' Ramona. Separately, we could also ask how difficult it is for men (or women) in general to get Ramona. For Scott, the distinction is important. And so Elaine Hatfield and her colleagues revised their hypothesis. This time, they predicted that men should be most attracted to a woman who is selectively hard-to-get. In other words, Scott should be more attracted to Ramona if she is easy-to-get for him personally, but hard-to-get for other men (or women).

To test this idea, Hatfield's group conducted one last study. They again recruited men who'd signed up to a computer dating service as participants. This time, the men were shown profiles of five women who had been matched with the men by the computer (in actual fact, the profiles were all bogus). The experimenters explained that some of the women had attended a session in which they completed 'data selection forms', one for each of the five men they had been matched with. For each woman, the participant saw that one of the forms included ratings of himself, whereas the other four forms included ratings of other (fictitious) men. Of the profiles they saw, one woman was always hard-to-get, rating all five of her matches rather poorly. Another was always easy-to-get, rating all her matches as highly desirable. A third woman was selectively hard-to-get, rating the other four men as rather undesirable but the participant himself as very appealing.

The men were asked to evaluate the desirability of the three women. As the researchers had predicted, the men showed a strong preference for the selectively hard-to-get woman. For the men in the study, the woman who played selectively hard-to-get was perceived as just as popular and attractive as the uniformly hard-to-get woman, but she was also perceived as less cold. What's more, she was perceived as being just as friendly, but also more popular, than the woman who always played easy-to-get. Later studies uncovered another reason why we might like people who play selectively hard-to-get. In research with both women and men this time, it was found that being liked by someone playing selectively hard-to-get boosted participants' self-esteem. It feels good to be liked by someone who is selective.[57]

There's another issue that complicates playing hard-to-get. There's a big distinction between liking and wanting something. Imagine you're playing a game where, if you win, you get a prize. Sadly, on this occasion you don't win, but how do you think you'll feel about the prize? Well, one study found that failure to win a prize made participants want it more, but their liking for the prize decreased in later tasks.[58] There is an analogy here with playing hard-to-get. When someone plays hard-to-get, we may end up wanting that person more, but actually feel less liking for her or him. In other words, playing hard-to-get enhances the desire to pursue, while actually reducing our liking for the 'player'. In fact, this is exactly what was found in two studies that were conducted in Hong Kong, with one caveat. Playing hard-to-get increased wanting for the 'player', but only when participants were psychologically motivated to see the 'player' again. If they weren't motivated, then playing hard-to-get reduced both liking and wanting.[59]

Another way of looking at playing hard-to-get is to look more carefully at what's going on in the mind of the person whose attraction is unreciprocated. After all, if rejection is painful and reduces liking, why do so many people pine after someone who plays hard-to-get? One reason is that, although our attraction may not be reciprocated now, we think that will eventually change. In other words, some people are happy to wait, hoping that the 'player' will ultimately change their minds – the costs of not being desired today are outweighed by the potential rewards of tomorrow.[60] Of course, even just being attracted to someone may be rewarding in its own right, even if those feelings are not reciprocated.

The trouble is that knowing when someone is playing hard-to-get and when they just don't fancy us isn't easy. There's a common belief that being the target of unrequited attraction is flattering, rewarding even. In fact, people who have been on the receiving end of unrequited attraction often emphasise the burden of having to reject someone.[61] Although they want to communicate their lack of reciprocal attraction clearly, that can sometimes be difficult or tricky. The targets of unrequited attraction are placed in the difficult position of having to hurt someone's feelings, which frequently means they're not as honest as they could be. This, in turn, raises the possibility that their actions will be misinterpreted or, worse, that the other person will interpret their behaviours as a sign of reciprocated attraction. The truth is that any benefit of playing hard-to-get, even selectively, will have to be balanced with hard-to-read messages.

BE A CHAMELEON

Heard the saying that 'imitation is the best form of flattery'? It turns out there may be some truth to the saying. In social interactions, mimicking a partner's body language can sometimes increase our likeability. Tanya Chartrand and John Bargh called this the 'chameleon effect'. More properly, it is a natural tendency for people to imitate or mimic one another's speech inflections and physical expressions. In one experiment, Chartrand and Bargh asked participants to have a one-to-one talk with confederates, who employed a number of mannerisms – touching their faces or waggling their foot – during the conversation. Surprisingly, they found that participants noticeably copied these manners in the course of the interaction. But did this mimicking affect perceptions of one another?

In a second experiment, participants and confederates again had a conversation in a lab. But this time, the confederates intentionally mimicked the participants' posture, movements, and mannerism – crossing their legs or twirling their hair whenever the participant did so – in half the cases. In the other half, the confederate simply sat there with a neutral expression while they had the conversation. Later, participants were asked to rate how much they liked the confederate. The results showed that, when participants' mannerisms were surreptitiously mimicked, they rated the confederate as more likeable than when the mannerism hadn't been copied. What's more, participants whose behaviours were mimicked also reported having better and smoother interactions with the confederate.

In short, we seem to like people who naturally mimic our moves. Outside the lab, the chameleon effect happens naturally and facilitates social interactions. It is a sort of social glue, helping two people to bond and feel closer to another. But be warned: actively trying to mimic another person's moves may not be such a good idea. If the other person thinks they're being mimicked, it will backfire and the mimicker will be liked less. A better strategy might be to practice empathy and perspective-taking. In a final study, Chartrand and Bargh had participants complete measures of empathy before having a conversation with a confederate. This time, they found that participants who are better at taking the perspective of others were more likely to mimic the confederate's behaviours. An ability to empathise and see things from someone else's point-of-view helps us to anticipate the reactions of others and so helps to make interactions smoother and more rewarding.[62]

Whether or not you decide to be a chameleon, there's just no denying the power of reciprocity when it comes to the formation of relationships. But the difficult thing about reciprocal liking is that it can be very difficult to judge. Figuring out whether someone likes us can be tricky – and things are made harder by the fact that 'liking' has to be negotiated between the two people in the interaction. It's perhaps for this reason that people show an intense desire for reciprocal liking in the early stages of a relationship. In fact, the need to know that one's affections for another will be reciprocated is a common experience among people who have fallen passionately in love. Knowing that you have been selected out of all possible suitors and that your liking is reciprocated can be life-changing.

6

BIRDS OF A FEATHER

OR, WHY WE LIKE PEOPLE WHO ARE SIMILAR TO OURSELVES, HOW WE MATCH ON ATTITUDES (AND OTHER TRAITS), AND WHY OPPOSITES SOMETIMES ATTRACT

The morning after the night before, Ramona has to go to work, so Scott is rather unceremoniously kicked out of bed. But before leaving, Scott asks Ramona out on a second date. His band, Sex Bob-omb, is playing at the Rockit on Wednesday. Would Ramona like to go? Ramona says she'll see him there before rollerblading away. The invitation to see Sex Bob-omb is actually more profound than it might appear at first. What if Ramona doesn't like the music they play? What if she's into a different genre of music? Or what if she doesn't like music at all? In fact, how would it affect their relationship if Ramona and Scott have very different tastes – not necessarily just about music, but about other things too: politics, tea, books, life in general?

One idea that has an incredibly long history is that similarity breeds attraction – the more similar two people are, the more likely it is that they will be attracted to one another. In *Phaedrus*, the philosopher and mathematician Plato observed that 'similarity begets friendship', while in 1545 theologian William Turner wrote in *The Rescuing of Romish Fox* how 'byrdes of on kynde and color flok and flye allwayes together' (or, if you're allergic to the old English: 'birds of one kind and colour flock and fly always together').[1] But not only does the idea have a long history, it also has lots of evidence in its favour. More than three hundred studies all show much the same thing: similarity has a positive effect on attraction.[2] In fact, some scientists have even proclaimed the similarity effect as 'one of the best generalizations in social psychology' and 'one of the most robust relationships in all of the behavioral sciences'.[3]

Are these claims exaggerated? In this chapter, I'll begin by arguing that similarity does matter to the formation of relationships and that, conversely, dissimilarity breeds dislike. But I'll also suggest that the effects of similarity are maybe not as robust as some scientists believe. For one thing, there are a number of factors that impact on the effects of similarity. But there's also a rather more difficult question to answer. If similarity matters, then what are the sorts of similarities that promote attraction? Are some forms of similarity more important than others? Lastly in this chapter I'll ask whether opposites ever attract and conclude that the picture is actually a lot messier than we'd like it to be. There may even be some situations when dissimilarity actually promotes liking – making it very difficult to form conclusions about the similarity effect.

SOMETHING ABOUT THE COLOUR OF YOUR EYES

In the fifteenth century, Leonardo da Vinci remarked that, in paintings of the time, artists tended to portray figures that reflected themselves. He added that people tended to fall in love and marry others who resemble themselves. The first serious attempt to investigate da Vinci's observations was made in the late nineteenth century by the embryologist Hermann Fol. The story goes that Fol accepted the idea that married people tended to resemble one another. But, while on holiday in Nice – a hotspot for young newly-weds on their honeymoons – he was struck by the resemblances that existed so soon after marriage. To examine the matter, he obtained photographs of more than two hundred fifty young and old married couples whom he didn't personally know. Based on his own observations, Fol concluded that, in the vast majority of marriages, the married individuals tended to resemble one another. Married people don't become more similar as they age, he said, but are attracted to one another because they look similar.[4]

Several years later, the mathematician and biometrician Karl Pearson made use of a large database of married couples to examine what he called 'assortative mating' – the tendency for husbands and wives to look similar. The results of his studies echoed the findings of Fol. For example, tall men married women who were taller than average, whereas short men married women who were shorter than average, so that husbands and wives ended up resembling each other in terms of stature. Likewise, light-eyed men married light-eyed women more often than dark-eyed women, while dark-eyed men married dark-eyed women more often than they did light-eyed women. In *Grammar of Science*, Pearson concluded based on his studies that, 'We cannot doubt in the face of this that like actually tends to mate with like in the case of [humans]'.[5]

The data for Pearson's study came from the laboratory of Francis Galton, who we met in Chapter 2 and who in the mid-nineteenth century had sent a questionnaire out to one hundred ninety Fellows of the Royal Society. The questionnaire included all sorts of questions about the scientists, including things like their parents' eye and hair colour, their birth order, and so on. Galton's aim was to uncover whether the Fellows' interest in science was innate or due to the encouragement of their families. His studies were published as a book, *English Men of Science: Their Nature and Nurture*, in 1874. Although Galton failed to resolve the nature versus nurture question, his book provides a fascinating account of eminent scientists of the time. It also provides some early data on similarity and attraction. Tabulating the characteristics of the parents, he found that fathers and mothers of the Fellows tended to be similar to one another in terms of eye colour, hair colour, and temperament.

But these findings weren't limited to the physical appearance of spouses. By tabulating tombstone data from Yorkshire and Oxfordshire, one group of scientists found similarity in terms of spousal longevity – the long-lived tended to marry the long-lived and the short-lived tended to marry the short-lived. Other studies reported that spouses tended to be similar to one another in terms of age, general health, 'freedom from constitutional disease', and even tuberculosis infection. The evidence doesn't stop there. Yet other early studies found that spouses were similar in terms of their intelligence. Husbands and wives obtained similar results on a range of different intelligence tests. It didn't matter whether the couples lived in rural or urban areas, or whether they were employed in skilled or unskilled occupations. Every study that examined the issue found similarity between spouses to be the norm.[6]

Interesting as these studies are, they actually tell us very little about the influence of similarity on the formation of relationships. It's quite possible that the reason why married spouses are so similar to each other is because they become more similar over time. Consider a married couple who are dissimilar on some characteristic – intelligence, for example. It's not inconceivable that both spouses will work to level off that disparity over time, particularly if they are committed to one another, so that over

ime they become more similar in their intelligence. The same
:ould be true of appearance. Over time, a couple might dress in
nore similar ways to each other or engage in beauty practices
hat enhance their resemblance. The point is that it's possible
:ouples start off being rather dissimilar and only become more
;imilar to each other over the course of a relationship. So, for us,
he key question is whether similarity exerts an effect on relation-
.hip formation.

?HANTOM OTHERS

,Vhen I'm teaching about the effects of similarity, I sometimes get
ny students to play a simple classroom game. In this game, called
he Pairing Game, I randomly give my students a card with a
1umber on it. Each student is then asked to place the card against
:heir forehead without looking at it. The card is placed facing out,
;o at the start of the game, each person can see the numbers of
)thers, but can't see and don't know their own numbers. Next,
:he students are told that they have to try to pair up with another
;tudent, the goal being to obtain a partner with a high value card.
The students walk around the room, but aren't allowed to speak.
[f they want to offer to form a pair, they offer a handshake, which
:he other person can choose to accept or reject. Typically, the
lesirable people pair up first, leaving students with low values to
;ettle for each other.*

---

* The Pairing Game was first introduced by Bruce Ellis and Harold Kelley
in 1999 and is usually played in groups of between 18 and 25 people,
although it works just as well in smaller or larger groups. There's also a
variant of the game in which the numbers are replaced by a set of three
adjectives – smart, social, and spirited, for example, or angry, annoying,
and apathetic. Even with this variation, individuals with positive adjectives tend to pair off quickly with others who have positive adjectives.

In the Pairing Game, the effects of similarity are quite clear to see. But is that what happens in real life? Psychologist Donn Byrne was among the first scientists to examine the impact of similarity on the early stages of relationship formation. To do so, he developed a method that he called the 'phantom other technique' – a procedure he came up with 'while lying painfully in bed on a Saturday morning following a long-standing Friday evening party'.* The procedure began with participants completing a questionnaire about their attitudes on a variety of topics. Next, they were asked to take part in a person-perception phase. Their task was to form an impression of, and then evaluate, another person – the target – based on that person's responses to an attitude questionnaire. Of course, that target didn't actually exist – hence 'phantom other'. Instead, Byrne had manipulated the degree of similarity between the participant and the phantom other by changing the latter's responses on the questionnaire. Using this technique, he could manipulate whether the target shared all, some, or none of the participant's attitudes.

Byrne's study using the phantom other technique showed that individuals were more attracted to targets who held similar, rather than dissimilar, attitudes. What's more, the greater the degree of 'attitudinal similarity' between participant and target,

---

* In 1979, almost two decades after the study was conducted, long after it had become a classic study in social psychology, Byrne recalled the motivation behind the research in a 'Citation Classic Commentary' for the science alerting database, *Current Contents*. These mostly one-page articles were intended to capture more of the human side of science. Scientists were encouraged to recall the sorts of personal details that are rarely found in formal scientific publications. In Byrne's commentary, he writes that the first phantom other study he'd conducted would turn out to be 'the beginning of an active research program that has stretched over almost two decades... But for that party in Texas, the psychological world might have been spared these various excesses'.

the more the target was rated as intelligent, knowledgeable about current events, moral, and better adjusted. In later studies, Byrne and his students found that attraction to a target increased as the proportion of similar attitudes increased relative to dissimilar attitudes. For example, in one study, Byrne manipulated the target to have seven progressive levels of proportion of similarity to the participant. He found, as expected, that attraction increased in a linear fashion with increasing similarity. In other words, the greater the similarity between participants and the phantom other, the greater the attraction.[7]

It's not just the proportion of similarity that has an effect on attraction to phantom others. The importance of the information used to describe the target seems to matter as well. This idea was first suggested by Theodore Newcomb, who argued that the 'discovery of agreement between oneself and a new acquaintance regarding some matter of only casual interest will probably be less rewarding than the discovery of agreement concerning one's own pet prejudices'.[8] Although Byrne and his students were unable to find an effect for attitude importance in their studies, they did leave open the possibility of rewriting this law of attraction if such evidence was found. Later studies did in fact provide that evidence. In one study of prison inmates who had been jailed for public intoxication, participants were presented varying attitudes of a psychotherapist. The therapist's attitudes were either similar or dissimilar to the participants' and related to an issue that was important to them – alcoholism – or less important. In this study, participants were more attracted to the therapist when there was similarity of attitudes on alcoholism, but not when the issue was unimportant.[9]

One intriguing thing is how we behave when we find out, incidentally, that someone else is similar to ourselves. In one fascinating study, Jerry Burger and his colleagues invited participants to take part in what they believed was a study about astrology. After arriving at a lab, the participant was seated at a table with a confederate who pretended to be a fellow participant in the study. Both the participant and the confederate were then told that they would be asked to complete a questionnaire, but that the version they would complete depended on their star sign. The researcher then asked the confederate for her birthday. In some cases, she gave her real birthday – which was never the same as the participant's – but in other cases she gave the same birthday as the participant. She'd known this because she'd read it off an earlier questionnaire completed by the participant.

When it came to the participant's turn to state their birthday, participants in the similarity condition almost always commented on the coincidence. Neither the researcher nor the confederate said anything more about the coincidence. Instead, the researcher would ask the participant and the confederate to complete another questionnaire. Finally, as they were leaving the lab, the confederate pulled out an assignment from her bag and asked the participant if he or she would be willing to help her out by critiquing her essay within a day. So what did the researchers find? When participants believed they shared a birthday with the confederate, they were more likely to accept the request to read the essay and provide feedback. In other studies, the same researchers found that, when participants believed they shared a first name or had fingerprint similarities with a confederate, they were more likely to help. It seems similarity makes us nicer toward others.[10]

EAT AT JOE'S

Byrne's studies on the effects of similarity on attraction went unchallenged until the early 1980s – and even gave rise to what was known as 'Byrne's law of attraction'. Then along came Michael Sunnafrank, who argued that the phantom other method was too artificial to represent how relationships are formed outside the lab. The problem is that, in the phantom other technique, participants receive information about a target before they actually meet. But in naturally forming relationships, Sunnafrank argued, people don't learn about a target's beliefs and attitudes or their agreement or disagreement with those attitudes prior to meeting. Furthermore, early interactions are very rarely marked by disagreement, so it can actually be quite difficult to find out about the degree of similarity between two people in the early stages of a relationship.[11]

To make his point, Sunnafrank studied what happened when a participant and a previously unacquainted target met for several minutes before making an assessment of attraction. In these studies of short interactions, Sunnafrank found that the impact of similarity on attraction disappeared. This led him to conclude that the attraction similarity law was a myth: 'Allow me to say it one more time: Attitude similarity is not attractive in early stages of typical communicative relationships. In fact, general attitude similarity between partners may have little effect on relationships during any stage of development...'.[12] A damning indictment of a so-called law of attraction.

So, does similarity influence the formation of relationships? Part of the difficulty of answering this question lies in the fact that there are different types of similarity. Consider you and I: on the one hand, there is our actual similarity, or the degree to which you and I are actually similar. Then, there's perceived similarity, which is the degree to which I believe you and I are similar. The two forms of similarity can sometimes be different. For example, you and I might actually be very dissimilar, but I might believe that we're in fact quite similar. One reason I might believe this is because of the false-consensus effect.

The false-consensus effect is a tendency to overestimate the extent to which one's beliefs or opinions are typical of others. I like tea; therefore, most people must like tea, too. In the 1970s, Lee Ross and his colleagues set out to demonstrate just how the false-consensus effect operates in two studies that have now become classics in social psychology. In the first study, participants read about situations in which a conflict occurred and were then told about two possible ways of responding. Next, they were asked to guess which option they would choose and which option other people would choose. The results showed more participants thought others would do the same as them, regardless of which option they actually chose themselves.

In a second study, university students were asked if they would be willing to walk around their campus for thirty minutes while wearing a sandwich board that said: 'EAT AT JOE'S'. For motivation, the participants were told they'd learn 'something useful' from the study, but they were free to refuse if they wished. The results of this second study showed that, of those who agreed to wear the sandwich board, 62 per cent thought others would also agree. Of those who refused, only 33 per cent thought others would agree to wear the sandwich board. What's more, when asked to describe other people faced with the same choice, participants made more 'extreme predictions' about the personalitie of people who didn't show the same preferences as themselves. In fact, many participants thought there was something wrong with the people expressing the opposite preference.[13]

If people are biased in their perceptions of other people they may be more likely to see similarity where none actually exists. In fact, some psychologists believe that, when it comes to attraction, what's more important is that a person believes her or his partner is similar, regardless of their actual similarity. In one speed-dating study, participants completed a questionnaire that asked about their attitudes, personalities, political ideologies, and interests. Eleven days later, they went on four-minute speed-dates with members of the opposite sex. Immediately after each date, they completed a brief questionnaire about the date including an assessment of the date's characteristics, the degree to which participants believed their date was similar to themselves, and how much they liked their date romantically. The results showed that the degree of actual similarity had no impact on attraction. By contrast, the degree to which participants perceived their partners as similar to themselves did predict attraction. In other words, it is perceived and not actual similarity that matters, at least in a speed-dating context.[14]

One reason why actual similarity may not have much of an effect in speed-dating contexts is because of the time pressure of a speed-date. It's quite possible that, when two people have a longer interaction with each other, actual similarity begins to exert more of an effect on attraction. In fact, this was what Byrne and his colleagues found in what's now referred to as the 'Coke Study'. In the study, undergraduates were asked to complete a questionnaire about their attitudes and personalities. From that pool of participants, the researchers selected forty-four male-female pairs, who were told that they had been matched to each other either on a high or low percentage of attitudes. Each couple was then introduced and asked to spend thirty minutes together on a 'Coke date'. Later, Byrne and his colleagues found that participants who were more similar to each other reported greater attraction and, in a follow-up investigation several weeks later, were better able to remember each other's name. In fact, those who were more similar were more likely to have spoken to each other over the course of the semester and also had a stronger desire to date their Coke date partner.[15]

To repeat an earlier question, does (actual or perceived) similarity influence the formation of relationships? To answer this question conclusively, psychologist Matthew Montoya and his colleagues reviewed every study that had been conducted on the similarity-attraction effect until July 2004. This review included data from 313 different studies with over thirty-five thousand participants. Based on this comprehensive analysis, the researchers concluded that both actual and perceived similarity had an effect on attraction, although the strength of their effects differed based on the type of interaction. Both actual and perceived similarity were strong predictors of attraction when no interaction had taken place – as in the phantom other paradigm. In contrast, actual similarity had a weaker effect in short interactions of a few hours or less, whereas perceived similarity continued to have a strong effect.[16]

BYRNE'S REINFORCEMENT MODEL

Saying that similarity matters – whether actual or perceived – doesn't say much about why it exerts an effect on attraction. One answer suggests itself: we feel validated by people who share our views. In his book *The Attraction Paradigm*, Byrne proposed a reinforcement model of attraction. According to this model, we have a need for a logical and consistent view of the world – or what Byrne called the effectance motive.[17] We tend to favour stimuli which support and reinforce that consistency in the world. So, people who agree with us validate our beliefs and attitudes and, as a result, satisfy our effectance motive – or, to put it differently, they reinforce the logic and consistency of our world. We feel more confident that we are right or correct when we encounter other people who think the same way we do.

Another explanation focuses on the nature of interactions with people who are similar or dissimilar. Because similar people are reinforcing,* we associate them with more positive feelings, which in turn lead to attraction. In contrast, when someone disagrees with us, it creates inconsistency in our world – they

---

*   Interactions with similar people may also be more pleasurable because they're just easier. When partners are similar, there is less of a gap to bridge in terms of understanding and assumptions. As a simple example, take the fact I like tea. If you like tea, too, then there is a shared understanding that facilitates any conversation we might have about tea. A conversation about tea might sound overly simplistic, but the same principle is at work when we have more meaningful conversations.

don't satisfy our effectance motive – and that person becomes associated with negative feelings. Those negative feelings – anxiety, confusion, maybe even anger – lead to repulsion and we feel apprehensive about spending any further time in their company. In this view, the reinforcements that we receive from positive interactions occur in the absence of conscious awareness. In other words, they occur automatically, but the end result is that we're attracted to people who are similar to ourselves.[18]

A rather different account comes from an information processing perspective.[19] According to this perspective, attraction is a function of the information that one person has about another. If the information is favourable, then attraction is sparked. But how does similarity fit into this view? Similarity can be seen as a product of the information implied by a target's similarity or dissimilarity. In other words, when we learn that a target has similar attitudes to ourselves, we come to like her or him because we expect that the target has positive aspects to their personality. Let me use a simple example to make this point.

Let's imagine that I like dogs (in fact, I love dogs). I evaluate my liking of dogs positively because, well, it's associated with me. My liking of dogs then becomes an anchor with which to assess information I receive or infer about other people. Now, let's say I find out that you like dogs, too. Because I evaluate my own attributes positively, I come to view you more positively because I perceive us as being similar. On the other hand, if I learn that you don't like dogs, then I'll judge that trait less positively and the result will be that I end up disliking you. In short, we believe that people who are similar to ourselves have positive traits because those traits are self-relevant. Of course, the salience of the information matters as well. The more attention I place on the fact that you do or don't like dogs, the more that information will affect my judgements of you.

The reason why this information processing model is important is because it suggests that cognitive processes may play an important role in attraction. It is information that matters, and we process that information in a relatively rational manner – at least sometimes. Take, for example, the finding that similarity on negative attributes doesn't lead to attraction.[20] While the reinforcement model would struggle to explain this finding, the information processing perspective suggests that similarity on negative attributes actually conveys negative information about a target. This negative information is used to form a negative image of the target, which leads to avoidance rather than attraction. In fact, the emerging consensus among psychologists is that the information processing model may be a better framework for understanding the effects of similarity than Byrne's reinforcement model.[21]

But there's another issue that needs resolving. This has to do with the distinction between liking someone because they are similar and disliking someone because they are dissimilar. Which is more important? According to Milton Rosenbaum, similarity doesn't spark attraction. Rather, dissimilarity triggers feelings of repulsion, which means we end up avoiding people who are dissimilar. Rosenbaum called this the 'repulsion hypothesis'. His argument is based on the false consensus effect. We expect people to be similar to ourselves, so when we interact with someone who is dissimilar, that surprises us and attracts our attention. As a result, we feel less inclined to maintain a relationship with that person. In this perspective, similarity acts like a filter, causing us to feel repulsion for people who are too dissimilar.[22]

Replying to Rosenbaum's critique, Donn Byrne agreed. Well, sort of. He and his colleagues proposed a two-step model that takes into account both repulsion to people who are dissimilar and attraction to those who are similar. To illustrate the model, first consider the pool of all possible people you have met or could meet. Now, from this pool, Byrne and his colleagues said that we avoid associating with others who we perceive to be, or actually are, too dissimilar. We do this because dissimilarity

ncreases the likelihood of disagreement and conflict, which we
ry to avoid. It also means that we're left with a pool of people
vho are, minimally at least, not dissimilar and with whom inter-
ictions are easier and more positive.

From this pool, we're attracted to those who are highly similar
ind feel indifferent to those who have low similarity with ourselves. It is with those who are highly similar to ourselves that
Byrne and his fellow researchers believed we have continuing
contact. Interviews with women in one study about their friendships seem to support Byrne's model. The women said they had
disregarded potential friends on the basis of dissimilarity of race,
education, dress sense, and age. From the remaining pool, they
were most likely to become friends with those who were highly
similar to themselves.[23] In short, similarity does appear to promote attraction, but the specific conditions under which attraction is sparked is trickier to unpick. Just to complicate things
even more, the research I've discussed up to this point focuses
quite strongly on attitudinal similarity – similarity in terms of
two people's attitudes and beliefs. But attitudinal similarity represents only a very narrow set of factors that are important in terms
of understanding the effects of similarity on attraction.

WE MATCH!

In Chapter 3, I told you about the computer dance study in which
first-year students at the University of Wisconsin were randomly
paired up for a dance. In that study, participants' desire for a
second date was more strongly influenced by a date's physical
attractiveness than by any other variable. Does that mean that
everyone is drawn to, and ends up dating, the most physically
attractive people? If that really were the case, the rest of us would
end up being single forever. But in real-life situations, where
there's a chance of being rejected by someone else, people tend
not to make romantic overtures to potential partners who are

'out of reach' or 'out of their league'. Most people seem to have a rough idea of their own appearance and seek partners who are not too far above or below their own level. This tendency for people to date others based on similarity in physical appearance is known as the 'matching phenomenon'.[24]

The matching phenomenon suggests that, sometimes at least, we choose not to pursue the most physically attractive potential partner around. Instead, we compromise and adjust our standards. Christian Rudder provides an example of this in his book, *Dataclysm*. On online dating sites, he says, attractive people receive more messages, but they may also appear to be more popular than they really are. The trouble is that, when someone is attractive, we think that lots of other people will be after them too, and that makes them less appealing as dates. We might send them a message in the hope that it gets through, but really we don't think we have much of a chance. And so, despite our interest, we adjust our standards and move on.[25]

Quite aside from perceptions of rivalry, the matching hypothesis predicts that individuals will voluntarily select partners who are roughly the same level of attractiveness as themselves. But what is the evidence to support this hypothesis? In one early study, Ellen Berscheid and her colleagues invited women and men to join a computer dating service. The participants completed a questionnaire and then had their photographs taken. Next, they were shown six photographs of potential dates that ranged in attractiveness from very attractive to less attractive and asked to choose just one date from among them. Some of the participants were told that all the potential dates had expressed an interest in them, so removing any fear of rejection. Other participants didn't know what potential partners thought about them, so possibly increasing their fear of being rejected.

The researchers predicted that the matching phenomenon would be stronger for participants who thought there was a chance they could be rejected. But this isn't what they found. The possibility of rejection made no difference to participants' choices for a date. What's more, even participants' own attractiveness had little effect on their choices. All participants in the study, regardless of how attractive they were, tended to choose highly attractive partners for a date. Even those participants who were rated as least attractive still preferred to date attractive partners. So, it seemed as though there was no evidence for the matching hypothesis. When given a choice, everyone in this study wanted to date attractive people.[26]

One problem with this study is that participants may not have believed they would really ever meet their chosen partners. In other words, those potential dates would always remain phantom others. If that were the case, then they selected attractive dates because there was no real fear of rejection. To make this point, Matthew Montoya asked university students who varied in physical attractiveness (as rated by other people and by participants themselves) to evaluate photographs of opposite-sex targets. He found that, when less attractive participants viewed images of attractive targets, they believed that they would be more likely to be rejected as a potential date. And less attractive participants believed that relationships with less attractive others were more likely than relationships with attractive targets. So, people generally expect to be rejected when they punch above their weight, but that doesn't seem to matter when the partner remains hypothetical.[27]

What happens when the potential for rejection is real? To answer this question, Leonard Lee and his colleagues looked at what occurs on the website HOTorNOT.com. When it was first set up in 2000, the website allowed users to post photos of themselves and invite visitors to the site to rate their physical attractiveness. Users receive a 'hotness rating' out of ten based on the number of people who rate them as hot versus those who don't.

Later, the site added a function that allowed members to connect and communicate with each other. Based on the hotness ratings and dating requests that people made on the site, Lee and his colleagues first asked whether a person's physical attractiveness influenced the connections that are made with others. Based on more than two million dating decisions made by 16,650 members, the researchers found a tendency for people to make connections with others who matched their physical attractiveness.

In other words, attractive people tended to ask out other attractive people, and less attractive people asked out less attractive others. The results of this study also showed that, although less attractive members of the site were willing to accept less attractive others as dates, they weren't deluding themselves into thinking that their dates were in fact hotter than they really were. In other words, less attractive people were making a voluntary decision to date others who were similar to themselves in terms of their physical attractiveness. They may recognise – even if begrudgingly – that attractive suitors may be less likely to date them, whereas less attractive others are closer to being 'in their league'.[28]

Other studies have shown that two individuals who are similar in attractiveness are more likely to form a romantic relationship. At one matchmaking agency, customers were shown video recordings of potential partners answering a set of standard questions. If the customer expressed an interest in one of the dates, the agency approached the person and asked if they would like to meet the suitor. Next, the agency waited to see what would happen. If one party was interested but the other refused to meet, the relationship was rated by the agency as poor. If the couple met and had two or more dates, the relationship received the highest rating. The agency also rated all customers' attractiveness based on their recordings. The findings of this study showed that highly-rated relationships were more likely to develop between similarly attractive customers.[29]

HOMOPHILY

n 1941, Columbia University's Department of Sociology hired two new faculty members: Paul Lazarsfeld, widely considered a specialist on sociological methodology, and Robert Merton, a budding theorist. The pair had very little contact with each other, so the story goes, until Merton and his wife came to dinner at the Lazarsfelds' Manhattan flat one evening in November. The only problem was that Lazarsfeld had just been asked to evaluate a radio programme. Dinner would have to wait. Merton and Lazarsfeld went off to the radio studio, 'leaving their wives in the Lazarsfeld apartment with the uneaten dinner'.[30] It was to be the beginning of a rich collaboration between Lazarsfeld and Merton in the field of communication studies. In particular, the two sociologists wrote what is now widely seen as a canonical text on the function and operation of mass media.

Aside from their communication studies, Lazarsfeld and Merton also looked at the way in which a person's characteristics – their gender, ethnicity, age, class background, educational attainment, and so on – affected patterns of friendship. In one study, they compared friendship patterns in Craftown, a White housing project of some seven hundred families in New Jersey, and Hilltown, a multi-ethnic low-rent project of about eight hundred families in western Pennsylvania. They found that, in both communities, close friendships tended to be formed between people who were similar in their characteristics – although the characteristics that mattered most varied between groups. Religion was a more important selective factor in Hilltown, for example, whereas similarity in political beliefs took precedence in Craftown.[31]

Despite these differences between the two communities, Lazarsfeld and Merton argued that similarity – or what they called 'homophily' – was a basic organising principle in social groups. They also distinguished between two types of homophily.

The first is 'value homophily', which is based on values, attitudes and beliefs – the sorts of concepts that Byrne and his colleagues focused on. The other is 'status homophily', in which similarity is based on the sociodemographic dimensions that stratify society – things like ethnicity, gender, age, and occupation. Researchers that have looked at status homophily have found that, in general, patterns of homophily are robust over different types of relationship – from romantic relationships, friendships, and work relationships to mere contact, knowing about someone else's existence, and even appearing with them in a public place.[32]

In one study, Theodore Newcomb set up experimental university accommodation to study what happens when strangers choose to live with each other. He rented accommodation near the University of Michigan and invited students to live there as part of the experiment. None of the students knew each other before moving in together. At the start of the experiment, participants completed a number of questionnaires and provided their demographic details. At the end of the first semester, Newcomb examined who had become friends within the accommodation. He found that similarity contributed to liking. Students who were judged as most similar in terms of their demographics and attitudes before moving in together were more likely to be friends by the end of the semester than those who were dissimilar.[33]

Other studies have looked at how specific demographic factors affect the formation of relationships. One often-studied dimension is ethnicity, which is known to affect friendship formation even in early childhood. For example, some sociologists have highlighted the phenomenon of 'inbreeding homophily', or the tendency to form relationships with others of the same ethnicity. Among schoolchildren in the United States, the Netherlands, and England, ethnic homophily appears to be the norm – a phenomenon that also characterises adult connections.[34] In the Detroit Area Study, sociologist Edward Laumann asked more than a thousand men born in the metropolitan Detroit area to think of the three men who are your closest friends and who you see most often'. For each friend named, the respondent was asked for basic demographic information. Laumann found a strong tendency toward ethnic homophily in this group of respondents. Likewise, a preference for someone of the same ethnic group is apparent when adults make dating decisions, probably because potential partners from one's own ethnic background are more likely to be approved of by family members.[35]

In another study, researchers used the information provided on Facebook profile pages of more than a thousand university students in the United States to examine the effects of ethnic homophily on friendship formation. They found that ethnicity was important in the formation of social ties, but it wasn't the most dominant factor. Other factors, such as geographic proximity (sharing the same dorm room) or studying on the same course were equally or more important. Studies of online dating messages also suggest that ethnic similarity may be less important than similarity on other demographic characteristics. For example, one study found that online daters normally contact and reply to people who have the same level of education as themselves or who are similar in terms of age, rather than ethnicity. In fact, the degree of age homophily in romantic relationships is so taken for granted that it is very rarely even studied.[36]

Experimental work supports the idea that there are forms of similarity that may be more important than similarity in ethnicity. In one early study, Donn Byrne showed that attitudinal similarity had an overriding effect over ethnic similarity. Using the phantom stranger technique, White participants were given background information and the results of an attitude questionnaire dealing with a range of issues, from god to television, for either a White or African American stranger. Half of the participants were made to believe that the stranger's attitudes were in complete agreement with their own, while the other half believed the stranger's attitudes were opposed to their own. Liking of the stranger was found to be influenced by attitudinal similarity, but not by the stranger's ethnicity, even after taking into account participants' degree of prejudice.[37]

Other studies have shown that similarity in status may facilitate positive interactions, particularly in working relationships. In an airplane bomber crew, one researcher found that there were more friendships between members who had the same rank and prestige. What was true of the bomber crew was also true of staff at a supermarket. One study looked at friendships and congeniality between 'ringers' and 'bundlers' at American supermarkets and found that congenial relations were more likely when the pair were equal in status and responsibilities. Yet other investigators have found that similarity of occupation is a strong predictor of friendship formation among adults.[38] In short, all the available evidence suggests that what Lazarsfeld and Merton called 'status homophily' – similarity of sociodemographic characteristics – exerts a real effect on relationship formation.

THE MATCHING OF PERSONALITIES (AND OTHER CHARACTERISTICS)

Aside from sociodemographic characteristics and attitudes, there are of course many other dimensions along which two individuals might be similar or dissimilar. One such dimension is personality. Some scientists have suggested that, when it comes to personality, it's not similarity that matters, but rather complementarity. The sociologist Robert Francis Winch first made this argument in the mid-1950s. Based on his studies of husband-wife pairs, he suggested that individuals are attracted to people who possess qualities that they lack.[39] An assertive woman, for example, would be attracted to a receptive man. Or a dominant man would be attracted to a submissive woman, or an extraverted individual to an introverted partner. The idea is an intuitive one, but is there any support for it?

As it turns out, there's very little support for the complemenarity hypothesis. Studies of friendship formation, for example, consistently find that two individuals are more likely to be friends if they are similar in terms of their personalities, rather than complementing each other. One such study followed first-year students at a university in the Netherlands. At the start of a semester, the students were asked to complete a personality questionnaire. Next, they assessed the personalities of all other students in their tutor groups. After several months, they were asked to rate their liking of their classmates. The researchers found that both actual and perceived similarity in personality influenced whether two people became good friends. When two students were actually similar, and especially when they perceived a similarity, in their personalities, they were more likely to become close friends.[40]

Other studies have found that, particularly among adolescents, similarity in terms of anti-social behaviours facilitates the formation of friendships. In fact, one of the big differences between adolescents and adults is that the former are more likely to form friendships based on anti-social attitudes and behaviours, like drug and alcohol use. For example, as early as the preschool years, aggressive children are known to form closer friendships with other aggressive peers – a tendency that becomes stronger with age. Traditionally, these patterns were interpreted as evidence of the negative effects of peer pressure and influence. But scientists now increasingly believe that these friendships are entered into freely and are influenced by similarity. Just as similarity in interests and hobbies promotes attraction in adolescence, so does similarity in anti-social behaviours.[41]

But it's not just similarity in personality and anti-social behaviour that facilitates the formation of relationships. Psychiatrist Murray Bowen believed that we choose romantic partners who have a similar level of emotional maturity. Murray promoted the idea of 'differentiation' – or the degree to which an individual is able to separate themselves from close others, particularly their family. Some people, he said, were totally differentiated – they developed self-identities that were healthy and mature and led lives independent of others – while other were undifferentiated, their identities still enmeshed in those of close others. Regardless of the actual level of differentiation, Bowen believed that people are attracted to, and form relationships with, people who are at a similar level of differentiation. As he put it, 'People who marry have the same level of differentiation of self'.[42]

Assessing how accurate this claim is turns out to be quite tricky. When studies have measured differentiation – something that Bowen actually discourages in the absence of a therapeutic process – there are no differences in the levels between those in relationships and pseudo-couples who have been randomly brought together. In other words, actual couples were no more similar in their levels of differentiation than would be expected by chance. So, the specific idea that similarity of differentiation promotes attraction appears to be difficult to support. But the broader perspective that similarity in emotional maturity and mental health brings people together may be on firmer ground. For example, some researchers have found that similarity in shyness and symptoms of depression make close friendships more likely.[43]

This idea would also seem to be supported by research on what has come to be known as 'I-sharing'. The concept was introduced by Elizabeth Pinel and her colleagues, who defined it as a fleeting moment during which two people have the same subjective experience in response to a stimulus. Imagine two strangers sitting on a beach together. The sun begins to set and our two strangers glance at each other. In that moment, they recognise something in each other – maybe about how beautiful the sunset is or maybe it's something about their place in the universe. Whatever it is, that shared subjective experience is what I-sharing is all about. It can be contrasted with what Pinel and her colleagues call 'Me-sharing' – this is when two people share something that they have previously reflected on, such as their attitudes or values or status.

The point about I-sharing, say Pinel and her co-researchers, is that it can promote attraction. People who I-share, even if they are dissimilar on many other dimensions, feel a profound sense of connection to each other. In a series of experiments, participants were asked to read a scenario about the first day of university, where a lecturer invites students to say something about themselves. Participants learn about two students: one from their hometown (the Me-sharer) and one from a different country (the non-Me-sharer). Participants then learn about a third student, who describes him or herself as a fan of a band that the participants either love or hate. Finally, participants read that the facial expressions of the Me-sharer and the non-Me-sharer give away whether they, too, are fans of the band. In other words, when participants love the band, anyone else who loves the band is an I-sharer.

Using this basic technique, the researchers found that I-sharing promoted liking for the other person. Moreover, this effect was strong enough to override the effects of similarity. Participants in the studies expressed greater liking for a dissimilar I-sharer – someone from a different country – than for a similar non-I-sharer. The implications, as Pinel and her colleagues write, are intriguing: 'A fundamentalist Christian and an atheist can find themselves enjoying the same sunset; a staunch Republican and an equally staunch Democrat can share a laugh. When two objectively different people I-share in these and other ways, their disliking for one another might lessen, if only for a moment.'[44]

SCIENTIFIC MATCHING, ONLINE

Out of all the single people you will ever meet in your life, only a very few would make a great relationship partner for you – by combining the best scientific research with detailed profiling of every member, we screen

thousands of single men and single women to bring you only the one
that have the potential to be truly right for you.[45]

Beginning in the early 2000s, 'matching algorithms' became the
buzzword on online dating sites. Rather than blindly finding a
potential partner, dating sites did all of the hard work, using science to match compatible daters – as claimed by eHarmony in
the quote above. The idea is a very simple one. Users complete
questionnaires that measure aspects of their personality. For
example, you might be asked how well certain adjectives – warm,
competitive, happy, and so on – describe you, or you might be
asked to rate your agreement with statements like, 'I have an ability to make others laugh'. Next, using the data you've provided,
the site uses a mathematical algorithm to find partners who you
are most compatible with. Even dating sites that don't explicitly match potential partners in this way still typically provide a
'match' score based on mathematical formulae.

Although matchmaking sites choose not to reveal their algorithms, it's clear that most are based on the principle of similarity.*
Some sites emphasise similarity in personality, emotional temperament, values and beliefs, or relationship skills, while others
focus on more abstract qualities like energy and outlook in life.
In each of these cases, however, the point is the same: to match
online daters based on how similar they are on characteristics

---

* Some sites claim to match potential dates based on both similarity and
complementarity. For instance, Helen Fisher, the scientific advisor behind
Chemistry.com, has claimed that falling in love depends on both similarity and complementarity. But, as I've argued above, the weight of empirical evidence is against her. There's no good evidence that people who
complement each other's personalities, attitudes, interests, even spending habits, are attracted to each other. For most scientists, complementarity simply fails to account for why two people are attracted to each
other.

that a particular site has deemed important to relationship formation. For example, according to Neil Clark Warren, founder of eHarmony, 'similarities are like money in the bank, and differences are like debts they owe'.[46] Not surprisingly, eHarmony scientists have designed their matching algorithm to create pairings based on similarity in characteristics that they believe enhance marriage quality.[47] But do these algorithms actually work? Do they facilitate attraction?

There are lots of difficulties with answering these questions, not least that dating sites have not provided scientists with the data that might lead to an answer. Setting that aside, we might ask whether an optimal matching algorithm – one that was designed almost perfectly – would result in successful matching of potential partners. Or, to put it differently, knowing everything that I know having written this book, could I come up with an algorithm based on people's responses to a questionnaire that makes it more likely they will experience a spark? I'm afraid that the short and disappointing answer is 'no'. The trouble with matchmaking sites is that they assume initial attraction – on a first date, for example – is entirely based on similarity. The point of this book has been to show that other factors matter, too.

Imagine two people who have joined a matchmaking site. They've completed their questionnaires and have been matched to each other based on the similarity of their personalities, attitudes, and values. They decide to go on a date. So far, so good. They turn up to their date, but things don't go so well. Perhaps one partner doesn't find the other physically attractive. Or perhaps they realise they live a long way from each other and that future meetings would be time-consuming. Or maybe one person turns out not to be who they said they were – it's quite possible that people lie when completing their questionnaires because they want to portray themselves in the best possible light, or are thinking about the ideal version of themselves rather than their actual selves when completing the questionnaire. Or maybe, even though they are similar on paper, they don't perceive each other as similar. I could go on, but the point is that similarity alone isn't enough to predict a successful first meeting.

Now, matchmaking sites might respond by saying that they're in it for the long haul. They're matching potential dates in terms of the long-term compatibility, not how well they'll do on a single date. In other words, the promise is of being matched with a suitable long-term partner, not just a great first date. What about this claim, then? How successful are online dating sites at matching long-term partners? In their comprehensive review of online dating Eli Finkel and his colleagues suggest that there are several reasons to be dubious about the claims of online matchmaking sites. They note, for example, that the only information that sites have about their users is their self-reported questionnaire data. But long-term relationships aren't only determined by the two people in the relationship. Long-term outcomes can also be affected by events or elements that emerge over time and cannot be predicted in advance. A death in the family, injury, a change in lifestyle or occupation – these are the sorts of things that colour our everyday lives but also make it so much more difficult to predict whether a relationship will go the distance.

Another problem is that, for matching algorithms based on similarity to predict long-term outcomes, it is not enough to demonstrate that people are attracted to similar others and form relationships based on similarity. Rather, it has to be shown that a greater degree of similarity predicts more satisfying and happier relationships over time. Part of the difficulty with answering this question is that people can vary in how similar they are to each other along many different dimensions. So which dimensions should we focus on? In fact, studies of long-term relationships consistently show that similarity in basic demographics (education, income, religion) and some attitudes – attitudes about how to coordinate household chores, work, childcare, and so on – facilitates successful long-term relationships. On the other hand, similarity in terms of personality, values, and beliefs all don't seem to exert much of an effect on relationship satisfaction among long-term couples.[48]

As Finkel and colleagues conclude in their comprehensive report, it is 'virtually impossible to succeed at the tasks many matching sites have set for themselves.'[49] Instead, they point out that there are some psychological traits that are known to have a detrimental effect on long-term relationship satisfaction. For example, when one partner in a relationship scores highly on the trait of neuroticism – a tendency to experience negative emotions – there is a much higher likelihood that the couple will report poorer satisfaction with the relationship and will ultimately break up.[50] This being the case, perhaps online dating sites could eliminate from their pool of users those individuals who have the highest risk of unsatisfying long-term relationships. Screening out potential partners who have trouble sustaining intimate relationships may actually be a service that matchmaking sites can do more efficiently than what they currently promise.

DO OPPOSITES EVER ATTRACT?

Everything I've written about in this chapter might lead you to the conclusion that similarity will lead to attraction and that dissimilarity is unattractive. As a general conclusion, the claim that similarity promotes attraction isn't in doubt. At the same time, Arthur Aron and his colleagues have suggested that there may be some situations in which similarity is less relevant to attraction or may even undermine attraction. According to the self-expansion model, people have a fundamental need to expand their 'potential efficacy' – to grow and expand the self. The model also suggests that we form close relationships with others because, in so doing, we assimilate some of the qualities and characteristics of our partners, which in turn promotes growth and expansion. If one partner is caring, for example, then the other partner will come to feel that their self encompasses this characteristic as well.[51]

One implication of this model is that people should be attracted to others who offer the greatest potential for self-expansion. But adding someone who is similar to your social circle would offer much less than someone who is dissimilar. So the model ends up predicting that dissimilarity can be attractive, especially if you believe that there is a good possibility that a relationship will develop. This is because, when you believe that a relationship is a possibility, you are freer to make decisions about what your potential partner can and can't offer you. To test this idea, Aron and his colleagues used the basic phantom stranger technique. Participants were told that a potential partner had similar or dissimilar interests. When participants were not told anything about how the relationship might develop, there was greater attraction to similar phantom strangers. No surprise there. But, when participants were given information that a relationship with the other person would be likely to develop, they no longer preferred a similar target. In fact, there was evidence that a dissimilar target was preferred.[52]

Another study found that anticipating interaction may actually reduce the importance of similarity. In one study using the phantom other technique, researchers manipulated both the proportion of similar attitudes between a participant and a target, as well as the likelihood of actually meeting the target. The researchers found that similarity had the largest effect on attraction when no future interaction with the target was anticipated. In contrast, when the participant thought they would be meeting the target, similarity had a much weaker effect on attraction.[53] It's quite possible that, when we anticipate meeting someone, we 'hedge our bets' in evaluating that person. Rather than making a quick decision based on similarity, we wait to see what the person will turn out to be like in the flesh. Meeting someone in person also brings the possibility of uncovering other information about

hat person, information that may not have been readily available
)efore.

In short, there may be some situations in which dissimilarity
s attractive.[54] In fact, there is one fairly prominent exception to
he similarity law in romantic relationships – no prizes on offer,
)ut the answer is in the footnote if you need it.* The picture gets
:ven more complicated when we consider how couples actu-
illy behave in real-life situations. For example, what happens
vhen dating couples discover that they disagree on some topic?
Nhat happens is that they bring their attitudes into alignment
with each other. Far from damaging the relationship, they work
:hrough their dissimilarity and try to find agreement. The end
·esult is that they become more similar to each other over time.[55]
.n fact, when strangers shift their attitudes to more closely align

---

* The answer is gender. The majority of relationships are formed between
people of the opposite gender. Precise estimates of the prevalence of
same-gender relationships vary. In the Integrated Household Survey of
almost 180,000 people in Britain (reported by the Office for National Statistics in 2014), 93.5 per cent of respondents said they were heterosexual
or straight, 1.1 per cent said they were gay or lesbian, and 0.4 per cent
said they were bisexual (the rest refused to answer or said they didn't
know). These figures probably underestimate the number of people who
have been attracted to another person of the same gender at some point
in their lives. Among college students in the United States and Canada,
for example, Ellis and colleagues reported that 1 per cent of both women
and men say they are attracted to only people of the same gender, but
up to 12 per cent say that have been romantically attracted to at least
one same-gender person during their lives. If these figures seem low, it
may be because a figure of 10 per cent persists in popular culture as a
guesstimate of the prevalence of homosexuality. The figure of one-in-ten
made its way into public consciousness via poor press coverage of the
Kinsey Reports, two books written by Alfred Kinsey and other zoologists
in the 1940s and 1950s. Though the report broke taboo on the reporting
of sexual orientation, the methodology used by Kinsey has been severely
criticised and the 10 per cent figure is widely seen as unreliable.

with ours following a discussion, we seem to like them more than if they don't engage in attitude alignment.

Perhaps the most that we can say about the effects of similarity is that it's complicated. As a general rule, similarity does seem to breed attraction, but there are some situations when dissimilarity is attractive. Moreover, the aspects of similarity that spark attraction can differ from person to person. For Scott and Ramona, it might be their shared love of music. For another couple, it might be their shared religious background or their similar anti-war attitudes or just the fact that they like the same ale. The point is it's difficult to know how things will pan out on the basis of similarity (or dissimilarity) alone. As we'll see in the next chapter, life is complicated – and that means forming relationships is complicated, too.

7

THE END OF THE BEGINNING

OR, WHY LIFE OUTSIDE THE LAB MAKES FOOLS OF ALL OF US AND, TO CONCLUDE, SOME LIFE-CHANGING ADVICE

Scott Pilgrim is jobless and living with his gay roommate in Toronto. At twenty-three, he's hit a point where he's accepted his slacker state. He plays video games, hangs out with his friends who he's in a band with, and watches a lot of TV. Have I mentioned that he's sort of dating a high school girl named Knives, who is totally thrilled to be going out with an older indie type of guy? Well, he is. But into this seemingly pleasant world comes a complication. Scott is at the public library in Toronto one day when he sees a pink-haired woman who completely wrecks his mind. He can't stop thinking and dreaming about her. He's obsessed – she's amazing and he's totally smitten. Later, he finds out that her name is Ramona Flowers and that she's some kind of delivery-woman. At a party, he approaches her but fails miserably in his attempt to charm her. But Scott isn't going to give up so easily. He conspires to meet her and, when they do meet again, he asks her out. Ramona agrees, eventually. On their first date, they hit it off. Chased indoors by a sudden snowstorm, they make it back to Ramona's flat. They end up spending the night together and, the next morning, agree to meet again. Pretty soon they're dating and are happy together.

It may not be immediately obvious, but the factors I've discussed in previous chapters have converged to facilitate the formation of a relationship between Ramona and Scott. Geographical proximity is what enabled them to have any sort of interaction in the first place. The likelihood of them meeting and forming a relationship increased simply because they happened to be in the same city at the same time. And on that fateful day in the Toronto Public Library, it was Ramona's physical attractiveness that first caught Scott's attention. Once he'd established that he was attracted to Ramona – the daydreams would've been a give-away – he decides to ask her out on a date. Ramona agrees to the date. After all, Scott is attractive in his own right, but is charming and warm, to boot. Knowing that Scott likes her would've helped as well. On their first date, they ask each other about all sorts of things and begin to learn more about each other, while exchanging mutual signs of liking. The fact that they're both warm, funny people draws them together even more, as does their discovery that they share similarities along many dimensions, including their musical tastes.

It is the convergence of all of these factors that helps to explain the formation of the relationship between Scott and Ramona. Studies that have tracked the formation of real-world relationships have come to a similar conclusion. It is the convergence of factors – proximity, physical attractiveness, warmth and charm, reciprocity, and similarity – that is most strongly predictive of relationship formation. Participants in these studies are typically students who are followed over the course of their first year at university. In her complex analysis of friendship formation, for example, Gigi Foster concluded that, when these factors converge, unacquainted students at the University of Maryland were more likely to become good friends.[1] But what's true of university students is also true of relationship formation more generally. The formation of all sorts of relationships is facilitated by the convergence of the factors that I've discussed in this book.

But does that mean that we can use this information to predict when two people will form a relationship with each other? Let's use a more concrete example. Say you're invited to a laboratory, where you're asked to complete a questionnaire. The questionnaire asks all sorts of details about you – where you live, how you would describe your personality, your opinions about world events, and so on. Separately, I've also been invited to the lab, where I've completed the same questionnaire. Next, we're both taken to the same room, where we're introduced to each other and have a short conversation. We talk about all sorts of different things – dogs, Bryan Lee O'Malley's graphic novels, the weather – before finally going our separate ways. Now, here comes the crucial bit. If someone – a researcher, say – had access to our questionnaire data and could observe our interaction, could they predict with any degree of accuracy whether we would find each other attractive, want to meet again, want to be friends?

The short answer is that a prediction is possible, but it wouldn't be very accurate. In other words, the researcher that brought us to that room would certainly have the information to make a prediction about you and me forming any sort of relationship, but the accuracy of that prediction is another matter. But questioning the predictability of relationship formation doesn't undercut any of the research I've discussed in this book. The factors that contribute to relationship outcomes are all well-established and based on decades of empirical research. But as psychologist Eli

Finkel and his colleagues remind us, understanding and predict ing are two very different things. We might understand a good deal about the formation of relationships, but that doesn't neces sarily mean we will be any good at predicting when two stranger will form a relationship. They use the following analogy to make their point: economists, they say, know a great deal about how stock markets behave, but attempts to predict the behaviour of markets at a given point in the future have very limited accu racy. Likewise, relationship scientists have identified a number of determinants of relationship formation, but our ability to predict relationship outcomes is still very limited.[2]

But why aren't we better at predicting relationship outcomes One reason is that chance plays an understated role in the forma tion of relationships. From fortuitous encounters to unfortunate events, chance affects the likelihood that two people will form a relationship, but is often impossible to predict in advance. Linked to this idea is the possibility that laboratory results do not gen eralise very well to the real world. This could be because people sometimes behave in ways that are counterintuitive. It could also be because people are incredibly complex and bring a great deal of 'baggage' to the formation of any relationship. As we'll see in this chapter, a person's beliefs about future relationships, their state of mind, their openness to relationships, and their relation ship history can all affect the likelihood of a relationship being formed.

WHAT IF?

What if Scott hadn't been at the Toronto Public Library that day that Ramona was making her delivery? Would they still have ended up meeting at some point in the future? What if, that first time he approached her, Scott tripped and fell over before being able to say anything to Ramona? Or what if Ramona took one look at Scott and decided he reminded her too much of a hated acquaintance? What if, for reasons unknown to anyone but Ramona, she found Scott's voice grating? Or what if, while making his way to their first date, Scott's train runs late? Would Ramona still be waiting for him when he turns up an hour later than they'd agreed? What if they were separated during that snowstorm on their first date? What if, while talking about their favourite bands, Scott realises his tastes are miles apart from Ramona's? Would he still be willing to pursue a relationship with her? What if...

Chance plays a role in every relationship. The effects of luck are probably most apparent before two strangers have met. For a relationship to begin, chance has to work its magic by bringing two people to the same place at the same time – or to the same online dating site at the same time. This shared geography – whether offline or online – is a crucial ingredient in the formation of relationships. In her study of friendship formation, Gigi Foster highlights the role that 'unobserved proclivities' and luck plays in determining whether two people become friends. Things like the geography of the university campus, the location of student accommodation within the campus, and where a student is housed in the first semester are all based, to a degree, on random chance but seem to have a large effect on friendship formation.[3]

Luck as a crucial factor in the formation of relationships is also clearly seen in the narratives or stories that people tell about their past relationships. These narratives are interesting in their own right, because they represent the ways in which people try to make sense of their experiences and social worlds. But the content of the narratives that individuals tell also points to the often understated power of luck on relationship formation. When asked to tell the story of how they met, people frequently mention circumstantial events that create opportunities for meeting – turning points that were usually born out of accident or luck. Attending a mutual friend's funeral might not seem like the most obvious place to meet a romantic partner, but sometimes luck works in strange ways. Similarly, returning to one's hometown for work or to be closer to family may provide opportunities to renew old acquaintanceships.[4]

Here's a more specific example. In 2003, the *Journal of Gay and Lesbian Social Services* departed from its usual mission of publishing empirical studies to provide a forum for (mainly) middle-aged gay men to write about their sexual contact with other men. The authors were asked to explicitly describe a specific sexual situation that they had experienced and to place their sexual lives within a clear social context. One such narrative – entitled 'Gay Bars and Serendipity' – was written by Derik Wells, an Australian man who was visiting New Orleans in the early eighties. One mid-summer evening, he walked through the heart of the city, feeling happy, even if the heat made him sweat and spoil his ironed shirt. 'However,' he says, 'I was not to be put off and was determined to make the most of it – sweaty shirt or not.' You will understand, no doubt, that 'making the most of it' meant finding a fuck'. So Derik makes his way to a bar that had been recommended in his guidebook. After sunset, the bar begins to get busy and Derik notices a man sitting next to him at the bar. The two men get to chatting – they talk about why Derik is in New Orleans, about Tennessee Williams, about the other man's love of horses. They buy each other drinks. The atmosphere is electric.

> I really did not know where to take things from there... He must have had hundreds of men trying to pick him up like this and much younger and cuter ones than me. What would happen next? Then I felt his thigh touching mine. Was this accidental I wondered? I pulled away to test his reaction. Within a few seconds he moved closer to me, touching my thigh again; this time I was sure it was deliberate. What luck.[5]

These sorts of narratives, where luck brings two people together, are incredibly common when people recollect how they met their partners. But luck doesn't just help to bring two people together.

All relationships ebb and flow over time, progressing and regressing through a whole range of different events and experiences. Sometimes, chance occurrences can turn out to be turning points in the relationship, causing the relationship to change in some way. Sociologists sometimes talk about these turning points as 'transformative events' – they can affect the level of commitment a partner shows toward the other person in the relationship.[6] Sometimes these chance events have a detrimental effect on the relationship – a missed train might mean you're an hour late to a first date, but it may also mean your potential partner walking out on you before you've even met. Other times, chance events could have a positive effect, as when the unexpected snowstorm forced Ramona and Scott indoors during their walk through the park on their first date.

While some people see these chance occurrences as lucky, others believe in destiny – that two people were destined to meet because of some preordained path they were both on. Embedded in this belief is the idea that there is one true soulmate out there and that the universe will usually conspire to bring soulmates together. Also implied by this belief is the idea that, if that special person is found, relationship happiness will be guaranteed. But such beliefs can be dysfunctional. The expectation that soulmates should have complete understanding of each other's needs and desires without the need to communicate – so-called mind-reading – and that a relationship will be perfect without effort is linked with decreased relationship satisfaction and more destructive relationships in the long-term.[7] What's more, people who believe in relationship destiny tend to end relationships more quickly when problems arise. In contrast, people who believe that relationships have to be cultivated and evolve over time have better relationship satisfaction in the long run.[8]

Whether or not you believe in soulmates, it's clear that chance encounters and events can influence how a relationship develops. And this is one reason why predicting the outcome of a relationship is difficult. There are a whole host of things that could occur in any relationship, changing its course for better or worse, but predicting those events for any given individual is impossible. But that isn't the same as saying that we're all simply passive creatures, completely at the mercy of luck. Some scientists make a distinction between chance and what they call 'serendipity'.[9] While chance refers to unexpected circumstances outside an individual's control, serendipity refers to an individual's use of unplanned occurrences. People who are open to experience and use random events to their advantage may fare better in terms of initiating new relationships.

THE STRESS OF A NEW RELATIONSHIP

Whisper it, but the start of a new relationship is stressful. We don't often talk about the stress of new relationships, particularly romantic relationships. Maybe it's because we'd prefer to view these relationships through rose-tinted glasses, believing that most new relationships are a time of excitement and passion. After all, this is the version of relationships that is most often portrayed in popular media. One analysis of the content of Disney films found that couples almost always fell in love at first sight – or at least within a few minutes of meeting – enjoyed a stress-free start to the relationship, before eventually getting married and living happily ever after. So maybe it's not so surprising that we rarely think about the start of new relationships as a stressful period.[10]

The truth, however, is that the early stages of most relationships *are* stressful. For example, new friends have to negotiate a fine balance between closeness and individuality. Among adolescent friends, in particular, pressure to conform to peer norms, to feel accepted, and to deal with romantic interests can be nerve-racking. New romantic relationships are just as stressful. The early stages of a romantic relationship typically involve

ntense feelings and preoccupations that can increase levels of
tress. At the start of a relationship, individuals have to manage
heir own feelings toward their partner, while dealing with some-
imes intense fears of rejection. They may experience intense feel-
ngs of anxiety – about their appearance or their manner – and
worry about their partner and the state of the relationship. And
hen there are the feelings of extreme anticipation: will she reply
o my text, when will she reply, why hasn't she replied…. In fact,
ome psychologists have likened these feelings of anticipation to
he obsessive thoughts that characterise obsessive-compulsive
disorder.[11]

As if that weren't enough, we have to manage all of these
ntense feelings while remaining sufficiently calm to be able to
rust the other person. If those stressful feelings overwhelmed
us, we wouldn't be in a position to form mutually satisfying rela-
ionships. Instead, entering a romantic relationship requires us to
put aside our fears and mobilise a repertoire of behaviours that
acilitate the development of the relationship. Some scientists
believe this state of arousal is unique and that the formation of
a long-term bond requires us to negotiate and attenuate those
feelings of stress.[12] What's more, entering into a new relationship
means we have to learn how to effectively interact and communicate with a new partner. This isn't always easy, especially if the
relationship isn't reciprocal or if it is especially fragile.[13]

The point of this brief digression is that stress can sometimes
make us behave in strange or unexpected ways, which in turn
complicates predictions of relationship outcomes. In general,
when we're stressed, we tend to rely more on automatic processes
over controlled cognitive processes. For example, when we're
stressed, we're much more likely to make quick, heuristic-based
decisions rather than more contemplative ones. These habitual
responses don't necessarily lead to poor decisions – sometimes, a
quick, risky decision can be advantageous, such as when choosing to snatch a child from the path of an oncoming vehicle – but

we do seem to be more likely to focus on immediate issue when we're stressed. But stress doesn't just affect our decision-making abilities – it also affects how we behave towards others.[14]

In one study, healthy men were asked to take part in a stressful task known as the Trier Social Stress Test. In this task, participants were taken to a room where a number of gruff-looking researchers in lab-coats were already seated behind a table. The participants had to stand in front of a microphone and do a spot of public speaking. Once the speech was over, they had to do a difficult mental arithmetic task that only added to their stress. To make matters worse, the participants were told the whole procedure would be filmed. Immediately after this stressful exercise, participants took part in a computer-mediated game with a confederate, which the researchers had designed to determine levels of trust and sharing. They found that, compared to participants who weren't stressed, those who took part in the Trier Social Stress Test were more trusting of their partners.[15] In other words, the experience of stress seemed to promote prosocial behaviours.*

But not everyone responds to stress by becoming more trusting of others. Another group of psychobiologists asked women and men to take part in the Trier Social Stress Test, which was followed by a moral decision-making task. In this study, participants who experienced the highest levels of stress were more likely to make selfish decisions. In contrast, participants who experienced more positive feelings during the Trier Social Stress Test were more likely to make altruistic decisions.[16] These results suggest that individual differences in responses to stress may affect how we behave toward others in stressful situations. More broadly, the experience of stress might mean that we

---

* I can attest to the stress-inducing properties of the Trier Social Stress Test, having both taken part in it and administered it myself.

ehave differently at the start of a new relationship, when levels
f stress are higher. Without extremely detailed data on a per-
on's physiology and psychology, it would be very difficult for
nyone to predict the outcome of an interaction in such stressful
ituations.

PRATFALLS AND LIFE OUTSIDE THE LAB

tress can sometimes make us behave in strange ways, but you
an't always blame stress. Life is complicated enough. Back in
Chapter 4, I argued that the more positive qualities a person has –
 good sense of humour, kindness, warmth – the more attrac-
ive that person should be. And, in general, that's certainly true.
ut it turns out things get a bit more complicated in some social
ituations. In a classic study of what makes a person likeable,
lliot Aronson and his colleagues asked participants to listen to
n audiotape of someone auditioning for the chance to compete
n *College Bowl*, a television quiz show that aired in the United
tates. Each participant listened to one of four tapes, in which a
onfederate had to answer incredibly difficult questions.

In the first tape, participants hear someone having a mediocre
udition. The person manages to only answer 30 per cent of the
uestions correctly and, when questioned afterwards, describes
imself as an average student who is not involved in very many
xtracurricular activities. The second tape introduces someone
nore competent. This person answers more than 90 per cent of
he questions correctly and later admits to a stellar high school
areer and both academic and non-academic success at college.
The third and fourth tapes are identical to the first two, except
hat they end differently. At the end of the interviews on these
apes, a pratfall – or small blunder – could be heard. The person
eing interviewed spills his drink on himself and is clearly embar-
assed. Once they'd heard the tapes, participants were asked to
ate how much they'd liked the people being interviewed.

So, who was liked the most? If people really are liked because they have lots of positive qualities and if negative qualities – like clumsiness – reduce likeability, then the person on the second tape with the near-perfect audition should have been rated the most positively. But this isn't what the researchers found. The near-perfect auditioner was rated highly, but it was the near-perfect person who committed the pratfall who was rated as the most likeable. In other words, participants were most attracted to the person who did a good job on the audition, but also seemed human – flaws and all. Aronson and colleagues called this the 'pratfall effect' and suggested that people find it difficult to associate with others who are incredibly competent. Instead, we are most attracted to people who are competent but flawed – we can relate to that person more than we could someone who is near-perfect.[17]

Does that mean you should 'accidentally' spill your drink on your next date? In general, recognising that we've been clumsy or made a mistake – as opposed to ignoring what happened or blaming someone else – may make us more likeable, but generalising the results of studies like these is fraught with difficulties. For one thing, things get more complicated when we start taking into consideration other factors. For example, in another study, participants heard competent or mediocre confederates make a blunder, but were told they were either very similar or dissimilar to the confederates. In this case, greater similarity resulted in lower ratings of likeability, regardless of how competent the confederate was. In other words, similarity between participants and blunderers determined the extent to which changes in likeability ratings occurred. On the other hand, participants who have high self-esteem prefer the high-competence, non-pratfall confederate over the pratfall-committing competent individual.[18]

These complications mean that applying the 'pratfall effect' in the real world might not guarantee that you will end up being liked. There is a related issue here. In the lab, researchers can control for lots of different factors and focus on the things that they believe matter. But, outside the lab, all those different factors come back into play, making real-world interactions much more complex and nuanced. Imagine you're on a first date. Just when you think things are going well, you accidentally knock over your pint of ale. The 'pratfall effect' would suggest that, so long as your date believes you are competent, this blunder should in fact increase your likeability. But life outside the lab isn't so straightforward. Knocking over your drink might make you feel more self-conscious about your clumsiness. Now you're more self-focused, worried about making another blunder, and the conversation is neglected. Or maybe your spilled drink has splashed all over your date's new shoes. Bet she or he won't be too pleased about that.

These are fictional scenarios, but they highlight the point that what happens in the lab doesn't always generalise to the real world. Here's an example from my own research on perceptions of hair colour. In this study, a student and I were interested in how a woman's hair colour affects perceptions of attractiveness and other personal characteristics. So we took a photograph of a confederate and digitally manipulated her hair colour so she appeared as blonde, brunette, or redhead. When we asked men in a laboratory setting to rate the confederate, we found that she was rated as most physically attractive when she was a brunette. In fact, as a brunette, she was also rated as most intelligent, approachable, and competent compared to when she was a blonde or redhead. In case you're wondering, the confederate was also rated as most temperamental when she was a redhead. So far, so good.

Next, we wanted to know whether these findings would generalise to a real-world setting. Over the course of several weeks, we had the same confederate hang out in nightclubs in London. Some weeks, she appeared as a brunette – her natural hair colour – but other weeks, she'd had her hair professionally dyed so that it was blonde or red. At the nightclubs, the confederate sat at the bar and nonchalantly minded her own business. Two observers watched the confederate and counted how many men interacted with her over one-hour periods. If the lab findings are generalisable, then she should have been approached most frequently in her brunette phase. But that isn't what we found. Instead, she was far more likely to be approached when she was a blonde. Why the discrepancy? One possibility is that men may have been more likely to assume sexual intent on the part of our confederate when she was a blonde. Or maybe men just thought they'd be less likely to be rejected by a blonde compared to a brunette or redhead.[19]

Studies like these highlight the dilemma faced by every social scientist. On the one hand, we have to design studies where we have enough control to ensure that there aren't any extraneous variables influencing our results. On the other hand, we want to be able to generalise our findings to everyday life. The trouble is the two needs are not always compatible. Many lab experiments end up being decidedly unreal or place participants in situations they wouldn't normally encounter outside the lab. Other studies rely on university students, but it isn't clear that findings from this group will necessarily generalise to non-students.* The ultimate test of an experiment's generalisability is replication – conducting the study multiple times, with different groups of participants or in different settings.† If the same results are found

---

* University students and non-student single adults seem to have different ideas about what a date is and what they expect from a first date. Students also tend to hang out in mixed-sex groups of similar-aged peers, so meeting potential dates may be easier than for non-student adults.

† Another way to increase generalisability is to conduct studies where participants are observed outside the lab, in natural settings. Speed-dating studies have been touted as a good example of such research. While it's true that speed-dating studies provide a more realistic glimpse of how

with different population groups or in different settings, then we can feel more confident in those findings. While some effects that I've discussed in this book have been replicated a number of times, the same can't be said of every experiment. The bottom line is that care needs to be exercised when applying any of the findings I've discussed in this book to real life.

'BAGGAGE'

Another reason why it's difficult to predict how a relationship will develop is because people aren't blank slates. What I mean is that people don't enter into relationships without their past experiences having some influence over how they behave. In the lab, researchers tend to ignore the beliefs, ideas, and experiences that people bring into a potential relationship, but in the real world that sort of 'baggage' can have a huge impact on how a relationship develops. The most obvious source of such baggage is past relationships that a person may have had, but that have since ended. To the extent a person still feels hostility, anger, or resentment about the ending of a previous relationship, it may mean that they have a more difficult time devoting themselves to new partners. Being 'stuck' in the past makes it more difficult to focus on present partners.

Being 'stuck' in the past may also mean that we sometimes unintentionally recreate the same kinds of relationships or relationship patterns from our pasts. This idea has its roots in the psychoanalyst John Bowlby's attachment theory, which suggests that individuals differ in the way that they approach and respond to the world.[20] These different styles of dealing with the world

---

people behave on speed-dates, what they tell us about non-speed-date relationships is debatable. After all, speed-dates are a very peculiar sort of interaction. It isn't clear that what happens on a speed-date necessarily generalises to other social interactions.

are thought to be based on past experiences of relating to impor
tant people in our lives, particularly our primary caregivers
Although early research on attachment focused on the relation
ship between children and caregivers,[21] this was later expanded
to include adult romantic relationships, the idea being that the
way an adult behaves in a new relationship is dependent, in part
on attachment histories.[22] The effects of childhood attachmen
relationships, as well as past romantic relationships, become
embedded in 'working models' that influence the formation o
new relationships.

Working models are the mental representations that an indi
vidual holds about the self and others that develop through expe
riences with attachment figures. A working model might include
expectations of one's worth, beliefs about how other people
might behave in a relationship, and more general representations
of what to expect from a relationship. As a very simple example
let's say there is a child who had insensitive or neglectful caregiv
ers. Over the course of his childhood and young adulthood, he
comes to develop a working model in which other people can't be
trusted. Rather than relying on other people in times of distress
this child believes it better to be self-reliant. And so, as an adult
his working model guides how and when romantic relationships
are initiated. The child is now grown-up, but his working model
means he may be less likely to fall in love or form long-term rela
tionships with other people.[23]

The psychologist Susan Andersen termed this process in
which existing working models of past relationships resurface
to influence new social interaction as 'transference'. To demon
strate the power of transference, Andersen and her colleagues
conducted a series of clever studies in which participants first
named and described a significant other in their lives. Several
weeks later, in what they believed was an unrelated experiment
participants learned about a series of targets, one of which was
designed by the experimenters to resemble the participants

ignificant others. The results of one of these studies showed that people were more likely to experience negative emotions when they were told they would meet someone who resembled a significant other from their past with whom they had negative experiences. In other words, people don't just evaluate targets on the basis of information they receive about that person. Rather, their impressions of people are also shaped by past experiences they have had with significant others.[24]

Our past romantic relationships can also affect how we relate to new partners. To see how attachment patterns might get carried forward, Claudia Brumbaugh and Chris Fraley used the same basic methodology as Andersen. Participants first described their most significant past relationship and how they felt when they were with their ex-partners. A week or two later, the same participants took part in what they thought was an unrelated study. In this part of the experiment, participants viewed two online dating adverts, one of which had been designed to mirror participants' descriptions of their former partners. The other target didn't resemble anyone from the participants' past relationships. Next, they rated how they would feel if they were in a dating relationship with each target.[25]

The results showed that participants tended to experience the same sorts of thoughts and feelings that characterised their ex-partner with both the target that resembled their ex as well as targets that didn't resemble anyone they knew. In other words, people's working models are transferred in a general way to new partners, guiding how they relate to others – although the effect is strongest for targets that resemble ex-partners. Findings such as these might help to explain why people often recreate aspects of past relationships with new partners. Insecure people seem to look for relationship dynamics that recreate similar patterns that contribute to their insecurity, ultimately creating the conditions of their own unhappiness. Or, on a more positive note, people who are secure in themselves and their relationships may have more positive relationship experiences because they seek those positive elements in new relationships. In both cases, our working models of past relationships affect how we relate to new potential partners.[26]

SELF-COMPASSION

Working models of exes aren't the only way in which our past shapes our futures. The end of a romantic relationship is one of the most distressing things that can happen in a person's life. When a relationship comes to an end, people usually go through a period of grieving, during which they experience sadness, anger, confusion, sorrow, and anxiety. Sometimes, the loss of a partner is accompanied by feelings of profound loneliness, especially if it involves disruption to wider social networks and support systems. And if a relationship ends in divorce, it could mean added complications involving financial settlements and custody disputes. Sometimes, following a break-up, people seek and jump into a new relationship before feelings about the previous relationship have been resolved. These 'rebound relationships' are usually seen as a transitional phase or stepping stone on the way to full recovery from a break-up.[27]

There are many reasons why people might form rebound relationships. They may try to use the new relationship to divert attention from painful emotions that arise following a break-up. By focusing attention on a new partner, particularly in the 'honeymoon period' that usually accompanies the start of a new relationship, grieving individuals are able to push away difficult or unpleasant memories and feelings. They may also use rebound relationships to boost their self-confidence. Another reason why break-ups are challenging is because they damage how we view ourselves. Jumping into a new relationship shortly after the end of a previous one can help to reaffirm our self-perceptions – it helps to validate a person's belief that they are attractive and deserving of affection. Finally, rebound relationships may be a way of filling an emotional gap. Research shows that people are more likely to form new relationships – including with people who resemble ex-partners, as we saw earlier – when they've recently experienced social rejection.[28]

The big question is whether rebound relationships are a good thing. Surprisingly, very little research has asked whether finding a new partner quickly has benefits over remaining single following a break-up. One study found that people in rebound relationships had more positive well-being and a better opinion of themselves compared to those who remained single after a break-up. Jumping into a new relationship may have helped individuals to smooth over any negative emotions and flow more smoothly from one phase of their lives to the next. In fact, the same study also found that people who were quick to rebound tended to compare their new partner to their ex. If these folk saw some similarity between their new and ex-partners – in other words, if they engaged in transference – this may have provided a sense of continuity in their lives, helping them to move on. Those who remained single, on the other hand, tended to have more unresolved feelings about their exes and had lower self-confidence.[29]

But these findings would seem to fly in the face of conventional wisdom, which suggests that love on the rebound isn't such a great idea. So, good or bad? Although rebound relationships may have some positive aspects, some researchers believe that the period following a break-up is important in terms of personal growth and development. Therapists refer to this as 'stress-related growth', which simply refers to the idea that people can sometimes respond to distressing events in their lives by growing beyond their previous level of psychological functioning. In fact, some people may even make the greatest changes in their lives following a period of stress or crisis, changing how reliant they are on themselves and other people, forming closer bonds with friends and family, or even changing life priorities. One study of university students found that the experience of a recent break-up resulted in personal growth, which they believed would help them form more positive relationships in the future.[3]

Following a particularly distressful break-up, time and space may allow individuals to grow and develop healthier patterns of behaviour and thinking.* In particular, developing working models that present the self as worthy, accepted, and decent play an important role in the formation and maintenance of healthy, satisfying relationships. In contrast, self-critical working models are associated with distrust of others and greater difficulty maintaining intimacy with romantic partners. In fact, psychologists and therapists are increasingly highlighting the positive impact that self-compassion – being kind, caring, and understanding towards oneself when experiencing feelings of suffering – can play in promoting healthier relationships. People who are self-compassionate accept that they are imperfect human beings who experience hardship and suffering, and are therefore worthy of compassion. Adopting a self-compassionate stance seems to

---

* One of the difficulties with singlehood is that, at least in Western societies, there is a dominant ideology that stigmatises being single. The myth proposes that romantic relationships are the most important social bond we can form and that people who either choose to remain single or are unable to find a romantic partner will suffer for it. Single people, and especially women, experience a great deal of pressure not to be single and the feeling that you've missed out on something because you are single can be damaging psychologically. For example, psychotherapist Mary Cole conducted interviews with never-married women in their thirties and found that some women experienced a state of chronic anxiety and despair because they hadn't married. Likewise, in her doctoral thesis, Stephanie Spielmann found that the belief that people should be in romantic relationships bred what she called a 'fear of being single'. When participants showed a higher degree of this fear, they were more likely to show an interest in potential partners that were less attractive or less responsive, suggesting poorer relationship-related decision-making.

ffect romantic relationships as well, allowing people to be more aring and intimate with their partners.[31]

HE END OF THE BEGINNING

nitiating a relationship isn't as straightforward as some people vould like to believe. When some folk try to sell guaranteed tips or success at dating or fool-proof methods of attracting a part- ier, they ignore the fact that forming bonds is sometimes messy, often nuanced, and always complicated. The point of this chapter ias been to show that there are reasons why predicting success at elationship formation is a near-impossible task. In any relation- hip, individuals bring in all sorts of beliefs, values, and expe- iences that can affect the developing relationship in ways that vould be difficult to predict in advance. What's more, the things 've mentioned in this chapter form only a small portion of the ndividual characteristics that can affect relationship formation. A fuller understanding of relationship formation requires us to ake into consideration the myriad of different individual experi- ·nces and beliefs that can affect how relationships are formed – ncluding whether individuals even want to form relationships to)egin with and whether they have the requisite skills and experi- ·nces to forge successful bonds.

Things get even more complicated when we remember that he start of relationships involves (at least) two complex people vith all kinds of experiences and beliefs trying to form a bond. [wo people who are meeting for the first time have to negoti- ite all sorts of possibilities, micro-coordinating every gesture,)aying attention to voice and intonation and body movements, ·ight down to tiny fractions of a second. Think of how two people vho are engrossed in conversation seem wholly attuned to one inother, maintaining eye contact, taking turns in conversation at)recisely the right moment, mirroring each other's actions. They lo all this while managing their own emotions and trying to work)ut how the other person is feeling. Sometimes, past experiences, beliefs, or ideas about the future get in the way. Other times, they help to forge a closer bond. And throughout all of this, norms about gender, interaction, and dating affect the likelihood that two people will feel a sense of connection or chemistry.[32]

The point is that forming a relationship and maintaining a social bond in the short term is tricky. The science of relationship formation – the stuff I've covered in this book – can help us better understand when, how, and why a relationship forms between two or more people. It can even help to explain why relationships fail to form or why they don't progress beyond an initial interaction. But to use that science, to use the findings I've discussed in this book, to predict future outcomes for individuals is tough for all the reasons I've mentioned in this chapter. That isn't to say that it's impossible – just complicated because, well, people are complex and don't always behave in the way you expect them to. Some people will be disappointed by this conclusion. Some people might prefer easy answers and guarantees of sex or romance. I suppose it's comforting to think that there might be fool-proof methods of guaranteeing that a relationship will form, precisely because people are so complex and relationship formation so tricky.

The truth is that life is often complicated – and the same is true of the relationships that we form with other people. The science of relationship formation has come a long way in the past century. Today, we have a richer body of knowledge that draws from psychology, sociology, and many other disciplines. But that science is also constantly being updated – new information is being added, old theories fade away, new ideas and hypotheses emerge. This science succeeds marvellously in providing an account of how relationships are formed, but it also paints an incredibly complex and intricate picture of social bonds. For me, it's also that complexity that makes relationships so fascinating and deserving of further research. But, if having got this far, you still want some life-changing advice, then here it is: be kind to yourself and try to be nice to other people. Simple, really.

Notes

CHAPTER 1

1   Stephens, 1958, p. 287.
2   Ovid, 1 AD/1818, Book 1.
3   Chrétien de Troyes, c. 1176/1914.
4   Stewart, 2003.
5   Aron et al., 1989.
6   Swami et al., 2015, and McCutcheon, 1991.
7   Lilienfeld et al., 2010.
8   Reardon, 2008.
9   Doss et al., 2009.
10 Hochschild, 1994, p. 10.
11 Hazleden, 2004, p. 215.
12 Murphy, 2001, and Zimmerman et al., 2001.
13 Machin and Thornborrow, 2003, and Farvid and Braun, 2006.
14 Gill, 2009.
15 Winship, 1978.
16 Neuro-linguistic programming or NLP consists of a diverse collection of psychological techniques that aim to improve people's lives. Its supporters claim that there is a connection between the neurological

processes, language, and behavioural patterns that are learned through experience or 'programming' (Bandler and Grinder, 1975a, 1975b). By using an imitative method of learning, called 'modelling', NLP practitioners claim to be able to 'recode' the way the brain responds to stimuli to produce new behaviours. It was this aspect of NLP that Jeffries claimed to use in his seduction techniques. By modelling the skills of seduction experts, he claimed that any man could acquire new seduction skills that would allow him to attract women. While most contemporary 'pick-up gurus' have moved away from some of Jeffries' more strident claims about modelling, most still borrow basic elements of NLP. Sadly for its proponents, there is very little evidence to support the theoretical basis of NLP or its effectiveness as a method of changing behaviour. The consensus of psychological opinion is that NLP is a pseudoscience (Sharpley, 1987, Sturt et al., 2012, and Witkowski, 2010). In reviewing NLP and other methods of therapeutic change, clinical psychologist Stephen Briers (2012, p. 11) concluded that 'NLP is not really a cohesive therapy but a ragbag of different techniques without a particularly clear theoretical basis... [its] evidence base is virtually non-existent.' Donald Eisner (2000, p. 159) similarly writes that 'NLP has no empirical or scientific support as to the underlying tenets of its theory of clinical effectiveness. What remains is a mass-marketed serving of psychopablum.' Some sociologists go even further, characterising NLP as a quasi-religion or 'psycho shamanism' (Tye, 1994).

17   See, for example, Rodríguez (2010), who places pick-up artistry on a continuum of sexist behaviours that includes rape and murder, and Marcotte (2014), who argues that pick-up artistry bleeds in to the men's rights movement, which contests claims that men have greater power or privilege than women do.

18   Mystery, 2007, pp. 3–4.

19   Denes, 2011.

20   Arrowsmith, 2014.

21   Thompson, 2014, and Rubin, 2014.

CHAPTER 2

1   Sprecher, 1998.

2   Bossard, 1932, pp. 219–222.

3   All the studies mentioned in this paragraph, and others, are reviewed in Katz and Hill, 1958.

4   Perry, 1969, p. 134.

5   Coleman, 1984, and Coleman and Haskey, 1986, p. 345.
6   Haandrikman et al., 2008.
7   Festinger et al., 1950.
8   Priest and Sawyer, 1967, Holahan and Wilcox, 1978, and Sacerdote and Marmaros, 2005.
9   Nahemow and Lawton, 1975.
10 Segal, 1974, Reagans, 2011, and Kraut et al., 2002.
11 Back et al., 2008, p. 440.
12 Bozon and Héran, 1988, 1989.
13 Lampard, 2007.
14 Rosenfeld and Thomas, 2012.
15 Korchmaros et al., 2015.
16 Baker, 2005, 2008.
17 Couch and Liamputtong, 2008, p. 273.
18 Moreland, 1987.
19 Gullahorn, 1952.
20 Walmsley and Lewis, 1993, and Latané et al., 1995.
21 Davie and Reeves, 1939, p. 517.
22 Nuttin, 1985.
23 Hoorens, 2014, and Pelham et al., 2002.
24 Titchener, 1910.
25 Zajonc, 1968.
26 Moreland and Beach, 1992.
27 Claypool et al., 2007, and Harmon-Jones and Allen, 2001.
28 Bornstein et al., 1987.
29 Bornstein, 1989, 2004.
30 Verrier, 2012.
31 Reis et al., 2011.
32 Mita et al., 1977.
33 Lorenz, 1943.
34 Bereczkei et al., 2002, 2004.
35 Fraley and Marks, 2010.
36 DeBruine, 2004.
37 Berscheid and Regan, 2005, p. 177.
38 Galton, 1908, pp. 315–316.
39 Swami and Garcia Hernandez, 2008.
40 Rentfrow et al., 2013, and Jokela et al., 2015.
41 Haandrikman and Hutter, 2012, pp. 252–253.
42 Parks, 2007.
43 Backstrom and Kleinberg, 2014.

44   Parks and Eggert, 1991.
45   Darley and Berscheid, 1967, and Tyler and Sears, 1977.
46   Berscheid et al., 1976.

CHAPTER 3

1   Swami et al., 2008.
2   Benson et al., 1976.
3   Landy and Sigall, 1974.
4   For all these effects and more, see Swami and Furnham, 2008a, Ch. 2.
5   Dion and Berscheid, 1974, Pellegrini and Long, 2007, and Bowker et al., 2012.
6   Greitemeyer and Kunz, 2013, and Wang et al., 2010.
7   Seidman and Miller, 2013.
8   Walster et al., 1966.
9   Asendorpf et al., 2011.
10   Sprecher and McKinney, 1987, Weeden and Sabini, 2007, Puts et al., 2012, and Brody and Weiss, 2013.
11   Aronson, 1969.
12   Hitsch et al., 2010a. Among site users who didn't post a photograph, users who described themselves as very attractive were still more likely to receive an initial message than those who stated their looks were average (Hitsch et al., 2010b).
13   Rudder, 2014, p. 188.
14   Taylor, 2005.
15   Alterovitz and Mendelsohn, 2009.
16   Strassberg and English, 2015. Similar findings have been reported on online dating sites, where a potential partner's physical attractiveness is about 1.3 times a stronger predictor of the decision to send an initial message for men compared to women, and a partner's income is about 1.9 times a stronger predictor for women compared to men (Hitsch et al., 2010b).
17   Ha et al., 2012
18   Swami and Tovée, 2006, and Smith et al., 2011.
19   Eastwick and Finkel, 2008.
20   Fletcher et al., 2014.
21   Wilbur and Campbell, 2010.
22   Moore et al., 2006, and Koyama et al., 2004.
23   Clark and Hatfield, 1989, 2003, and Clark, 1990.
24   Hald and Høgh-Olesen, 2010.

5 Conley et al., 2013.
6 Conley, 2011, p. 310.
7 Conley et al., 2014.
8 Schützwohl et al., 2009, and Regan, 1998.
9 Bzdok et al., 2011.
10 Tsukiura and Cabeza, 2011.
11 Lemay et al., 2010.
12 Dion et al., 1972.
13 Swami, 2012, and Andersen and Bem, 1981.
14 Feingold, 1992, p. 304.
15 Langlois et al., 2000.
16 Snyder et al., 1977.
17 Brand et al., 2012.
18 Bar et al., 2006, Willis and Todorov, 2006, and Olivola and Todorov, 2010.
19 Carney et al., 2007, and Naumann et al., 2009.
20 Lorenzo et al., 2010, p. 1777.
21 Todorov and Porter, 2015.
22 Ellison et al., 2006.
23 Marek et al., 2004, and Human et al., 2013.
24 Pinquart and Pfeiffer, 2012.
25 Eastwick et al., 2014.

CHAPTER 4

1 Fletcher et al., 1999.
2 Eastwick and Finkel, 2008.
3 Eastwick et al., 2011.
4 Fletcher et al., 1999, 2000.
5 Eastwick et al., 2014.
6 Rudder, 2014, Ch. 5.
7 Shaw Taylor et al., 2010.
8 Swami et al., 2010, and Swami, 2011.
9 Lewandowski et al., 2007.
10 Kniffin and Wilson, 2004, p. 93ff.
11 DiDonato et al., 2013.
12 Li et al., 2009. Humour seems to be one area where there are clear sex differences. In heterosexual relationships, women tend to show a preference for men who can make them laugh, whereas men tend to prefer women who laugh at their jokes. In both newspaper personal ads (Provine, 2000) and online dating profiles (Wilbur and Campbell, 2011),

women more than men seek partners who can make them laugh, while men more than women tend to offer the ability to make others laugh. In the early stages of a relationship, men tend to produce more humour and the amount of laughter that a woman produces is a very good predictor of mutual interest in dating (Grammer and Eibl-Eibesfeldt 1990). Why this sex difference exists is difficult to answer. Evolutionary psychologists argue that humour is an 'honest' signal of intelligence – because it is difficult to fake – and so should be preferred by people who value long-term relationships, which they argue happen to be women more than men. On the other hand, feminist scholars remind us that we live in a patriarchal world, where women are expected to recognise men's superior joke-making abilities and laugh at their jokes. As Jennifer Hay (2000, p. 711–712) put it, "women have to understand male humor, men do not have to understand women's". For what it's worth Freud (1905) believed that women didn't need a sense of humour as much as men because they have fewer feelings to repress.

13 Urbaniak and Kilmann, 2003, p. 416.

14 Barclay, 2010.

15 Burger and Cosby, 1999.

16 Ahmetoglu and Swami, 2012.

17 One complicating factor in all this is the gendered nature of expectations that we have about potential partners. In many societies, traits typically and traditionally cited as masculine include assertiveness, dominance, and aggression – precisely those characteristics that don't sit well with 'niceness'. So being 'nice' may require (some) men to transgress socially-constructed ideals of masculinity or at the very least to precariously negotiate how they present their masculinity. Doing so, in turn, may make them less desirable as potential partners, particularly to the extent that women endorse gendered norms of behaviour and value assertiveness and dominance over niceness. There is some evidence to support this idea. In a sample of adults, Jeffrey Hall and Melanie Canterberry (2011) first measured the degree to which women and men preferred assertive 'courtship strategies'. This included things that are popular with pick-up artists, like refusing to back down even if an advance has been rejected, negging (see How to Get Beautiful Women into Bed in Chapter 1), and making aggressive sexual comments. They also measured the degree to which participants endorsed negative attitudes toward women who are viewed as collectively trying to destroy male privilege and patriarchal power. These researchers found that women who scored highly on this measure of sexism were more

receptive to assertive courtship strategies and (among non-college adult) men who were more sexist were more likely to say they would use these aggressive strategies. In other words, the more women and men accepted male privilege and patriarchal attitudes, the more accepting they were of male-led, assertive dating strategies. The point is that socially-constructed gendered norms can complicate relationship formation between women and men.

18   Cited in Urbaniak and Kilmann, 2003, p. 414.

19   Ford, 2012.

20   The classic case being the narcissist – someone who shows high levels of self-importance, superiority, entitlement, and arrogance, combined with a willingness to manipulate and exploit others. There's actually evidence to suggest that, for first impressions, narcissists are perceived as very attractive, mainly because they put a lot of time and effort into their appearance – female narcissists wear more make-up and reveal more cleavage than women who score lower on narcissism, whereas male narcissists were more likely to build up their muscle mass compared to less narcissistic men (Vazire et al., 2008). In the very short term, particularly in initial interactions, narcissists can even seem more well-adjusted, entertaining, and generally nicer. Part of the reason for this is that narcissists may come across as being extraverted and their extraverted behaviour may make a good first impression (Holtzman et al., 2010). But over the long term, narcissists find it difficult to maintain a favourable reputation and tend to be perceived as less adjusted, less warm, and more hostile and arrogant. Not surprisingly, the evidence shows that narcissists don't like long-term, committed relationships and don't do well in them anyway (Morf and Rhodewalt, 2001).

21   Barclay and Haber, 1965.

22   Aron and Aron, 1986, pp. 101–103.

23   Aron, 1970.

24   Dutton and Aron, 1974.

25   Lewandowski and Aron, 2004, Stephan et al., 1971, and Valins, 1966.

26   Meston and Frohlich, 2003. Among individuals who went on the ride with their significant other, there were no differences in attractiveness or dating desirability ratings between persons entering and exiting the ride. Curiously, the researchers also found that physiological arousal didn't increase ratings of the attractiveness of seatmates on the roller coaster rides. They argued that people are simply less attractive post-ride: "Sweating, messy hair, and 'postanxiety expressions' may have made partners appear less physically attractive".

27 Harris et al., 2000, and Cohen et al., 1989.
28 Dienstbier, 1979.
29 White et al., 1981.
30 Pennebaker et al., 1979.
31 Brehm, 1966.
32 Putnam et al., 2001.
33 Lyvers et al., 2011.
34 Johnco et al., 2010.
35 Jones et al., 2003.
36 Markham, 2005, pp. 5ff.
37 Swami et al., 2007, and Swami, 2009.
38 Penton-Voak et al., 2007.
39 Swami, 2011.
40 Swami and Furnham, 2008b.
41 Shakespeare (c. 1597/2000, 2.6.33–39).

CHAPTER 5

1   Backman and Secord, 1959. The effect held only after the first discus sion, but not for the rest of the five weeks. Presumably, subsequen group discussions provided participants with more honest informatior about whether they were liked or disliked by other group members. I a variation of this procedure, researchers found that, when participant were shown positive ratings of themselves made by fellow group mem bers, they showed a stronger desire to remain in the group and wor with other members and were also more attracted to other group mem bers (Dittes, 1959, and Dittes and Kelley, 1956).
2   Lehr and Geher, 2006.
3   Kenny and Nasby, 1980.
4   Newcomb, 1961, and Walster et al., 1966.
5   Folkes and Sears, 1977.
6   Kenny and Nasby, 1980, and Kenny, 1994.
7   Eastwick et al., 2007.
8   Curtis and Miller, 1986.
9   Jones, 1964.
10 Brehm, 1966.
11 Brehm and Cole, 1966. When a group of researchers later replicated this study, they found that participants were more likely to believe that the target had an ulterior motive in the high-importance condition wher they brought the participant a soda (Worchel et al., 1976). In othe

words, it seems that when we believe there is an ulterior motive for a behaviour, we're less likely to express liking.

2   Pruitt, 1968.

3   Montoya and Horton, 2012a.

4   Scheflen, 1965.

5   Clore et al., 1975a, 1975b.

6   Perper, 1989.

7   Moore, 1985, and Moore and Butler, 1989. By contrast, rejection behaviours are often the opposite of courting behaviours. They include leaning away from the man, crossing her arms over her chest, sneering or frowning, and picking at her nails or teeth (Moore, 1998).

8   Walsh and Hewitt, 1985, Maxwell et al., 1985, Moore and Butler, 1989.

9   Abbey, 1982, Abbey and Melby, 1986, and Abbey et al., 2005.

0   Vorauer and Ratner, 1996.

1   Abbey, 1987. Men also believe that women share the same thresholds – their beliefs serve as a "model for the attribution of the appetite of others" (Shotland and Craig, 1988, p. 66). The result is that men end up misperceiving the behaviours of women and, in some cases, it leads to sexual aggression. Sensitivity training could help men to better perceive women's behaviours (Moore, 1997).

2   I've taken these examples from a study by Bale and colleagues (2006), in which they argue that chat-up lines are a way in which men can display characteristics that they think women will find desirable – their wealth or knowledge, for example. In the study, these researchers found that the chat-up lines that were rated by women as most likely to lead to further conversation were those that followed a helpful behaviour by the man (although this may be because the woman feels obliged not to end the conversation) and those that demonstrated good character or wealth. Chat-up lines in which men used pre-planned jokes, jokes that were sexual in nature, or in which the man made fun of the woman – so-called "negging" – were all rated as ineffective.

3   Walle, 1976.

4   Wiseman, 2011.

5   Baddeley, 2010, p. 112.

6   Wade et al., 2009.

7   Mac an Ghaill et al., 2013, p.82. The names are pseudonyms and the spelling hasn't been changed from the original.

8   TextPlus, 2012.

9   Turkle, 2011.

0   Cupples and Thompson, 2010.

31 Laursen, 2005.

32 Knobloch and Miller, 2008. In fact, research consistently shows that ambiguity and uncertainty has a negative effect on performance for both individuals in a relationship. One example comes from research on individuals who are forced to conceal their sexual orientation. Supporters of policies that force gay and lesbian individuals to hide their sexual orientation in the workplace argue that working with openly gay individuals hurts performance. In fact, studies have shown that, when participants work with openly gay partners, they perform better on tasks than when they are left to guess the sexual orientation of their partner (Everly et al., 2012). In most situations, uncertainty and ambiguity hurt social interactions.

33 Berger and Calabrese, 1975.

34 Berger and Kellerman, 1983, and Afifi and Lucas, 2008.

35 Kellerman and Berger, 1984.

36 Douglas, 1987.

37 Baxter and Wilmot, 1984.

38 Bell and Buerkel-Rothfuss, 1990.

39 Baxter and Montgomery, 1996, and Tormala et al., 2012.

40 Baxter and Wilmot, 1985. Another "taboo topic" in close relationships is sex. Couples very rarely ask direct questions about a partner's sexual health and instead rely on observable, outward signals – what they look like, where they're socialising, how they're dressed (Cleary et al., 2002). This reliance on a "relational radar" – an intuition about someone – is often flawed, but sadly seems to trump frank discussions about sexual history and safe sex (Cline et al., 1992).

41 Altman and Taylor, 1973.

42 Taylor, 1968.

43 Berg and Clark, 1986.

44 Altman et al., 1981. These ideas are formalised in Altman's theory of privacy regulation, which has a good deal of support. In one study, a researcher recorded conversations between new acquaintances who met once a week over a month-long period to have a 30-minute conversation. The conversations became deeper over time, which would seem to suggest that self-disclosure occurred gradually. But the researchers also found cyclical patterns in how open or closed the participants were with one another (Vanlear, 1991). In fact, those periods of openness, when we disclose more personal information with a partner, are often retrospectively viewed as turning points in a relationship (Baxter and Erbert, 1999).

45 Dindia and Allen, 1992.
46 Derlega et al., 1985.
47 O'Sullivan, 2005.
48 Utz, 2015.
49 Forest and Wood, 2015.
50 Kleiman et al., 2015.
51 Davis and Perkowitz, 1979, p. 546.
52 Sprecher et al., 2013. In a follow-up study, Sprecher and her colleagues found that, when one person self-discloses and the other listens, it's the listener who more rapidly forms positive interpersonal impressions of the discloser. There is something in disclosing personal information to someone that seems to breed trust and liking (Sprecher et al., 2015).
53 Berg and Archer, 1980.
54 Aron et al., 1997.
55 Slatcher, 2010, and Welker et al., 2014.
56 Walster et al., 1973, p. 115.
57 Matthews et al., 1979.
58 Litt et al., 2010.
59 Dai et al., 2014.
60 Aron et al., 1998.
61 Baumeister et al., 1993.
62 Chartrand and Bargh, 1999.

CHAPTER 6

1 Plato, 360 BC/1960, p. 837, and Turner, 1545.
2 Montoya et al., 2008.
3 Layton and Insko, 1974, p. 149, and Berger, 1975, p. 281.
4 The story is recounted in *Studies in the Psychology of Sex* by Havelock Ellis (1906/2001, p. 201).
5 Pearson, 1900, p. 431.
6 Cooperative Study, 1903, and Jones, 1929.
7 Byrne, 1961, 1962, and Byrne and Nelson, 1965.
8 Newcomb, 1956, p. 578.
9 Cheney, 1975.
10 Burger et al., 2004. In another study, participants were asked to read a three-page profile about Grigori Rasputin, the infamous mystical faith healer who became a trusted friend of the Russian Tsar during the First World War. The profile was rather unflattering: Rasputin was described as unscrupulous and selfish, exploiting the Russian aristocracy for his

own gain. While all participants read the same profile, some were le
to believe that Rasputin shared the same birthday as themselves. Late
when asked to evaluate Rasputin's character, participants who believe
they shared a birthday with Rasputin rated him less harshly (Finch an
Cialdini, 1989).

11   Sunnafrank and Miller, 1981.

12   Sunnafrank, 1992, p. 164.

13   Ross et al., 1977.

14   Condon and Crano, 1988, and Tidwell et al., 2013.

15   Byrne et al., 1970.

16   Montoya et al., 2008. One reason why the distinction between perceive
and actual similarity matters is because of their effects on developin
relationships. If there is a discrepancy between actual and perceive
similarity, it could put strain on a relationship when the dissimilarity i
eventually uncovered. Someone who finds out that their perceptions c
similarity were wrong might feel surprised or disappointed. They ma
even feel that their partner has been disingenuous or deceitful, whic
results in anger and conflict (Sunnafrank, 1992).

17   Byrne, 1971.

18   Byrne and Clore, 1970.

19   Ajzen, 1974, and Kaplan and Anderson, 1973.

20   Novak and Lerner, 1968. In this study, the researchers used the phar
tom other technique and varied how similar the target was to the pa
ticipant. However, some participants saw a version of the phantor
target's survey in which they'd written: 'I don't know if this is relevan
or not, but last fall I had kind of a nervous breakdown and I had to b
hospitalized for a while. I've been seeing a psychiatrist ever since. A
you probably noticed, I'm pretty shaky right now.' When the participant
saw this information and when they were similar to the target, they like
the phantom other less. The researchers concluded that, although sim
larity generally sparks attraction, the effects are diminished when th
nature of that information is negative. It's possible that reading abou
someone else's suffering reminds us of our own vulnerability and, i
those cases, dissimilarity may be more comforting than similarity.

21   Montoya and Horton, 2012b.

22   Rosenbaum, 1986.

23   Byrne et al., 1986, Smeaton et al., 1989, and Gouldner and Strong, 1987

24   Rosenfeld, 1964.

25   Rudder, 2014, p. 50. In contrast, Rudder believes, someone who appear
unconventional or less attractive by mainstream standards may b

perceived as having fewer suitors. In other words, there is less competition and having fewer rivals means the chances of dating 'success' are higher. Rudder gives the example of a man who, while browsing through profiles, chances upon an unconventional-looking woman: 'I can imagine our man browsing her profile, circling his cursor, thinking to himself: *I bet she doesn't meet many guys who think she's awesome. In fact, I'm actually into her quirks, not in spite of them. This is my diamond in the rough,* and so on'. In fact, one study of online daters found that users were more likely to receive responses from a potential date when the two were similar in terms of their physical attractiveness. Less attractive users contacting attractive dates were less likely to receive a reply (Taylor et al., 2011).

6   Berscheid et al., 1971.
7   Montoya, 2008.
8   Lee et al., 2008.
9   Folkes, 1982.
10 Rogers, 1994, p. 244.
11 Lazarsfeld and Merton, 1954.
12 McPherson et al., 2001.
13 Newcomb, 1961.
14 Burgess et al., 2011, and McPherson and Smith-Lovin, 1987, and Marsden, 1988.
15 Laumann, 1973, and Liu et al., 1995.
16 Wimmer and Lewis, 2010, Skopek et al., 2010, and Kalmijn, 1998.
17 Byrne and Wong, 1962.
18 Adams, 1953, and Homans, 1961.
19 Winch, 1955.
20 Selfhout et al., 2009.
21 Haselager et al., 1998, Gifford-Smith and Brownell, 2003, and Davis, 1981.
22 Bowen, 1978, and Bowen and Kerr, 1988, p. 225.
23 Miller et al., 2004, and Haselager et al., 1998.
24 Pinel et al., 2006, p. 245.
25 eHarmony, 2011.
26 Warren, 2002, p. 116.
27 Carter and Buckwalter, 2009.
28 Houts et al., 1996, Weisfeld et al., 1992, and Montoya et al., 2008.
29 Finkel et al., 2012, p. 49.
30 Kelly and Conley, 1987.
31 Aron et al., 2006.
32 Aron and Aron, 1986.

53 Layton and Insko, 1974.

54 Likewise, some evolutionary psychologists have claimed that human beings, like many other species of animal, seek genetic dissimilarity in a partner. The argument is that inbreeding increases the risk of children being born with physical and mental disorders, whereas outbreeding – or choosing partners on the basis of genetic dissimilarity – promotes the likelihood of healthy children. In humans specifically, this idea has been applied to a set of genes central to immune functioning called the major histocompatibility complex or MHC for short. When infants inherit different copies of MHC genes from their parents, they tend to have healthier immune systems. So, according to psychologists, human beings may have evolved to identify and prefer to mate with individuals whose MHC genes are different to their own (Grob et al., 1998). In support of this idea, early studies found that, when asked to smell t-shirts worn by others with similar or dissimilar MHC genes, participants preferred the odour of MHC-dissimilar others (Thornhill et al., 2003). But not everyone is convinced. For one thing, even if people prefer the odour of MHC-dissimilar others, they seem to prefer the faces of MHC-similar others (Roberts and Little, 2008). Moreover, evidence that real couples actually make partner decisions based on MHC-similarity is inconsistent (Havlicek and Roberts, 2009).

55 Davis and Rusbult, 2001.

CHAPTER 7

1 Foster, 2005.

2 Finkel et al., 2012.

3 Foster, 2005, p. 1462.

4 Dailey et al., 2013.

5 Wells, 2003, p. 56. Narratives by other authors are contained in the same issue of the journal.

6 Conville, 1987.

7 Franiuk et al., 2002, and Eidelson and Epstein, 1982.

8 Knee et al., 2001. An interesting question is where such beliefs come from. Some scientists point to the way in which popular media construct the idea that the 'right person' is just waiting out there for you. In popular movies, television programmes – particularly those aimed at women – ideas of romance often include themes of love at first sight and meeting 'the one and only' (Carpenter, 1998). Other studies have found that individuals who have a preference for romance media are more likely to believe in the idea of a predestined soulmate and also

hold more dysfunctional beliefs about relationships, including the idea
that soulmates should be able to mind-read (Holmes, 2007).

9   Lieblich et al., 2008.

10   Tanner et al., 2003.

11   Seiffge-Krenke, 2011, and Leckman and Mayes, 1999.

12   Carter and Porges, 2011.

13   One way of understanding the stressful nature of new relationship is to
look at what happens to levels of cortisol, a hormone that is secreted
in response to stress. One study compared new lovers in the first six
months of their relationships with singles and individuals in long-term
romantic relationships. It was found that the new lovers had higher
cortisol levels than the other two groups, suggesting that they may
have been experiencing greater levels of stress (Marazziti and Canale,
2004). Another study found that women exhibited an increase in
cortisol levels simply after being asked to think about their partners
(Loving et al., 2009). However, other research has shown that levels
of daily cortisol production are attenuated among new lovers in the
first three months of the relationship compared with singles (Weisman
et al., 2015). One explanation for these contrasting findings is that
stable, mutually-satisfying relationships may help to reduce levels of
stress, whereas fragile relationships continue to be a source of stress.
In the longer-term, stable and positive relationships are associated with
lower cortisol levels for both women and men (Maestripieri et al., 2013).

14   Starcke and Brand, 2012.

15   von Dawans et al., 2012.

16   Starcke et al., 2011.

17   Aronson et al., 1966.

18   Kiesler and Goldberg, 1968, and Mettee and Wilkins, 1972. There's also
some evidence that the pratfall effect is strongest when men rate other
men. Women seem to prefer the competent non-blunderer, regardless
of that person's gender (Deaux, 1972). In any case, no one seems to like
the mediocre blunderer.

19   Swami and Barrett, 2011.

20   Bowlby, 1969.

21   In seminal work, Mary Ainsworth and her students (1978) observed
interactions between mothers and their babies in their homes. In
the most famous part of the research, they watched how the babies
responded to a separation from their mothers in a procedure called
the 'strange situation'. In this procedure, the mother and baby enter a
toy-filled room, where a researcher greets them and invites the baby to
play with the toys. The baby is then observed as the mother leaves the

room three times for several minutes, leaving the child either alone or with the researcher. Based on these observations, Ainsworth and her students identified three patterns of behavioural reactions. The first called 'secure attachment', described babies who explored the room while the caregiver was present, was upset when the caregiver left the room, and was generally happy when the caregiver returned. Babies who were 'anxiously attached' didn't explore very much, were wary of the strange researcher, and were highly distressed when the caregiver left, but were ambivalent when she returned. Finally, 'anxious-avoidant insecure attachment' describes babies that avoided or ignored the caregiver, showed little emotion when the caregiver left or returned, and chose not to explore regardless of who was in the room. These attachment patterns that are formed in infancy seem to persist into adulthood. In one large, nationally representative survey of adults in the United States, 59 per cent of respondents were found to be securely attached, 25 per cent were anxious-avoidant, and 11 per cent were anxiously attached (Mickelson et al., 1997).

22   Hazan and Shaver, 1987.

23   Bowlby, 1973, and Simpson, 1990.

24   Andersen and Cole, 1990, and Andersen and Baum, 1994.

25   Brumbaugh and Fraley, 2006.

26   Johnson, 2004. This isn't to say that people's attachment styles in relationships can never change. People who are insecure can become more secure if their partner is secure, but the process is long and depends on the two people in the relationship establishing mutual trust in each other (Kirkpatrick and Hazan, 1994).

27   Sbarra and Emery, 2005.

28   Spielmann et al., 2009, Slotter et al., 2010, and Maner et al., 2007.

29   Brumbaugh and Fraley, 2015.

30   Tedeschi et al., 1998, and Tashiro and Frazier, 2003.

31   Neff and Beretvas, 2013. There are a number of intervention programmes that may help people develop self-compassion, such as Jon Kabat-Zinn's (1991) Mindfulness-Based Stress Reduction programme. Mindfulness teaches people to focus attention on the emotions, thoughts, and sensations that occur in the present moment, so that they can be accepted with kindness and without judgement. Mindfulness programmes are often taught by health professionals to help people deal with stress and mental suffering, but they may also offer individuals and couples a way of developing self-compassion (Carson et al., 2004).

32   McFarland et al., 2013.

References

Abbey, A. (1982). Sex differences in attributions for friendly behavior: Do males misperceive females' friendliness? *Journal of Personality and Social Psychology*, *42*, 830–538.

Abbey, A. (1987). Misperceptions of friendly behavior as sexual interest: A survey of naturally occurring incidents. *Psychology of Women Quarterly*, *11*, 173–194.

Abbey, A., & Melby, C. (1986). The effects of nonverbal cues on gender differences in perceptions of sexual intent. *Sex Roles*, *32*, 297–313.

Abbey, A., Zawacki, T., & Buck, P. O. (2005). The effects of past sexual assault perpetration and alcohol consumption on men's reactions to women's mixed signals. *Journal of Social and Clinical Psychology*, *24*, 129–155.

Adams, S. (1953). Status congruency as a variable in small group performance. *Social Forces*, *32*, 16–22.

Afifi, W. A., & Lucas, A. A. (2008). Information seeking in the initial stages of relational development. In S. Sprecher, A. Wenzel, & J. Harvey (Eds.), *Handbook of relationship initiation* (pp. 135–151). New York, NY: Psychology Press.

Ahmetoglu, G., & Swami, V. (2012). Do women prefer 'nice guys'? The effect of male dominance behavior on women's ratings of sexual attractiveness. *Social Behavior and Personality*, *40*, 667–672.

Ainsworth, M. D. S., Blehar, M., Waters, E., & Wall, S. (1978). *Patterns of attachment*. Hillsdale, NJ: Erlbaum.

Ajzen, I. (1974). Effects of information on interpersonal attraction: Similarity versus affective value. *Journal of Personality and Social Psychology, 29* 374–380.

Alterovitz, S. S.-R., & Mendelsohn, G. A. (2009). Partner preferences across th life span: Online dating by older adults. *Psychology and Aging, 24*, 513–517

Altman, I., & Taylor, D. A. (1973). *Social penetration: The development of inter personal relationships*. New York, NY: Holt, Rinehart, and Winston.

Altman, I., Vinsel, A., & Brown, B. H. (1981). Dialectic conceptions in socia psychology: An application to social penetration and privacy regulation In L. Berkowitz (Ed.), *Advances in experimental social psychology* (Vol. 14 pp. 107–160). New York, NY: Academic Press.

Andersen, S. M., & Baum, A. (1994). Transference in interpersonal relations Inferences and affect based on significant-other representations. *Journal o Personality, 62*, 459–497.

Andersen, S. M., & Bem, S. L. (1981). Sex typing and androgyny in dyadic inter action: Individual differences in responsiveness to physical attractiveness *Journal of Personality and Social Psychology, 41*, 74–86.

Anderen, S. M., & Cole, S. W. (1990). "Do I know you?": The role of significan others in general social perception. *Journal of Personality and Social Psychol ogy, 59*, 384–399.

Aron, A. (1970). *Relationship variables in human heterosexual attractior* (Unpublished doctoral dissertation). University of Toronto, Toronto Canada.

Aron, A., & Aron, E. N. (1986). *Love and the expansion of self: Understandin attraction and satisfaction*. New York, NY: Hemisphere.

Aron, A., & Aron, E. N. (1989). *The heart of social psychology: A backstage viev of a passionate science* (2nd ed.). Lexington, MA: Lexington Books.

Aron, A., Aron, E. N., & Allen, J. (1998). Motivations for unreciprocated love *Personality and Social Psychology Bulletin, 24*, 787–796.

Aron, A., Dutton, D. G., Aron, E. N., & Iverson, A. (1989). Experiences of fall ing in love. *Journal of Social and Personal Relationships, 6*, 243–257.

Aron, A., Melinat, E., Aron, E. N., Vallone, R. D., & Bator, R. J. (1997). The experimental generation of interpersonal closeness: A procedure and some preliminary findings. *Personality and Social Psychology Bulletin, 23* 363–377.

Aron, A., Steele, J. L., Kashdan, T. B., & Perez, M. (2006). When similars de not attract: Tests of a prediction from the self-expansion model. *Persona Relationships, 13*, 387–396.

Aron, E. N., & Aron, A. (1996). Love and expansion of the self: The state of the model. *Personal Relationships*, *3*, 45–58.

Aronson, E. (1969). Some antecedents of interpersonal attraction. In W. J. Arnold, & D. Levine (Eds.), *Nebraska symposium on motivation* (Vol. 17, pp. 142–177). Lincoln, NE: University of Nebraska Press.

Aronson, E., Willerman, B., & Floyd, J. (1966). The effect of a pratfall on increasing interpersonal attractiveness. *Psychonomic Science*, *4*, 227–228.

Arrowsmith, A. (2014). Rethinking misogyny: Men's perceptions of female power in dating relationships. Ph.D. Thesis, University of Sussex.

Asendorpf, J. B., Penke, L., & Back, M. D. (2011). From dating to mating and relating: Predictors of initial and long-term outcomes of speed-dating in a community sample. *European Journal of Personality*, *25*, 16–30.

Back, M. D., Schmulke, S. C., & Egloff, B. (2008). Becoming friends by chance. *Psychological Science*, *19*, 439–440.

Backman, C. W., & Secord, P. F. (1959). The effect of perceived liking on interpersonal attraction. *Human Relations*, *12*, 379–384.

Backstrom, L., & Kleinberg, J. (2014). Romantic partnerships and the dispersion of social ties: A network analysis of relationship status on Facebook. In Association for Computing Machinery (Ed.), *Proceedings of the 17th ACM Conference on Computer Supported Work and Social Computing* (pp. 831–841). New York, NY: Association for Computing Machinery.

Baddeley, G. (2010). *Goths: Vamps and dandies*. London: Plexus.

Baker, A. J. (2005). *Double click: Romance and commitment among online couples*. Cresskill, NJ: Hampton Press.

Baker, A. J. (2008). Down the rabbit hole: The role of place in the initiation and development of online relationships. In A. Barak (Ed.), *Psychological aspects of cyberspace: Theory, research, applications* (pp. 163–184). Cambridge: Cambridge University Press.

Bale, C., Morrison, R., & Caryl, P. G. (2006). Chat-up lines as male sexual displays. *Personality and Individual Differences*, *40*, 655–664.

Bandler, R., & Grinder, J. (1975a). *The structure of magic I: A book about language and therapy*. Palo Alto, CA: Science and Behavior Books.

Bandler, R., & Grinder, J. (1975b). *The structure of magic II: A book about communication and change*. Palo Alto, CA: Science and Behaviour Books.

Bar, M., Neta, M., & Linz, H. (2006). Very first impressions. *Emotion*, *6*, 269–278.

Barclay, A. M., & Haber, R. N. (1965). The relation of aggressive to sexual motivation. *Journal of Personality*, *33*, 462–475.

Barclay, P. (2010). Altruism as a courtship display: Some effects of third-party generosity on audience perceptions. *British Journal of Psychology*, *101*, 123–135.

Baumeister, R. F., Wotman, S. R., & Sillwell, A. M. (1993). Unrequited love: C heartbreak, anger, guilt, scriptlessness, and humiliation. *Journal of Persona ity and Social Psychology, 64*, 377–394.

Baxter, L. A., & Erbert, L. A. (1999). Perceptions of dialectical contradiction in turning points of development in heterosexual romantic relationship *Journal of Social and Personal Relationships, 16*, 547–569.

Baxter, L. A., & Montgomery, B. M. (1996). *Relating: Dialogues and dialectic* New York, NY: Guilford.

Baxter, L. A., & Wilmot, W. W. (1984). "Secret tests": Social strategies for acqui ing information about the state of the relationship. *Human Communicatic Research, 2*, 171–201.

Baxter, L. A., & Wilmot, W. W. (1985). Taboo topics in close relationships. *Jou nal of Social and Personal Relationships, 2*, 253–269.

Bell, R. A., & Buerkel-Rothfuss, N. L. (1990). (S)he loves, (s)he loves me nc Predictors of relational information-seeking in courtship and beyond. *Con munication Quarterly, 38*, 64–82.

Benson, P. L., Karabenick, S. A., & Lerner, R. M. (1976). Pretty pleases: Th effects of physical attractiveness, race, and sex on receiving help. *Journal c Experimental Social Psychology, 12*, 409–415.

Bereczkei, T., Gyuris, P., Koves, P., & Bernath, L. (2002). Homogamy, genet similarity, and imprinting: Parental influence on mate choice preference *Personality and Individual Differences, 33*, 677–690.

Bereczkei, T., Gyuris, P., & Weisfeld, G. E. (2004). Sexual imprinting i human mate choice. *Proceedings of the Royal Society of London B, 27* 1129–1134.

Berg, J. H., & Archer, R. L. (1980). Disclosure concern: A second look at likin for the norm-breaker. *Journal of Personality, 48*, 245–257.

Berg, J. H., & Clark, M. S. (1986). Differences in social exchange between int mate and other relationships: Gradually evolving or quickly apparent? I V. J. Derlega, & B. A. Winstead (Eds.), *Friendships and social interactic* (pp. 1101–1128). New York, NY: Springer-Verlag.

Berger, C. R. (1975). Task performance and attributional communica tion as determinants of interpersonal attraction. *Speech Monographs, 4* 1053–1070.

Berger, C. R., & Calabrese, R. J. (1975). Some explorations in initial interactior and beyond: Toward a developmental theory of interpersonal communica tion. *Human Communication Research, 1*, 99–112.

Berger, C. R., & Kellerman, K. (1983). To ask or not to ask: Is that a question In R. N. Bostrom (Ed.), *Communication Yearbook 7* (pp. 342–368). Newbur Park, CA: Sage.

Berscheid, E., Dion, K., Walster, E., & Walster, G. W. (1971). Physical attractiveness and dating choice: A test of the matching hypothesis. *Journal of Experimental Social Psychology*, 7, 173–189.

Berscheid, E., Graziano, W., Monson, T., & Dermer, M. (1976). Outcome dependency: Attention, attribution, and attraction. *Journal of Personality and Social Psychology*, 34, 978–989.

Berscheid, E., & Regan, P. (2005). *The psychology of interpersonal relationships*. Upper Saddle River, NJ: Pearson Education.

Bornstein, R. F. (1989). Exposure and affect: Overview and meta-analysis of research, 1968–1987. *Psychological Bulletin*, 106, 265–289.

Bornstein, R. F. (2004). Mere exposure effect. In R. F. Pohl (Ed.), *Cognitive illusions: A handbook on fallacies and biases in thinking, judgement and memory* (pp. 215–234). Hove: Psychology Press.

Bornstein, R. F., Leone, D. R., & Galley, D. J. (1987). The generalizability of subliminal mere exposure effects: Influence of stimuli perceived without awareness on social behavior. *Journal of Personality and Social Psychology*, 53, 1070–1079.

Bossard, J. H. S. (1932). Residential propinquity as a factor in marriage selection. *American Journal of Sociology*, 38, 219–224.

Bowen, M. (1978). *Family therapy in clinical practice*. New York, NY: Jason Aronson.

Bowker, J. C., Spencer, S. V., Thomas, K. K., & Gyoerkoe, E. A. (2012). Having and being an other-sex crush during early adolescence. *Journal of Experimental Child Psychology*, 111, 629–643.

Bowlby, J. (1969). Disruption of affectional bonds and its effects on behavior. *Canada's Mental Health Supplement*, 59, 12.

Bowlby, J. (1973). *Attachment and loss: Volume 2. Separation: Anxiety and anger*. New York, NY: Basic Books.

Bozon, M., & Héran, F. (1988). La Découverte du Conjoint II: Les scènes de rencontre dans l'éspace social. *Population*, 43, 121–150.

Bozon, M., & Héran, F. (1989). Finding a spouse: A survey of how French couples meet. *Population*, 44, 91–121.

Brand, R. J., Bonatsos, A., D'Orazio, R., & DeShong, H. (2012). What is beautiful is good, even online: Correlations between photo attractiveness and text attractiveness in men's online dating profiles. *Computers in Human Behavior*, 28, 166–170.

Brehm, J. W. (1966). *A theory of psychological reactance*. New York, NY: Academic Press.

Brehm, J. W., & Cole, A. H. (1966). Effect of favor which reduces freedom. *Journal of Personality and Social Psychology*, 3, 420–426.

Briers, S. (2012). *Brilliant cognitive behavioural therapy: How to use CBT t* *change your mind and your life* (2nd ed.). Harlow: Pearson.

Brody, S., & Weiss, P. (2013). Slimmer women's waist is associated with bette erectile function in men independent of age. *Archives of Sexual Behavio 42*, 1191–1198.

Brumbaugh, C. C., & Fraley, R. C. (2006). Transference and attachment: Hov do attachment patterns get carried forward from one relationship to th next. *Personality and Social Psychology Bulletin, 32*, 552–560.

Brumbaugh, C. C., & Fraley, R. C. (2015). Too fast, too soon? An empirica investigation into rebound relationships. *Journal of Social and Person Relationships, 32*, 99–118.

Burger, J. M., & Cosby, M. (1999). Do women prefer dominant men? The case the missing control condition. *Journal of Research in Personality, 33*, 358–368

Burger, J. M., Messian, N., Patel, S., del Prado, A., & Anderson, C. (2004). Wha a coincidence! The effects of incidental similarity on compliance. *Personalit and Social Psychology Bulletin, 30*, 35–43.

Burgess, S., Sanderson, E., & Umaña-Aponte, M. (2011). School ties: An analy sis of homophily in an adolescent friendship network. *The Centre for Marke and Public Organisation Working Paper Series No. 11/267*. Bristol: Universit of Bristol Press.

Byrne, D. (1961). Interpersonal attraction and attitude similarity. *Journal c Abnormal and Social Psychology, 62*, 713–715.

Byrne, D. (1962). Response to attitude similarity-dissimilarity as a function o affiliation need. *Journal of Personality, 30*, 137–149.

Byrne, D. (1971). *The attraction paradigm*. New York, NY: Academic Press.

Byrne, D. (1979). Citation classic commentary: Interpersonal-attraction an attitude similarity. *Current Contents, 16*, 222.

Byrne, D., & Clore, G. L. (1970). A reinforcement model of evaluative response *Personality: An International Journal, 1*, 103–128.

Byrne, D., Clore, G. L., & Smeaton, G. (1986). The attraction hypothesis: D similar attitudes affect anything? *Journal of Personality and Social Psychol ogy, 51*, 1167–1170.

Byrne, D., Ervin, C. R., & Lamberth, J. (1970). Continuity between the experi mental study of attraction and real-life computer dating. *Journal of Personal ity and Social Psychology, 16*, 157–165.

Byrne, D., & Nelson, D. (1965). Attraction as a linear function of proportion of positive reinforcements. *Journal of Personality and Social Psychology, 659*–663.

Byrne, D., & Wong, T. J. (1962). Racial prejudice, interpersonal attraction, and assumed dissimilarity of attitudes. *Journal of Abnormal and Social Psychol ogy, 65*, 246–253.

Bzdok, D., Langner, R., Caspers, S., Kurth, F., Habel, U., Zilles, K., Laird, A., & Eickhoff, S. B. (2011). ALE meta-analysis on facial judgements of trustworthiness and attractiveness. *Brain Structure and Function, 215*, 209–223.

Carney, D. R., Colvin, R. C., & Hall, J. A. (2007). A thin slice perspective on the accuracy of first impressions. *Journal of Research in Personality, 41*, 1054–1072.

Carpenter, L. M. (1998). From girls into women: Scripts from sexuality and romance in *Seventeen* magazine. *The Journal of Sex Research, 35*, 158–168.

Carson, J. W., Carson, K. M., Gil, K. M., & Baucom, D. H. (2004). Mindfulness-based relationship enhancement. *Behavior Therapy, 35*, 471–494.

Carter, C. S., & Porges, S. W. (2011). The neurobiology of social bonding and attachment. In J. Decety, & J. T. Cacioppo (Eds.), *The Oxford handbook of social neuroscience* (pp. 151–163). New York, NY: Oxford University Press.

Carter, S. R., & Buckwalter, J. G. (2009). Enhancing mate selection through the Internet: A comparison of relationship quality between marriages arising from an online matchmaking system and marriages arising from unfettered selection. *Interpersona: An International Journal on Personal Relationships, 3*, 105–125.

Catron, M. L. (2015, January 9). To fall in love with anyone, do this. *New York Times*. Retrieved from http://www.nytimes.com

Chartrand, T. L., & Bargh, J. A. (1999). The chameleon effect: The perception-behavior link and social interaction. *Journal of Personality and Social Psychology, 76*, 893–910.

Cheney, T. (1975). Attitude similarity, topic importance, and psychotherapeutic attraction. *Journal of Counseling Psychology, 22*, 2–5.

Cherry, F. (1995). *The stubborn particulars of social psychology: Essays on the research process*. London: Routledge.

Chrétien de Troyes (1176/1914). *Chrétien de Troyes: Arthurian romances*. Translated by W. W. Comfort. London: Everyman's Library.

Clark, R. D., III. (1990). The impact of AIDS on gender differences in willingness to engage in casual sex. *Journal of Applied Social Psychology, 20*, 771–782.

Clark, R. D., III, & Hatfield, E. (1989). Gender differences in receptivity to sexual offers. *Journal of Psychology and Human Sexuality, 2*, 39–55.

Clark, R. D., III, & Hatfield, E. (2003). Love in the afternoon. *Psychological Inquiry, 14*, 227–231.

Claypool, H. M., Hugenberg, K., Housley, M. K., & Mackie, D. M. (2007). Familiar eyes are smiling: On the role of familiarity in the perception of facial affect. *European Journal of Social Psychology, 37*, 856–866.

Cleary, J., Barhman, R., MacCormack, T., & Herold, E. (2002). Discussing sexual health with a partner: A qualitative study with young women. *Canadian Journal of Human Sexuality*, *11*, 117–132.

Cline, R. J. W., Johnson, S. J., & Freeman, K. E. (1992). Talk among sexual partners about AIDS: Interpersonal communication for risk reduction or risk enhancement? *Health Communication*, *4*, 39–56.

Clore, G., Wiggens, N. H., & Itkin, S. (1975a). Judging attraction from nonverbal behavior: The gain phenomenon. *Journal of Consulting and Clinical Psychology*, *43*, 491–497

Clore, G., Wiggens, N. H., & Itkin, S. (1975b). Gain and loss in attraction: Attributions from nonverbal behavior. *Journal of Personality and Social Psychology*, *31*, 706–712.

Cohen, B., Waugh, G., & Place, K. (1989). At the movies: An unobtrusive study of arousal-attraction. *The Journal of Social Psychology*, *129*, 691–693.

Cole, M. L. (1999). *The experience of never-married women in their thirties who desire marriage and children* (Unpublished doctoral dissertation). Institute for Clinical Social Work.

Coleman, D. A. (1984). *Reading Marriage Survey, 1974*. Colchester: UK Data Archive.

Coleman, D. A., & Haskey, J. C. (1986). Marital distance and its geographical orientation in England and Wales, 1979. *Transaction of the Institute of British Geographers*, *11*, 337–355.

Condon, J. W., & Crano, W. D. (1988). Inferred evaluation and the relation between attitude similarity and interpersonal attraction. *Journal of Personality and Social Psychology*, *54*, 789–797.

Conley, T. D. (2011). Perceived proposer personality characteristics and gender differences in acceptance of casual sex offers. *Journal of Personality and Social Psychology*, *100*, 309–329.

Conley, T. D., Rubin, J. D., Matsick, J. L., Ziegler, A., & Moors, A. C. (2014). Proposer, gender, pleasure, and danger in casual sex offers among bisexual women and men. *Journal of Experimental Social Psychology*, *55*, 80–88.

Conley, T. D., Ziegler, A., & Moors, A. C. (2013). Backlash from the bedroom: Stigma mediates gender differences in acceptance of casual sex. *Psychology of Women Quarterly*, *37*, 392–407.

Conville, R. L. (1987). Relational transitions: Inquiry into their structure and function. *Journal of Social and Personal Relationships*, *5*, 422–437.

Cooperative Study (1903). Assortative mating in man: A cooperative study. *Biometrika*, *2*, 481–498.

Couch, D., & Liamputtong, P. (2008). Online dating and mating: The use of the Internet to meet sexual partners. *Quality Health Research*, *18*, 268–279.

Cupples, J., & Thompson, L. (2010). Heterotextuality and digital foreplay. *Feminist Media Studies, 10*, 1–17.

Curtis, R. C., & Miller, K. (1986). Believing another likes or dislikes you: Behaviors making the beliefs come true. *Journal of Personality and Social Psychology, 51*, 284–290.

Dai, X., Dong, P., & Jia, J. S. (2014). When does playing hard to get increase romantic attraction? *Journal of Experimental Psychology: General, 143*, 521–526.

Dailey, R. M., Brody, N., LeFebvre, L., & Crook, B. (2013). Charting changes in commitment: Trajectories of on-again/off-again relationships. *Journal of Social and Personal Relationships, 30*, 1020–1044.

Darley, J. M., & Berscheid, E. (1967). Increased liking as a result of the anticipation of personal contact. *Human Relations, 20*, 29–40.

Davie, M. E., & Reeves, R. J. (1939). Propinquity of residence before marriage. *American Journal of Sociology, 44*, 510–517.

Davis, D. (1981). Implications for interaction versus effectance as mediators of the similarity-attraction relationship. *Journal of Experimental Social Psychology, 17*, 96–117.

Davis, D., & Perkowitz, W. T. (1979). Consequences of responsiveness in dyadic interactions. In W. Ickes, & E. G. Knowles (Eds.), *Personality, roles, and social behavior* (pp. 85–140). New York, NY: Springer-Verlag.

Davis, J. L., & Rusbult, C. E. (2001). Attitude alignment in close relationships. *Journal of Personality and Social Psychology, 81*, 65–84.

Deaux, K. (1972). To err is humanizing: But sex makes a difference. *Representative Research in Social Psychology, 3*, 20–28.

DeBruine, L. M. (2004). Facial resemblance increases the attractiveness of same-sex faces more than other-sex faces. *Proceedings of the Royal Society of London B, 271*, 2085–2090.

Denes, A. (2011). Biology as consent: Problematizing the scientific approach to seducing women's bodies. *Women's Studies International Forum, 34*, 411–419.

Derlega, V. J., Winstead, B. A., Wong, P. T. P., & Hunter, S. (1985). Gender effects in an initial encounter: A case where men exceed women in disclosure. *Journal of Social and Personal Relationships, 2*, 25–44.

DiDonato, T. E., Bedminster, M. C., & Machel, J. J. (2013). My funny valentine: How humor styles affect romantic interest. *Personal Relationships, 20*, 374–390.

Dienstbier, R. A. (1979). Attraction increases and decreases as a function of emotion-attributed and appropriate social cues. *Motivation and Emotion, 3*, 201–218.

Dindia, K., & Allen, M. (1992). Sex differences in self-disclosure: A meta-analysis. *Psychological Bulletin, 112*, 106–124.

Dion, K., & Berscheid, E. (1974). Physical attractiveness and peer perception among children. *Sociometry, 37*, 1–12.

Dion, K., Berscheid, E., & Walster, E. (1972). What is beautiful is good. *Journal of Personality and Social Psychology, 24*, 285–290.

Dittes, J. E. (1959). Attractiveness of group as a function of self-esteem and acceptance by group. *Journal of Abnormal and Social Psychology, 59*, 77–82.

Dittes, J. E., & Kelley, H. H. (1956). Effects of different conditions of acceptance upon conformity to group norms. *Journal of Abnormal and Social Psychology, 53*, 100–107.

Doss, B. D., Rhoades, G. K., Stanley, S. M., & Markman, H. J. (2009). Marital therapy, retreats, and books: The who, what, when, and why of relationship help-seeking. *Journal of Marital and Family Therapy, 35*, 18–29.

Douglas, W. (1987). Affinity testing in initial interactions. *Journal of Social and Personal Relationships, 4*, 3–15.

Dutton, D. G., & Aron, A. P. (1974). Some evidence for heightened sexual attraction under conditions of high anxiety. *Journal of Personality and Social Psychology, 30*, 510–517.

Eastwick, P. W., & Finkel, E. J. (2008). Sex differences in mate preferences revisited: Do people know what they initially desire in a romantic partner? *Journal of Personality and Social Psychology, 94*, 245–264.

Eastwick, P. W., Finkel, E. J., & Eagly, A. H. (2011). When and why do ideal partner preferences affect the process of initiating and maintaining romantic relationships? *Journal of Personality and Social Psychology, 101*, 1012–1032.

Eastwick, P. W., Finkel, E. J., Mochon, D., & Ariely, D. (2007). Selective versus unselective romantic desire: Not all reciprocity is created equal. *Psychological Science, 18*, 317–319.

Eastwick, P. W., Luchies, L. B., Finkel, E. J., & Hunt, L. L. (2014). The predictive validity of ideal partner preferences: A review and meta-analysis. *Psychological Bulletin, 140*, 623–665.

eHarmony (2011). Scientific match making. Retrieved from http://www.eharmony.com/why/science

Eidelson, R. J., & Epstein, N. (1982). Cognition and relationship maladjustment: Development of a measure of dysfunctional relationship beliefs. *Journal of Consulting and Clinical Psychology, 50*, 715–720.

Eisner, D. (2000). *The death of psychotherapy: From Freud to alien abductions.* Santa Barbara, CA: Praeger.

Ellis, B. J., & Kelley, H. H. (1999). The pairing game: A classroom demonstration of the matching phenomenon. *Teaching of Psychology, 26*, 118–121.

Ellis, H. (1906/2001). *Studies in the psychology of sex: Sexual selection in man.* Honolulu, HI: University Press of the Pacific.

llis, L., Robb, B., & Burke, D. (2005). Sexual orientation in United States and Canadian students. *Archives of Sexual Behavior, 34*, 569–581.

llison, N., Heino, R., & Gibbs, J. (2006). Managing impressions online: Self-presentation processes in the online dating environment. *Journal of Computer-Mediated Communication, 11*, 415–441.

verly, B. A., Shih, M. J., & Ho, G. C. (2012). Don't ask, don't tell? Does disclosure of gay identity affect partner performance? *Journal of Experimental Social Psychology, 48*, 407–410.

arvid, P., & Braun, V. (2006). 'Most of us guys are raring to go, anytime, anyplace, anywhere': Male and female sexuality in *Cleo* and *Cosmo*. *Sex Roles, 55*, 295–310.

ein, E., & Schneider, S. (1996). *The rules: Time-tested secrets for capturing the heart of Mr. Right*. New York, NY: Warner Books.

eingold, A. (1992). Good-looking people are not what we think. *Psychological Bulletin, 111*, 304–341.

estinger, L., Schachter, S., & Back, K. W. (1950). *Social pressures in informal groups: A study of human factors in housing*. Stanford, CA: Stanford University Press.

inch, J. F., & Cialdini, R. B. (1989). Another indirect tactic of (self-)image management: Boosting. *Personality and Social Psychology Bulletin, 15*, 222–232.

inkel, E. J., Eastwick, P. W., Karney, B. R., Reis, H. T., & Sprecher, S. (2012). Online dating: A critical analysis from the perspective of psychological science. *Psychology Science in the Public Interest, 13*, 3–66.

isher, H. E. (2009). *Why him? Why her?* New York, NY: Henry Holt.

letcher, G. J. O., Kerr, P. S. G., Li, N. P., & Valentine, K. A. (2014). Predicting romantic interest and decisions in the very early stages of mate selection: Standards, accuracy, and sex differences. *Personality and Social Psychology Bulletin, 40*, 540–550.

letcher, G. J. O., Simpson, J. A., & Thomas, G. (2000). Ideals, perceptions, and evaluations in early relationship development. *Journal of Personality and Social Psychology, 79*, 933–940.

letcher, G. J. O., Simpson, J. A., Thomas, G., & Giles, L. (1999). Ideals in intimate relationships. *Journal of Personality and Social Psychology, 76*, 72–89.

olkes, V. S. (1982). Forming relationships and the matching hypothesis. *Personality and Social Psychology Bulletin, 8*, 631–636.

olkes, V. S., & Sears, D. O. (1977). Does everybody like a liker? *Journal of Experimental Social Psychology, 13*, 505–519.

ord, K. A. (2012). Thugs, nice guys, and players: Black college women's partner preferences and relationship expectations. *Black Women, Gender, and Families, 6*, 23–42.

Forest, A. L., & Wood, J. V. (2012). When social networking is not working: Individuals with low self-esteem recognise but do not reap the benefits of self-disclosure on Facebook. *Psychological Science, 12*, 295–302.

Foster, G. (2005). Making friends: A nonexperimental analysis of social pair formation. *Human Relations, 58*, 1443–1465.

Fraley, R. C., & Marks, M. J. (2010). Westermarck, Freud, and the incest taboo: Does familial resemblance activate sexual attraction? *Personality and Social Psychology Bulletin, 36*, 1202–1212.

Franiuk, R., Cohen, D., & Pomerantz, E. M. (2002). Implicit theories of relationships: Implications for relationship satisfaction and longevity. *Personal Relationships, 9*, 345–367.

Freud, S. (1905). *Der Witz und seine Beziehung zum Unbewußten [The joke and its relation to the unconscious]*. Leipzig: Denicke.

Freud, S. (1913). *Totem und Tabu: Einige Übereinstimmungen im Seelenleben der Wilden und der Neurotiker [Totem and taboo: Resemblances between the mental lives of savages and neurotics]*. Leipzig: Hugo Heller and Cie.

Freud, S. (1916). *Vorlesungen zur Einführung in die Psychoanalyse [Introduction to Psychoanalysis]*. Leipzig: Hugo Heller and Cie.

Galton, F. (1874). *English men of science: Their nature and nurture*. London: Macmillan and Co.

Galton, F. (1908). *Memories of my life*. London: Methuen.

Gifford-Smith, M. E., & Brownell, C. A. (2003). Childhood peer relationships: Social acceptance, friendships, and peer networks. *Journal of School Psychology, 41*, 235–284.

Gill, R. (2009). Mediated intimacy and postfeminism: A discourse analytic examination of sex and relationships advice in a women's magazine. *Discourse and Communication, 3*, 345–369.

Gouldner, H., & Strong, M. S. (1987). *Speaking of friendship: Middle-class women and their friends*. New York, NY: Greenwood Press.

Grammer, K., & Eibl-Eibesfeldt, I. (1990). *The ritualisation of laughter*. Bochum, Germany: Brockmeyer.

Greitemeyer, T., & Kunz, I. (2013). Name-valence and physical attractiveness in Facebook: Their compensatory effects on friendship acceptance. *Journal of Social Psychology, 153*, 257–260.

Grob, B., Knapp, L. A., Martin, R. D., & Anzenberger, G. (1998). The major histocompatibility complex and mate choice: Inbreeding avoidance and selection of good genes. *Experimental and Clinical Immunogenetics, 15*, 119–129.

Gullahom, J. T. (1952). Distance and friendship as factors in the gross interaction matrix. *Sociometry, 15*, 123–134.

a, T., van den Berg, J. E. M., Engels, R. C. M. E., & Lichtwarck-Aschoff, A. (2012). Effects of attractiveness and status in dating desire in homosexual and heterosexual men and women. *Archives of Sexual Behavior, 41,* 673–682.

aandrikman, K., Harmsen, C., van Wissen, L. J. G., & Hutter, I. (2008). Geography matters: Patterns of spatial homogamy in the Netherlands. *Population, Space, and Place, 14,* 387–405.

aandrikman, K., & Hutter, I. (2012). "That's a different kind of person": Spatial connotations and partner choice. *Population, Space, and Place, 18,* 241–259.

ald, G. M., & Høgh-Olesen, H. (2010). Receptivity to sexual invitation from strangers of the opposite gender. *Evolution and Human Behavior, 31,* 453–458.

all, J. A., & Canterberry, M. (2011). Sexism and assertive courtship strategies. *Sex Roles, 65,* 840–853.

armon-Jones, E., & Allen, J. J. B. (2001). The role of affect in the mere exposure effect: Evidence from psychophysiological and individual differences approaches. *Personality and Social Psychology Bulletin, 27,* 889–898.

arris, R. J., Hoekstra, S. J., Scott, C. L., Sanborn, F. W., Karafa, J. A., & Brandenburg, J. D. (2000). Young men's and women's different autobiographical memories of the experience of seeing frightening movies on a date. *Media Psychology, 2,* 245–268.

aselager, G. J. T., Hartup, W. W., van Lieshout, C. F. M., & Riksen-Walraven, J. M. A. (1998). Similarities between friends and nonfriends in middle childhood. *Child Development, 69,* 1198–1208.

avlicek, J., & Roberts, S. C. (2009). MHC-correlated mate choice in humans: A review. *Psychoneuroendocrinology, 34,* 497–512.

ay, J. (2000). Functions of humor in the conversations of men and women. *Journal of Pragmatics, 32,* 709–742.

azan, C., & Shaver, P. (1987). Romantic love conceptualized as an attachment process. *Journal of Personality and Social Psychology, 52,* 511–524.

azleden, R. (2004). The pathology of love in contemporary relationship manuals. *Sociological Review, 52,* 201–217.

itsch, G. J., Hortaçsu, A., & Ariely, D. (2010a). Matching and sorting in online dating. *American Economic Review, 100,* 130–163.

itsch, G. J., Hortaçsu, A., & Ariely, D. (2010b). What makes you click? Mate preferences in online dating. *Quantitative Marketing and Economics, 8,* 393–427.

ochschild, A. R. (1994). The commercial spirit of intimate life and the abduction of feminism: Signs from women's advice books. *Theory, Culture, and Society, 11,* 1–24.

Holahan, C. J., & Wilcox, B. L. (1978). Residential satisfaction and friendshi formation in high- and low-rise student housing: An interactional analysi: *Journal of Educational Psychology, 70,* 237–241.

Holmes, B. M. (2007). In search of my "one-and-only": Romance-related medi and beliefs in romantic relationship destiny. *The Electronic Journal of Cor munication, 17,* article 10.

Holtzman, N. S., Vazire, S., & Mehl, M. R. (2010). Sounds like a narcissis Behavioral manifestations of narcissism in everyday life. *Journal of Researc in Personality, 44,* 478–484.

Homans, G. C. (1961). *Social behavior: Its elementary forms.* New York, NY Harcourt Brace.

Hoorens, V. (2014). What's really in a name-letter effect? Name-letter prefer ences as indirect measures of self-esteem. *European Review of Social Psy chology, 25,* 228–262.

Houts, R. M., Robins, E., & Huston, T. L. (1996). Compatibility and the develop ment of premarital relationships. *Journal of Marriage and the Family, 58,* 7–2(

Human, L. J., Sandstrom, G. M., Biesanz, J. C., & Dunn, E. W. (2013). Firs impressions leave a lasting impression: The long-term effects of distinctiv self-other agreement on relationship development. *Social Psychological an Personality Science, 4,* 395–402.

Johnco, C., Wheeler, L., & Taylor, A. (2010). They do get prettier at closing time A repeated measures study of the closing-time effect and alcohol. *Socic Influence, 5,* 261–271.

Johnson, S. (2004). Attachment theory: A guide for healing couple relation ships. In W. S. Rhodes & J. A. Simpson (Eds.), *Adult attachment: Theor research, and clinical implications* (pp. 367–387). New York, NY: Guilford.

Jokela, M., Bleidorn, W., Lamb, M. E., Gosling, S. D., & Rentfrow, P. J. (2015) Geographically varying associations between personality and life satisfac tion in the London metropolitan area. *Proceedings of the National Academ of Sciences of the United States of America, 112,* 725–730.

Jones, B. T., Jones, B. C., Thomas, A. P., & Piper, J. (2003). Alcohol consumptio increases attractiveness ratings of opposite-sex faces: A third route to risk sex. *Addiction, 98,* 1069–1075.

Jones, E. E. (1964). *Ingratiation: A social psychological analysis.* New York, NY Appleton-Century-Crofts.

Jones, H. E. (1929). Homogamy in intellectual abilities. *American Journal o Sociology, 35,* 369–382.

Kabat-Zinn, J. (1991). *Full catastrophe living: Using the wisdom of your body an mind to face stress, pain, and illness.* New York, NY: Dell Publishing.

Kalmijn, M. (1998). Intermarriage and homogamy: Causes, patterns, an trends. *Annual Review of Sociology, 24,* 395–421.

Kaplan, M. F., & Anderson, N. H. (1973). Information integration theory and reinforcement theory as approaches to interpersonal attraction. *Journal of Personality and Social Psychology, 28*, 301–312.

Katz, A. M., & Hill, R. (1958). Residential propinquity and marital selection: A review of theory, method, and fact. *Marriage and Family Living, 20*, 27–35.

Kellerman, K. A., & Berger, C. R. (1984). Affect and the acquisition of social information: Sit back, relax, and tell me about yourself. In R. N. Bostrom (Ed.), *Communication Yearbook 8* (pp. 412–445). Newbury Park, CA: Sage.

Kelly, E. L., & Conley, J. J. (1987). Personality and compatibility: A prospective analysis of marital stability and marital satisfaction. *Journal of Personality and Social Psychology, 52*, 27–40.

Kenny, D. A. (1994). *Interpersonal perception: A social relations analysis.* New York, NY: Guilford.

Kenny, D. A., & Nasby, W. (1980). Splitting the reciprocity correlation. *Journal of Personality and Social Psychology, 38*, 249–256.

Kiesler, C. A., & Goldberg, G. N. (1968). Multi-dimensional approach to the experimental study of interpersonal attraction: Effect of a blunder on the attractiveness of a competent other. *Psychological Reports, 22*, 693–705.

Kirkpatrick, L. A., & Hazan, C. (1994). Attachment styles and close relationships: A four-year prospective study. *Personal Relationships, 1*, 123–142.

Kleiman, E. M., Kashdan, T. B., Monfort, S. S., Machell, K. A., & Goodman, F. R. (2015). Perceived responsiveness during an initial social interaction with a stranger predicts a positive memory bias one week later. *Cognition and Emotion, 29*, 332–341.

Knee, C. R., Nanayakkara, A., Vietor, N. A., Neighbors, C., & Patrick, H. (2001). Implicit theories of relationships: Who cares if romantic partners are less than ideal? *Personality and Social Psychology Bulletin, 27*, 808–819.

Kniffin, K. M., & Wilson, D. S. (2004). The effect of nonphysical traits on the perception of physical attractiveness: Three naturalistic studies. *Evolution and Human Behavior, 25*, 88–101.

Knobloch, L. K., & Miller, L. E. (2008). Uncertainty and relationship initiation. In S. Sprecher, A. Wenzel, & J. Harvey (Eds.), *Handbook of relationship initiation* (pp. 121–134). New York, NY: Psychology Press.

Korchmaros, J. D., Ybarra, M. L., & Mitchell, K. J. (2015). Adolescent online romantic relationship initiation: Differences by sexual and gender identification. *Journal of Adolescence, 40*, 54–64.

Koyama, N. F., McGain, A., & Hill, R. A. (2004). Self-reported mate preferences and 'feminist' attitudes regarding marital relations. *Evolution and Human Behavior, 25*, 327–335.

Kraut, R. E., Fussell, S. R., Brennan, S. E., & Siegel, J. (2002). Understanding effects of proximity on collaboration: Implications for technologies to support remote collaborative work. In P. J. Hinds, & S. Kiesler (Eds.), *Distributed work* (pp. 137–164). Cambridge, MA: Massachusetts Institute of Technology Press.

Lampard, L. (2007). Couples' places of meeting in late 20th century Britain: Class, continuity and change. *European Sociological Review, 23*, 357–371.

Landy, D., & Sigall, H. (1974). Beauty is talent: Task evaluation as a function of the performer's physical attractiveness. *Journal of Personality and Social Psychology, 29*, 299–304.

Langlois, J. H., Kalakanis, L., Rubenstein, A. J., Larson, A., Hallam, M., & Smoot, M. (2000). Maxims or myths of beauty? A meta-analytic and theoretical review. *Psychological Bulletin, 126*, 390–423.

Latané, B., Liu, J. H., Nowak, A., Bonavento, M., & Zheng, L. (1995). Distance matters: Physical space and social impact. *Personality and Social Psychology Bulletin, 21*, 795–805.

Laumann, E. O. (1973). *Bonds of pluralism: The form and substance of urban social networks*. New York, NY: Wiley.

Laursen, D. (2005). Please reply! The replying norm in adolescent SMS communication. In R. Harper, L. Palen, & A. Taylor (Eds.), *The inside text: Social, cultural, and design perspectives on SMS* (pp. 53–73). Dordrecht: Springer.

Layton, B. D., & Insko, C. A. (1974). Anticipated interaction and the similarity attraction effect. *Sociometry, 37*, 149–162.

Lazarsfeld, P. F., & Merton, R. K. (1954). Friendship as a social process: A substantive and methodological analysis. In M. Berger (Ed.), *Freedom and control in modern society* (pp. 18–66). New York, NY: van Nostrand.

Leckman, J. F., & Mayes, L. C. (1999). Preoccupations and behaviors associated with romantic and parental love. Perspectives on the origin of obsessive-compulsive disorder. *Child and Adolescent Psychiatric Clinics of North America, 8*, 635–665.

Lee, L., Loewenstein, G. F., Ariely, D., Hong, J., & Young, J. (2008). If I'm not hot, are you hot or not? Physical-attractiveness evaluations and dating preferences as a function of one's own attractiveness. *Psychological Science, 19*, 669–677.

Lehr, A. T., & Geher, G. (2006). Differential effects of reciprocity and attitude similarity across long- versus short-term mating contexts. *The Journal of Social Psychology, 146*, 423–439.

Lemay, E. P., Jr., Clark, M. S., & Greenberg, A. (2010). What is beautiful is good because what is beautiful is desired: Physical attractiveness stereotyping as projection of interpersonal goals. *Personality and Social Psychology Bulletin, 36*, 339–353.

Lewandowski, G. W., Aron, A., & Gee, J. (2007). Personality goes a long way: The malleability of opposite-sex physical attractiveness. *Personal Relationships, 14,* 571–585.

Lewandowski, G. W., Jr., & Aron, A. P. (2004). Distinguishing arousal from novelty and challenge in initial romantic attraction between strangers. *Social Behavior and Personality, 32,* 361–372.

Li, N. P., Griskevicius, V., Durante, K. M., Jonason, P. K., Pasisz, D. J., & Aumer, K. (2009). An evolutionary perspective on humor: Sexual selection or interest indication? *Personality and Social Psychology Bulletin, 35,* 923–936.

Lieblich, A., Zilber, T. B., & Tuval-Mashiach, R. (2008). Narrating human actions: The subjective experience of agency, structure, communion, and serendipity. *Qualitative Inquiry, 14,* 613–631.

Lilienfeld, S. O., Lynn, S. J., Ruscio, J., & Beyerstein, B. L. (2010). *50 great myths of popular psychology.* Chichester: Wiley-Blackwell.

Litt, A., Khan, U., & Shiv, B. (2010). Lusting while loathing: Parallel counterdriving of wanting and liking. *Psychological Science, 21,* 118–125.

Liu, J. H., Campbell, S. M., & Condie, H. (1995). Ethnocentrism in dating preferences for an American sample: The in-group bias in social context. *European Journal of Social Psychology, 25,* 95–115.

Lorenz, K. (1943). The innate forms of potential experience. *Zietschrift für Tierpsychologie, 5,* 234–409.

Lorenzo, G. L., Biesanz, J. C., & Human, L. J. (2010). What is beautiful is good and more accurately understood: Physical attractiveness and accuracy in first impressions of personality. *Psychological Science, 21,* 1777–1782.

Loving, T. J., Crockett, E. E., & Paxson, A. A. (2009). Passionate love and relationship thinkers: Experimental evidence for acute cortisol elevations in women. *Psychoneuroendocrinology, 34,* 939–946.

Lyvers, M., Cholakians, E., Puorro, M., & Sundram, S. (2011). Beer goggles: Blood alcohol concentration in relation to attractiveness ratings for unfamiliar opposite sex faces in naturalistic settings. *The Journal of Social Psychology, 151,* 105–112.

Mac an Ghaill, M., Haywood, C., & Bright, Z. (2013). Making connections: Speed dating, masculinity, and interviewing. In B. Pini, & B. Pease (Eds.), *Men, masculinities, and methodologies* (pp. 77–89). Basingstoke: Palgrave Macmillan.

Machin, D., & Thornborrow, J. (2003). Branding and discourse: The case of *Cosmopolitan. Discourse and Society, 14,* 453–471.

Maestripieri, D., Klimczuk, A. C., Seneczko, M., Traficonte, D. M., & Wilson, M. C. (2013). Relationship status and relationship instability, but not dominance, predict individual differences in baseline cortisol levels. *PLoS ONE, 8,* e840003.

Maner, J. K., DeWall, N., Baumeister, R. F., & Schaller, M. (2007). Does social exclusion motivate interpersonal reconnection? Resolving the "porcupine problem". *Journal of Personality and Social Psychology*, *92*, 42–55.

Marazziti, D., & Canale, D. (2004). Hormonal changes when falling in love. *Psychoneuroendocrinology*, *29*, 931–936.

Marcotte, A. (2014, May 25). How 'pick-up artist' philosophy and its more misogynist backlash shaped mind of alleged killer Elliot Rodger. *American Prospect*. Online at: www.prospect.org

Marek, C. I., Wanzer, M. B., & Knapp, J. L. (2004). An exploratory investigation of the relationship between roommates' first impressions and subsequent communication patterns. *Communication Research Reports*, *21*, 210–220.

Markham, A. N. (2005). "Go ugly early": Fragmented narrative and bricolage as interpretive method. *Qualitative Inquiry*, *11*, 813–839.

Marsden, P. (1988). Homogeneity in confiding relations. *Social Networks*, *10*, 57–76.

Matthews, K. A., Rosenfeld, D., & Stepan, W. G. (1979). Playing hard-to-get: A two-determinant model. *Journal of Research in Personality*, *13*, 234–244.

Maxwell, G. M., Cook, M. W., & Burr, R. (1985). The encoding and decoding of liking from behavioral cues in both auditory and visual channels. *Journal of Nonverbal Behavior*, *9*, 239–263.

McCutcheon, L. E. (1991). A new test of misconceptions about psychology. *Psychological Reports*, *68*, 647–653.

McFarland, D. A., Jurafsky, D., & Rawlings, C. (2013). Making the connection: Social bonding in courtship situations. *American Journal of Sociology*, *118*, 1596–1649.

McPherson, M., & Smith-Lovin, L. (1987). Homophily in voluntary organizations: Status distance and the composition of face-to-face groups. *American Sociological Review*, *52*, 370–379.

McPherson, M., Smith-Lovin, L., & Cook, J. M. (2001). Birds of a feather: Homophily in social networks. *Annual Review of Sociology*, *27*, 415–444.

Meston, C. M., & Frohlich, P. F. (2003). Love at first fright: Partner salience moderates roller-coaster-induced excitation transfer. *Archives of Sexual Behavior*, *32*, 537–544.

Mettee, D. R., & Wilkins, P. C. (1972). When similarity "hurts": Effects of perceived ability and a humorous blunder on interpersonal attractiveness. *Journal of Personality and Social Psychology*, *22*, 246–258.

Mickelson, K. D., Kessler, R. C., & Shaver, P. R. (1997). Adult attachment in a nationally representative sample. *Journal of Personality and Social Psychology*, *73*, 1092–1106.

Miller, R. B., Anderson, S., & Keala, D. K. (2004). Is Bowen's theory valid? A review of basic research. *Journal of Marital and Family Therapy*, *30*, 453–466.

Mita, T. H., Dermer, M., & Knight, J. (1977). Reversed facial images and the mere-exposure effect. *Journal of Personality and Social Psychology*, *35*, 597–601.

Montoya, R. M. (2008). I'm hot, so I'd say you're not: The influence of objective physical attractiveness on mate selection. *Journal of Personality and Social Psychology*, *34*, 1315–1331.

Montoya, R. M., & Horton, R. S. (2012a). The reciprocity of liking effect. In M. Paludi (Ed.), *The psychology of love* (pp. 39–57). Santa Barbara, CA: Praeger.

Montoya, R. M., & Horton, R. S. (2012b). A meta-analytic investigation of the processes underlying the similarity-attraction effect. *Journal of Social and Personal Relationships*, *30*, 64–94.

Montoya, R. M., Horton, R. S., & Kirchner, J. (2008). Is actual similarity necessary for attraction? A meta-analysis of actual and perceived similarity. *Journal of Social and Personal Relationships*, *25*, 889–922.

Moore, F. R., Cassidy, C., Law Smith, M. J., & Perrett, D. I. (2006). The effects of female control of resources on sex-differentiated mate preferences. *Evolution and Human Behavior*, *27*, 193–205.

Moore, M. (1985). Nonverbal courtship patterns in women: Context and consequences. *Ethology and Sociobiology*, *6*, 237–247.

Moore, M. (1997). Nonverbal courtship signaling: Flunking flirting 101. Paper presented at the joint annual meeting of the Society for the Scientific Study of Sexuality and the American Association of Sex Educators, Counselors, and Therapists, Arlington, VA, November 16.

Moore, M. (1998). Nonverbal courtship patterns in women: Rejection signaling – an empirical investigation. *Semiotica*, *118*, 201–214.

Moore, M., & Butler, D. (1989). Predictive aspects of nonverbal courtship behavior in women. *Semiotica*, *76*, 205–215.

Moreland, R. L. (1987). The formation of small groups. *Review of Personality and Social Psychology*, *8*, 80–110.

Moreland, R. L., & Beach, S. R. (1992). Exposure effects in the classroom: The development of affinity among students. *Journal of Experimental Social Psychology*, *28*, 255–276.

Morf, C. C., & Rhodewalt, F. (2001). Unraveling the paradoxes of narcissism: A dynamic self-regulatory processing model. *Psychological Inquiry*, *12*, 177–196.

Murphy, K. (2001). What does John Gray have to say to feminism? *Continuum: Journal of Media and Cultural Studies*, *15*, 159–167.

Mystery (2007). *The Mystery Method: How to get beautiful women into bed.* New York: St. Martin's Press.

Nahemow, L., & Lawton, M. (1975). Similarity and propinquity in friendship formation. *Journal of Personality and Social Psychology*, *32*, 205–213.

Naumann, L. P., Vazire, S., Rentfrow, P. J., & Gosling, S. D. (2009). Personalit judgments based on physical appearance. *Personality and Social Psycholog Bulletin, 35*, 1661–1671.

Neff, K. D., & Beretvas, S. N. (2013). The role of self-compassion in romanti relationships. *Self and Identity, 12*, 78–98.

Newcomb, T. M. (1956). The prediction of interpersonal attraction. *America Psychologist, 11*, 575–586.

Newcomb, T. M. (1961). *The acquaintance process.* New York, NY: Holt, Rine hart, and Winston.

Novak, D. W., & Lerner, M. J. (1968). Rejection as a consequence of perceive similarity. *Journal of Personality and Social Psychology, 9*, 147–152.

Nuttin, J. M. (1985). Narcissism beyond Gestalt and awareness: The name lette effect. *European Journal of Social Psychology, 15*, 353–361.

Office for National Statistics (2014). *Integrated Household Survey – January t December 2013.* London: Office for National Statistics.

Olivola, C. Y., & Todorov, A. (2010). Fooled by first impressions? Reexaminin the diagnostic value of appearance-based inferences. *Journal of Experimen tal Social Psychology, 46*, 315–324.

O'Malley, B. L. (2004). *Scott Pilgrim's precious little life.* Portland, OR: Oni Press

O'Sullivan, P. B. (2005). Masspersonal communication: Rethinking the mas interpersonal divide. Paper presented at the Annual Meeting of the Interna tional Communication Association, New York, NY, May 22.

Overbury, T. (1613/2010). *The wife, a poem: Express'd in a compleat wife. Wit an elegy on the untimely death of the author, poyson'd in the tower.* Londor Gale ECCO Print Editions.

Ovid (1 AD/1818). *Metamorphoses.* Translated by S. Garth et al. Cambridge MA: Internet Classics Archive.

Ovid (1 AD/2014). *The metamorphoses* (2nd ed.). Translated by A. S. Kline. Lon don: CreateSpace Independent Publishing Platform.

Parks, M. R. (2007). *Personal relationships and personal networks.* Mahwah, N Lawrence Erlbaum.

Parks, M. R., & Eggert, L. L. (1991). The role of social context in the dynam ics of personal relationships. In W. H. Jones, & D. Perlman (Eds.), *Advance in personal relationship: A research annual* (Vol. 2, pp. 1–34). London: Jessic Kingsley.

Pearson, K. (1900). *Grammar of science* (2nd ed.). London: Adam and Charle Black.

Pellegrini, A. D., & Long, J. D. (2007). An observational study of early hetero sexual interaction at middle school dances. *Journal of Research on Adoles cence, 17*, 613–638.

elham, B. W., Mirenberg, M. C., Jones, J. T. (2002). Why Susie sells seashells by the seashore: Implicit egotism and major life decisions. *Journal of Personality and Social Psychology, 82*, 469–487.

ennebaker, J., Dyer, M., Caulkins, R., Litowitz, D., Ackreman, P. L., Anderson, D. B., & McGraw, K. M. (1979). Don't the girls get prettier at closing time: A country and western application to psychology. *Personality and Social Psychology Bulletin, 5*, 122–125.

enton-Voak, I., Rowe, A., & Williams, J. (2007). Through rose-tinted glasses: Relationship satisfaction and representations of partners' facial attractiveness. *Journal of Evolutionary Psychology, 5*, 169–181.

erper, T. (1989). Theories and observations on sexual selection and female choice in human beings. *Medical Anthropology, 11*, 409–454.

erry, P. J. (1969). Working-class isolation and mobility in rural Dorset, 1837–1936: A study of marriage distances. *Transaction of the Institute of British Geographers, 46*, 121–141.

inel, E. C., Long, A. E., Landau, M. J., Alexander, K., & Pyszczysnki, T. (2006). Seeing I to I: A pathway to interpersonal connectedness. *Journal of Personality and Social Psychology, 90*, 243–257.

inquart, M., & Pfeiffer, J. P. (2012). What is essential is invisible to the eye: Intimate relationships of adolescents with visual impairment. *Sexuality and Disability, 30*, 139–147.

lato (360 BC/1960). *Phaedrus.* Translated by R. G. Bury. Cambridge, MA: Harvard University Press.

riest, R. F., & Sawyer, J. (1967). Proximity and peership: Bases of balance in interpersonal attraction. *American Journal of Sociology, 72*, 633–649.

rovine, R. R. (2000). *Laughter: A scientific investigation.* New York, NY: Viking.

ruitt, D. G. (1968). Reciprocity and credit building in a laboratory dyad. *Journal of Personality and Social Psychology, 8*, 143–147.

utnam, S. K., Du, J., Sato, S., & Hull, E. M. (2001). Testosterone restoration of copulatory behavior correlates with medical preoptic dopamine release in castrated male rats. *Hormones and Behavior, 39*, 216–224.

uts, D. A., Welling, L. L. M., Burriss, R. P., & Dawood, K. (2012). Men's masculinity and attractiveness predict their partners' reported orgasm frequency and timing. *Evolution and Human Behavior, 33*, 1–9.

eagans, R. (2011). Close encounters: Analyzing how social similarity and propinquity contribute to strong network connections. *Organization Science, 22*, 835–849.

eardon, K. (2008). *Top tips for girls: Real advice from real women for real life.* London: Headline.

Regan, P. C. (1998). Willingness to compromise ideal mate selection standards as a function of sex, mate value, and relationship context. *Journal of Personality and Social Psychology, 24*, 1294–1303.

Reis, H. T., Maniaci, M. R., Caprariello, P. A., Eastwick, P. W., & Finkel, E. J. (2011). Familiarity does indeed promote attraction in live interaction. *Journal of Personality and Social Psychology, 101*, 557–570.

Rentfrow, P. J., Gosling, S. D., Jokela, M., Stillwell, D. J., Kosinski, M., & Potter, J. (2013). Divided we stand: Three psychological regions of the United States and their political, economic, social, and health correlates. *Journal of Personality and Social Psychology, 105*, 996–1012.

Roberts, S. C., & Little, A. C. (2008). Good genes, complementary genes, and human mate choice. *Genetica, 132*, 309–321.

Rodríguez, G. (2010, December). From misogyny to murder: Everyday sexism and femicide in cross-cultural context. *Center for the Study of Women Update*. Online at: http://escholarship.org/uc/item/5tw6h8nk

Rogers, E. M. (1994). *A history of communication study: A biographical approach.* New York, NY: Free Press.

Rosenbaum, M. E. (1986). The repulsion hypothesis: On the nondevelopment of relationships. *Journal of Personality and Social Psychology, 51*, 1156–1166.

Rosenfeld, H. M. (1964). Social choice conceived as a level aspiration. *Journal of Abnormal and Social Psychology, 68*, 491–499.

Rosenfeld, M. J., & Thomas, R. J. (2012). Searching for a mate: The rise of the Internet as a social intermediary. *American Sociological Review, 77*, 523–547.

Ross, L., Greene, D., & House, P. (1977). The false consensus effect: An egocentric bias in social perception and attributional processes. *Journal of Experimental Social Psychology, 13*, 279–301.

Rubin, G. (2014, November 23). I took a class on how to pick up women. I learned more about male anxiety. *The Guardian*. Online at: www.theguardian.com.

Rudder, C. (2014). *Dataclysm: Who we are (when we think no one's looking).* London: Fourth Estate.

Sacerdote, B., & Marmaros, D. (2005) How do friendships form? *The Quarterly Journal of Economics, 121*, 79–119.

Sbarra, D. A., & Emery, R. E. (2005). The emotional sequelae of nonmarital relationship dissolution: Analysis of change and intraindividual variability over time. *Personal Relationships, 12*, 213–232.

Schachter, S., & Singer, J. E. (1962). Cognitive, social, and physiological determinants of emotional state. *Psychological Review, 69*, 379–399.

Scheflen, A. E. (1965). Quasi-courtship behavior in psychotherapy. *Psychiatry, 28*, 245–257.

chützwohl, A., Fuchs, A., McKibbin, W. F., & Shackelford, T. K. (2009). How willing are you to accept sexual requests from slightly unattractive to exceptionally attractive imagined requestors? *Human Nature, 20*, 282–293.

egal, M. (1974). Alphabet and attraction: An unobtrusive measure of the effect of propinquity in a field setting. *Journal of Personality and Social Psychology, 30*, 654–657.

eidman, G., & Miller, O. S. (2013). Effects of gender and physical attractiveness on visual attention to Facebook profiles. *Cyberpsychology, Behavior, and Social Networking, 16*, 20–24.

eiffge-Krenke, I. (2011). Coping with relationship stressors: A decade review. *Journal of Research on Adolescence, 21*, 196–210.

elfhout, M., Denissen, J., Branje, S., & Meeus, W. (2009). In the eye of the beholder: Perceived, actual, and peer-rated similarity in personality, communication, and friendship intensity during the acquaintance process. *Journal of Personality and Social Psychology, 96*, 1152–1165.

hakespeare, W. (*c.* 1597/2000). *The merchant of Venice.* London: Wordsworth Classics.

harpley, C. F. (1987). Research findings on neurolinguistic programming: Nonsupportive data or an untestable theory? *Journal of Counselling Psychology, 34*, 103–107.

haw Taylor, L., Fiore, A. T., Mendelsohn, G. A., & Cheshire, C. (2010). A second chance to make a first impression: Factors affecting the longevity of online dating relationships. Paper presented at the Fourth International AAAI Conference on Weblogs and Social Media, Washington, DC, May 26.

hotland, R. L., & Craig, J. M. (1988). Can men and women differentiate between friendly and sexually interested behavior? *Social Psychology Quarterly, 51*, 66–73.

impson, J. A. (1990). Influence of attachment styles on romantic relationships. *Journal of Personality and Social Psychology, 59*, 971–980.

kopek, J., Schulz, F., & Blossfeld, H. (2010). Who contacts whom? Educational homophily in online mate selection. *European Sociological Review, 27*, 180–195.

latcher, R. B. (2010). When Harry and Sally met Dick and Jane: Creating closeness between couples. *Personal Relationships, 17*, 279–297.

lotter, E. B., Gardner, W. L., & Finkel, E. J. (2010). Who am I without you? The influence of romantic breakup on the self-concept. *Personality and Social Psychology Bulletin, 36*, 147–160.

meaton, G., Byrne, D., & Murnen, S. K. (1989). The repulsion hypothesis revisited: Similarity irrelevance or dissimilarity bias? *Journal of Personality and Social Psychology, 56*, 54–59.

Smith, C. A., Konik, J. A., & Tuve, M. V. (2011). In search of looks, status, o something else? Partner preferences among butch and femme lesbians an heterosexual men and women. *Sex Roles, 64*, 658–668.

Snyder, M., Tanke, E. D., & Berscheid, E. (1977). Social perception and inter personal behavior: On the self-fulfilling nature of social stereotypes. *Journe of Experimental Social Psychology, 35*, 656–666.

Spielmann, S. (2013). *Settling for less out of fear of being single*. Unpublishe doctoral thesis, University of Toronto.

Spielmann, S. S., MacDonald, G., & Wilson, A. E. (2009). On the reboun Focusing on someone new helps anxiously attached individuals let go c ex-partners. *Personality and Social Psychology Bulletin, 35*, 1382–1394.

Sprecher, S. (1998). Insiders' perspectives on reasons for attraction to a clos other. *Social Psychology Quarterly, 61*, 287–300.

Sprecher, S., & McKinney, K. (1987). Barriers in the initiation of intimate het erosexual relationships and strategies for intervention. *Journal of Socie Work and Human Sexuality, 5*, 97–110.

Sprecher, S., Treger, S., & Wondra, J. D. (2015). Effects of self-disclosure ro on liking, closeness, and other impressions in get-acquainted interaction *Journal of Social and Personal Relationships, 30*, 497–514.

Sprecher, S., Treger, S., Wondra, J. D., Hilaire, N., & Wallpe, K. (2013). Takin turns: Reciprocal self-disclosure promotes liking in initial interactions. *Jour nal of Experimental Social Psychology, 49*, 860–866.

Starcke, K., & Brand, M. (2012). Decision making under stress: A selectiv review. *Neuroscience and Biobehavioral Reviews, 36*, 1228–1248.

Starcke, K., Polzer, C., Wolf, O. T., & Brand, M. (2011). Does stress alter every day moral decision-making? *Psychoneuroendocrinology, 36*, 210–219.

Steig, W. (1942). *The lonely ones*. New York, NY: Duell, Sloan, and Pearce.

Steig, W. (1990). *Shrek!* New York, NY: Farrar, Straus, and Giroux.

Stephan, W. A., Berscheid, E., & Walster, E. (1971). Sexual arousal an interpersonal perception. *Journal of Personality and Social Psychology, 2(* 93–101.

Stephens, W. C. (1958). Cupid and Venus in Ovid's *Metamorphoses*. *Trans actions and Proceedings of the American Philological Association, 8S* 286–300.

Stewart, D. E. (2003). *The arrow of love: Optics, gender, and subjectivity in med eval love poetry*. Cranbury, NJ: Rosemont.

Strassberg, D. S., & English, B. L. (2015). An experimental study of men's an women's personal ads. *Archives of Sexual Behavior, 44*, 2249–2255.

Strauss, N. (2005). *The Game: Penetrating the Secret Society of Pickup Artist* London: Canongate Books.

turt, J., Ali, S., Robertson, W., Metcalfe, D., Grove, A., Bourne, C., & Bridle, C. (2012). Neurolinguistic programming: A systematic review of the effects on health outcomes. *British Journal of General Practice, 62*, e757–764.

unnafrank, M. (1992). On debunking the attitude similarity myth. *Communication Monographs, 59*, 164–179.

unnafrank, M. J., & Miller, G. R. (1981). The role of initial conversations in determining attraction to similar and dissimilar strangers. *Human Communication Research, 8*, 16–25.

unnafrank, M. J., & Miller, G. R. (1992). The role of initial conversations in determining attraction to similar and dissimilar strangers. *Human Communication Research, 8*, 16–25.

wami, V. (2007). *The missing arms of Vénus de Milo: Reflections on the science of attractiveness*. Brighton: Book Guild.

wami, V. (2009). An examination of the love-is-blind bias among gay men and lesbians. *Body Image, 6*, 149–151.

wami, V. (2011). Love at first sight? Individual differences and the psychology of initial romantic attraction. In T. Chamorro-Premuzic, S. von Stumm, & A. Furnham (Eds.), *Handbook of individual differences* (pp. 747–772). Oxford, UK: Wiley-Blackwell.

wami, V. (2012). Physical attractiveness and personality. In T. Cash (Ed.), *Encyclopedia of body image and human appearance* (pp. 622–628). Oxford: Elsevier.

wami, V., & Barrett, S. (2011). British men's hair color preferences: An assessment of courtship solicitation and stimulus ratings. *Scandinavian Journal of Psychology, 52*, 595–600.

wami, V., Chan, F., Wong, V., Furnham, A., & Tovée, M. J. (2008). Weight-based discrimination in occupational hiring and helping behaviour. *Journal of Applied Social Psychology, 38*, 968–981.

wami, V., & Furnham, A. (2008a). *The psychology of physical attraction*. Hove: Routledge.

wami, V., & Furnham, A. (2008b). Is love really so blind? *The Psychologist, 21*, 108–111.

wami, V., Furnham, A., Chamorro-Premuzic, T., Akbar, K., Gordon, N., Harris, T., Finch, J., & Tovée, M. J. (2010). More than just skin deep? Personality information influences men's ratings of the attractiveness of women's body sizes. *The Journal of Social Psychology, 150*, 628–647.

wami, V., Furnham, A., Georgiades, C., & Pang, L. (2007). Evaluating self and partner physical attractiveness. *Body Image, 4*, 97–101.

wami, V., & Garcia Hernandez, E. (2008). A beauty-map of London: Ratings of the physical attractiveness of women and men in London's boroughs. *Personality and Individual Differences, 45*, 361–366.

Swami, V., Stieger, S., Haubner, T., Voracek, M., & Furnham, A. (2009). Evalu ating the physical attractiveness and oneself and one's romantic partner Individual and relationship correlates of the love-is-blind bias. *Journal o Individual Differences, 30*, 35–43.

Swami, V., & Tovée, M. J. (2006). The influence of body weight on the physi cal attractiveness preferences of feminist and non-feminist heterosexua women and lesbians. *Psychology of Women Quarterly, 30*, 252–257.

Swami, V., Tran, U. S., Thorn, L., Nader, I. W., von Nordheim, L., Pietschnig, J Stieger, S., Husbands, D., & Voracek, M. (2015). Are the scope and natur of psychology properly understood? An examination of beliefs in myths o popular psychology among university students. In A. M. Columbus (Ed.) *Advances in psychology research, Volume 101* (pp. 3–29). Hauppage, N Nova Science Publishers.

Tanner, R. L., Haddock, S. A., Zimmerman, T. S., & Lund, L. K. (2003). Image of couples and families in Disney feature-length animated films. *America Journal of Family Therapy, 31*, 355–373.

Tashiro, T., & Frazier, P. (2003). "I'll never be in a relationship like that again" Personal growth following romantic relationship breakups. *Personal Rela tionships, 10*, 113–128.

Taylor, D. A. (1968). Some aspects of the development of interpersonal rela tionships: Social penetration processes. *The Journal of Social Psychology, 7 79*–90.

Taylor, L. D. (2005). All for him: Articles about sex in American lad magazines *Sex Roles, 52*, 153–163.

Taylor, L. S., Fiore, A. T., Mendelsohn, G. A., & Cheshire, C. (2011). "Out of m league": A real-world test of the matching hypothesis. *Personality and Socia Psychology Bulletin, 37*, 942–954.

Tedeschi, R. G., Park, C. L., & Calhoun, L. G. (1998). *Posttraumatic growth* Mahwah, NJ: Erlbaum.

TextPlus (2012). *It's prom party time!* Available online at: http://www.textplu .com/its-prom-party-time/

Thompson, N. (2014, July 25). Confessions of an ex-pickup artist. *Vice.* Onlin at: www.vice.com

Thornhill, R., Gangestad, S. W., Miller, R., Scheyd, G., McCollough, J. K., & Frank lin, M. (2003). Major histocompatibility complex genes, symmetry, and bod scent attractiveness in men and women. *Behavioral Ecology, 14*, 668–678.

Tidwell, N. D., Eastwick, P. W., & Finkel, E. J. (2013). Perceived, not actual, sim ilarity predicts initial attraction in a live romantic context: Evidence from the speed-dating paradigm. *Personal Relationships, 20*, 199–215.

Titchener, E. B. (1910). *Textbook of psychology.* New York: Macmillan.

odorov, A., & Porter, J. M. (2015). Misleading first impressions: Different for different facial images of the same person. *Psychological Science, 25*, 1404–1417.

ormala, Z. L., Jia, J. S., & Norton, M. I. (2012). The preference for potential. *Journal of Personality and Social Psychology, 103*, 567–583.

sukiura, T., & Cabeza, R. (2011). Remembering beauty: Roles of orbitofrontal and hippocampal regions in successful memory encoding of attractive faces. *NeuroImage, 54*, 653–660.

urkle, S. (2011). *Alone together: Why we expect more from technology and less from each other.* London: Basic Books.

urner, W. (1545). *The rescuing of Romish Fox.* Winchester: Gardiner.

versky, A., & Kahneman, D. (1973). Availability: A heuristic for judging frequency and probability. *Cognitive Psychology, 5*, 207–232.

ye, M.J.C. (1994). Neurolinguistic programming: Magic or myth? *Journal of Accelerative Learning and Teaching, 19*, 309–342.

yler, T. R., & Sears, D. O. (1977). Coming to like obnoxious people when we must live with them. *Journal of Personality and Social Psychology, 35*, 200–211.

rbaniak, G. C., & Kilmann, P. R. (2003). Physical attractiveness and the 'nice guys paradox': Do nice guys really finish last? *Sex Roles, 49*, 413–426.

tz, S. (2015). The function of self-disclosure on social network sites: Not only intimate, but also positive and entertaining self-disclosures increase the feeling of connection. *Computers in Human Behavior, 45*, 1–10.

alins, S. (1966). Cognitive effects of false heart rate feedback. *Journal of Personality and Social Psychology, 4*, 400–408.

anlear, C. A. (1991). Testing a cyclical model of communicative openness in relationship development: Two longitudinal studies. *Communication Monographs, 58*, 337–361.

azire, S., Naumann, L. P., Rentfrow, P. J., & Gosling, S. D. (2008). Portrait of a narcissist: Manifestations of narcissism in physical appearance. *Journal of Research in Personality, 42*, 1439–1477.

errier, D. (2012). Evidence for the influence of the mere-exposure effect on voting in the Eurovision Song Contest. *Judgement and Decision Making, 7*, 639–643.

on Dawans, B., Fischbacher, Y., Kirschbaum, C., Fehr, E., & Heinrichs, M. (2012). The social dimension of stress reactivity: Acute stress increases prosocial behavior in humans. *Psychological Science, 23*, 651–660.

orauer, J. D., & Ratner, R. K. (1996). Who's going to make the first move? Pluralistic ignorance as an impediment to relationship formation. *Journal of Social and Personal Relationships, 13*, 483–506.

Wade, T. J., Butrie, L. K., & Hoffman, K. M. (2009). Women's direct opening line are perceived as most effective. *Personality and Individual Differences, 52*, 74–7*

Walle, A. (1976). Getting picked up without being put down: Jokes and the ba rush. *Journal of the Folklore Institute, 13*, 210–217.

Walmsley, D. J., & Lewis, G. J. (1993). *People and environment: behav ioural approaches in human geography.* London: Longman Scientific an Technical.

Walsh, D. G., & Hewitt, J. (1985). Giving men the come-on: Effect of eye contac and smiling in a bar environment. *Perceptual and Motor Skills, 61*, 873–87*

Walster, E., Aronson, V., Abrahams, D., & Rottman, L. (1966). Importance physical attractiveness in dating behavior. *Journal of Personality and Soci Psychology, 4*, 508–516.

Walster, E., Walster, G. W., Piliavin, J., & Schmidt, L. (1973). "Playing hard t get": Understanding an elusive phenomenon. *Journal of Personality an Social Psychology, 26*, 113–121.

Wang, S. S., Moon, S.-I., Kwon, K. H., Evans, C. A., & Stefanon, M. A. (2010 Face off: Implications of visual cues on initiating friendship on Faceboo *Computers in Human Behavior, 26*, 226–234.

Warren, N. C. (2002). *Date… or soul mate? How to know if someone is wort pursuing in two dates or less.* Nashville, TN: Nelson Books.

Weeden, J., & Sabini, J. (2007). Subjective and objective measures of attractive ness and their relation to sexual behavior and sexual attitudes in universit students. *Archives of Sexual Behavior, 36*, 79–88.

Weisfeld, G. E., Russell, R.J.H., Weisfeld, C. C., & Wells, P. A. (1992). Correlate of satisfaction in British marriages. *Ethology and Sociobiology, 13*, 125–145

Weisman, O., Schneiderman, I., Zagoory-Sharon, O., & Feldman, R. (2015 Early stage romantic love is associated with reduced daily cortisol produc tion. *Adaptive Human Behavior and Physiology, 1*, 41–53.

Welker, K. M., Slatcher, R. B., Baker, L., & Aron, A. (2014). Creating positiv out-group attitudes through intergroup couple friendships and implica tions for compassionate love. *Journal of Social and Personal Relationship 31*, 706–725.

Wells, D. (2003). Gay bars and serendipity. *Journal of Gay and Lesbian Socia Services, 15*, 53–63.

Westermarck, E. (1891). *The history of human marriage.* London: Macmillan.

White, G. L., Fishbein, S., & Rutstein, J. (1981). Passionate love and misattribu tion of arousal. *Journal of Personality and Social Psychology, 41*, 56–62.

Wilbur, C. J., & Campbell, L. (2010). What do women want? An interactionis account of women's mate preferences. *Personality and Individual Difference 49*, 749–754.

Wilbur, C. J., & Campbell, L. (2011). Humor in romantic contexts: Do men participate and women evaluate? *Personality and Social Psychology Bulletin*, *37*, 918–929.

Willis, J., & Todorov, A. (2006). First impressions: Making up your mind after a 100-ms exposure to a face. *Psychological Science*, *17*, 592–598.

Wimmer, A., & Lewis, K. (2010). Beyond and below racial homophily: ERG models of a friendship network documented on Facebook. *American Journal of Sociology*, *116*, 583–642.

Winch, R. F. (1955). The theory of complementary needs in mate selection: A test of one kind of complementariness. *American Sociological Review*, *20*, 52–56.

Winship, J. (1978). A woman's world: *Woman* – An ideology of femininity. In Centre for Contemporary Culture Studies (Ed.), *Women take issue: Aspects of women's subordination* (pp. 133–154). Birmingham: Hutchinson.

Wiseman, R. (2011). *Quirkology: The science of everyday lives*. London: Pan.

Witkowski, T. (2010). Thirty-five years of research on Neuro-Linguistic Programming – NLP Research Data Base: State of the art or pseudoscientific decoration? *Polish Psychological Bulletin*, *41*, 58–66.

Worchel, S., Andreoli, V. A., & Archer, R. (1976). When is a favor a threat to freedom: The effects of attribution and importance of freedom on reciprocity. *Journal of Personality*, *44*, 294–310.

Zajonc, R. B. (1968). Attitudinal effects of mere exposure. *Journal of Personality and Social Psychology*, *9*, 1–27.

Zimmerman, T., Holm, K., & Starrels, M. (2001). A feminist analysis of self-help bestsellers for improving relationships: A decade review. *Journal of Marital and Family Therapy*, *27*, 165–175.

INDEX